THE SEX SECTOR

The economic and social bases of
prostitution in Southeast Asia

THE SEX SECTOR

The economic and social bases of prostitution in Southeast Asia

Edited by Lin Lean Lim

International Labour Office · Geneva

Lim, Lin Lean (ed.)
The sex sector: The economic and social bases of prostitution in Southeast Asia
Geneva, International Labour Office, 1998
/Prostitution/,/woman worker/,/children/,/Indonesia/,/Malaysia/,/Philippines/,/Thailand/.
02.04.1
ISBN 92-2-109522-3

ILO Cataloguing in Publication Data

Printed and bound in Great Britain by
Biddles Ltd, Guildford and King's Lynn   BID

PREFACE

The subject of prostitution has always been controversial. But behind the often emotive or sensationalized treatment of the subject are critical issues relating to basic human rights, employment and working conditions, gender discrimination and commercial exploitation, especially of the child victims of prostitution. All of these issues fall within the ILO's areas of concern and mandate and, with the growing scale, economic importance and increasing international dimensions of prostitution in many countries throughout the world, they have assumed greater significance and urgency. Hence the publication of this study by the ILO.

While the issues deserve attention, for the ILO, as for anyone with integrity and a social conscience, there are serious dilemmas because of the wide range of circumstances of those in prostitution and the multiple and complex issues involved. The study shows that some go into prostitution as a matter of free personal choice or the right to sexual liberation, others are pressured because of dire economic conditions or the lack of remunerative alternatives, and yet others are forced through deception, violence or debt bondage. Partly depending upon the mode of entry into prostitution, the terms and conditions of work can range from decent and lucrative to severely exploitative and abusive. Where prostitutes are considered as workers with rights under standard labour legislation, the concern would be to ensure that they, like other legitimate workers, are entitled to proper working conditions and protection from exploitation and discrimination. It is, however, outside the purview of the ILO to take a position on whether prostitution should be legalized. The question of legalization is thorny because the human rights concerns are difficult to disentangle from concerns over morality, criminality and public health threats. Many of these concerns would stretch the ILO's jurisdiction beyond its current mandate.

Where the ILO does take a clear stand is in maintaining that child prostitution is a serious human rights violation and an intolerable form of child labour. In the case of adults, we can concede that it may be possible to make a distinction between prostitution as a freely chosen form of work and prostitution through coercion. But among children, all prostitution must by definition be deemed involuntary and the aim is its total elimination. The chapter on child prostitution in this study drives home the point that child and adult prostitution are quite different; child prostitution is much more serious with life-long and life-threatening consequences for its young victims. The commercial sexual exploitation of children will be part of a new ILO Convention to be considered in 1998 for the prevention of the most extreme forms of child labour.

The book includes country case studies from Indonesia, Malaysia, the Philippines and Thailand. It is important to stress that the choice of these countries was not by any means intended to suggest that they have a unique prostitution problem. Prostitution and its attendant problems are universal. As data quoted in the first chapter show, the sex sector is large in many other parts of Asia and the Pacific, not to mention the rest of the world. Research in the four Southeast Asian countries was influenced by geographical proximity (the ILO expert was then based in Bangkok) and by the collaboration of national researchers, who are all experienced and well-respected in their own countries. The country case studies are illustrative of the situation in many countries which have a significant sex sector. The value of these case studies lies in their description of the economic and social structures and vested interests that maintain the sex sector, and the problems confronting policy makers and legislators attempting to adopt and enforce a clear-cut legal stance and to implement effective social programmes. Parts of the descriptions are admittedly graphic, even sordid. But they are based on surveys conducted for the study and are included to depict the realities of the occupation and the sector.

The book concludes with a discussion of policy and programme "lessons" and advocates the elimination of child prostitution, but does not commit itself to a particular legal position on adult prostitution. It suggests that having a clear legal stance and consistently following through with appropriate policies and programmes is important. But it does not prescribe whether adult prostitution should be prohibited, legalized and regulated, or decriminalized. In the final analysis, we believe that a well-researched and intellectually honest exposition will help to clarify the many controversial and complex issues and, therefore, provide a more solid and informed basis for those attempting to arrive at their own legal and policy approach to prostitution.

ACKNOWLEDGEMENTS

I would like to acknowledge the role of Mr. Robert Wihtol, who helped conceive the research design and survey questionnaire and was closely involved as a joint coordinator for the project. While professional responsibilities in a new job prevented Mr. Wihtol from participating in the writing of the book, his invaluable contributions are gratefully acknowledged.

The project was funded by the Canada-ASEAN Women's Initiative Fund under the ASEAN Regional CIDA Programme and implemented in coordination with the Institute for Population and Social Research of Mahidol University, Thailand. The active support and encouragement of Mr. Apichat Chamratrithirong, Director of the Institute for Population and Social Research, deserves special mention. Sincere appreciation also goes out to all the national consultants; without their professionalism, enthusiasm and patience the book would not have been completed.

The portions of the book dealing with child prostitution owe much to the encouragement and materials provided by Ms. Pannada Boonpala and Ms. Nelien Haspels of the ILO International Programme for the Elimination of Child Labour.

I would also like to express my gratitude to the reviewers for their invaluable comments and suggestions; to Mr. Ali Taqi, Mr. Werner Sengenberger, Mr. Gek-Boo Ng, Mr David Freedman and Ms. Alice Ouédraogo for their encouragement and support; and to Mr. John Rodwan and Mr. John Myers for final editing.

CONTENTS

Tables

The sex sector

THE ECONOMIC AND SOCIAL BASES OF PROSTITUTION IN SOUTHEAST ASIA

1

Lin Lean Lim

Introduction

Prostitution – the provision of sexual services for reimbursement or material gain – has a long history. It has strong economic foundations as well as social bases involving unequal relations between men and women and between parents and children. In the last three to four decades, prostitution has undergone dramatic changes in some Southeast Asian countries. The scale of prostitution has been enlarged to an extent where we can justifiably speak of a commercial sex sector that is integrated into the economic, social and political life of these countries. The sex business has assumed the dimensions of an industry and has directly or indirectly contributed in no small measure to employment, national income and economic growth. The organizational structures and relations within the sex sector have become very diversified and complex. They involve a growing number of vested and powerful interests and networks of dependencies. The prostitutes are mainly women, but homosexual and heterosexual men also provide sexual services. Child prostitution involves young girls and an increasing number of boys.

The growing scale, economic significance and increasing international dimension of prostitution have heightened concerns related to public morality and social welfare, the violation of the human rights of the prostitutes, their working conditions, the commercial sexual exploitation of the child victims of prostitution and public health threats. The danger of an extending chain of transmission of HIV/AIDS has been especially worrying. The sex sector tends to be rife with economic exploitation and corruption and often is connected to organized crime and drug abuse. Yet governments have found it exceedingly difficult to tackle the problems, in large measure because of the sensitivity and complexity of the issues involved and the range of circumstances of those working in the sex sector. The sex sector is not recognized as an economic sector in official statistics, development plans or government budgets. It has only been in recent years that some aspects of the commercial sex sector, in particular child prostitution and sex-related tourism, have attracted large-scale attention and prompted public discussion and national and international action.

A major difficulty is that measures targeting the sex sector have to consider moral, religious, health, human rights and criminal issues in addressing a phenomenon that is mainly economic in nature and that has its foundations in deeply ingrained patriarchal views. On the one hand, societies frown upon or condemn sexual relations outside marriage. On the other hand, there is concern for those working in the sector, especially children, who are seen as "unfortunate victims", "highly vulnerable" or "deviant" and who are therefore in need of assistance to "rehabilitate" or "resocialize" them or to prevent them from being drawn into prostitution. But economic considerations and vested interests remain strong. In developing countries, macroeconomic policies, such as for the promotion of tourism or export of labour (which have been linked to the growth of the sex sector), tend to take priority over policies to deal with prostitution. Viable and remunerative employment alternatives for the poorly educated and unskilled are not easy to provide, especially in contexts of growing materialism and rising costs of living. Furthermore, many groups, sometimes including government and law and order officials, have an interest in maintaining the sex sector.

Powerful lobbies, which include the lucrative entertainment businesses, have been pushing for the political acceptance of the hugely profitable sex industry. One of the arguments they use is that prostitution is the "oldest profession", a "universal and inevitable social evil" based on patriarchal assumptions about differences in male and female sexuality. Anti-prostitution groups, including some human rights and feminist groups, have been highlighting the human rights abuses and exploitative working conditions within the sex sector and have been questioning the ideological bases for the existence of prostitution. They attack the patriarchal assumptions that men and women have different sexual needs and that men, being naturally sexually aggressive, should have access to prostitutes if "innocent" women are to maintain their chastity. They are also concerned that an important reason for prostitution is the fact that children, especially girls, are often brought up to feel that it is their duty or moral obligation to repay their parents by earning money in any way they can.

Unless policy makers deal with the economic and social bases of prostitution, sanctions and measures targeted at individual prostitutes are not likely to be effective or may even be inappropriate. Policy makers also have to grapple with the dilemma that while both adults and children are involved in prostitution, legislation and policies often cannot be the same for adult and child prostitution. In the case of adults, prostitution could be viewed as a matter of personal choice and a form of work, in which case the policy issues are mainly concerned with whether prostitution should be recognized as a legal occupation with protection under labour law and social security and health regulations. In the case of children, commercial sexual exploitation clearly constitutes a form of coercion and violence against children, and amounts to forced labour and a contemporary form of slavery. Many prostitutes actually become involved in the sex sector while still children. However, the reasons for entering the sector differ greatly for adults and children. Some adults make a relatively "free" personal choice or choose to work as prostitutes as their right to sexual liberation; others "choose" sex work because of economic pressures or because there are no better-paying alternatives; and yet others are overtly pressured by third parties in the form of deception, violence and/or debt bondage. The working conditions of prostitutes vary greatly and depend in part on the method of entry into the sex sector. For some, working conditions and remuneration could be better than what could be expected in other occupations open to them. For others, however, working conditions are clearly exploitative and the women and children are subject to various forms of abuse. Legislation, policies and programmes would need to address these different groups differently.

This study elaborates on these various perspectives by focusing on the commercial sex sector in four Southeast Asian countries: Indonesia, Malaysia, the Philippines and Thailand. The choice of these countries was not intended to suggest that they have a unique prostitution problem or that their social, moral or economic values are especially aberrant; it was mainly influenced by collaborators in the research project. The national case studies are illustrative of the situation in many countries which have a significant sex sector. The study describes the organizational structures and arrangements within the commercial sex sector and shows how increasingly complex and significant the sector is in the national economies of these countries and in the international economy. It also examines how these structures, the economic interests behind the sex industry and social relations between the sexes and generations interact with human rights, workers' rights, morality, criminality, health threats and other considerations to influence the legal stance adopted by governments and the kinds of social programmes used to target the sex sector. The four national case studies include the results of small surveys of individual prostitutes to illustrate the situation of the women workers and how they are affected by the economic and social foundations of the sector. A separate chapter on child prostitution is included to show that, while in the case of adults it may be possible to make a distinction between "voluntary" prostitution and prostitution through coercion, in the case of children it is clearly a serious human rights violation and an intolerable form of child labour. Yet child prostitution is also part of the commercial sex sector, with strong economic and social bases and vested interests involved.

Many current studies highlight the pathetic stories of individual prostitutes, especially of women and children deceived or coerced into the sector. Such an approach tends to sensationalize the issues and to evoke moralistic, rather than practical, responses. This study aims, therefore, to illustrate with new data the wide range of circumstances of those in prostitution; to draw attention to the economic and social bases that sustain the sex sector; to discuss from a basically dispassionate viewpoint the issues and concerns; and to draw out the relevant implications and suggestions for legislation, policies and programmes affecting the sector in general and child prostitution in particular. The discussion of the legal and policy issues and concerns have relevance and applicability beyond the four Southeast Asian countries covered.

The organizational structures and heterogeneity of the sex sector

In Indonesia, Malaysia, the Philippines and Thailand, the magnitude of prostitution in terms of employment and economic turnover has expanded. The organizational structures and relations within the sex sector have become very diversified and complex. The sector responds to the changing tastes and sophistication of customers, the constraints imposed by recent legislation and its enforcement, and the growing number of national and international interests involved. The arrangements for commercial sex have become more diversified, to cater to specific market niches. The operations can be distinguished in terms of being "organized" or "unorganized". The organized establishments have a proprietor or manager and defined work relations with the commercial sex workers, and they often use intermediaries such as pimps or *mamasans* (female managers) who are paid to put the sex workers in touch with clients. In the unorganized activities, the prostitutes work on their own to find and contact their clients, although they often rely on someone to protect them from harassment.

In Indonesia, most major cities have established official brothel complexes and small towns have ubiquitous small-scale operations. Other areas, such as Indramayu in West Java and Wonogiri in Central Java, have a long history of supplying large numbers of women as prostitutes to the cities. More recently, with the development of a "growth triangle" involving economic arrangements between Indonesia, Singapore and Malaysia, a sex industry has developed on the island of Batam to cater mainly to higher-income clients from nearby Singapore and Malaysia.

The official brothel complexes in Indonesia are a form of legalized prostitution. They have their origins in the government's promotion of brothels in the nineteenth century and are now under the control of local councils, which normally comprise the regional administrators, the local prosecutor, the police chief and the military commander. Under the system of localizing prostitution to particular areas, the council not only regulates but also participates in the management of prostitution. The women working in these complexes are subject to very strict rules and regulations and are supposed to be there only temporarily while undergoing rehabilitation and resocialization. While working as prostitutes, they have to attend, and pay for, compulsory education, skills training and mental and social guidance classes. Other parts of the organized sex sector include massage parlours, call-girl establishments and nightclubs. In the unorganized sector, there are street walkers, independent call-girls and those who operate out of places such as hotel lobbies, bars and discotheques. Prostitutes also operate in the vicinity of railway stations, roadside rest-stops for long distance truck drivers, military bases, timber and mining camps and universities.

In Malaysia, the sex sector appears to have grown along with the national economy. But increasingly strict law enforcement (stimulated in part by growing religious fundamentalism and in part by public concern over the reported rising number of teenagers entering the sex sector) has forced the legal "frontline" establishments, such as *karaoke* (sing along) lounges, nightclubs, pubs and coffee houses, to keep the business of commercial sex separate from their legitimate operations. These establishments earn their income from the sale of drinks and door entry charges for entertainment, and provide an access route for clients to arrange sexual transactions. The guest relations officers, or GROs as they are popularly called, are employed by these establishments to provide company to men; sexual relations are not officially part of their job and it is up to them to negotiate their own arrangements. The commercial sex which takes place elsewhere is not supposed to be the concern of the establishment. Frequent police raids have forced the illegal operations to become more innovative and discreet, to make use of modern technology, especially the mobile telephone, or to be constantly on the move. Pimps with mobile phones deliver sex workers to clients. Taxi drivers are also an important link between prostitutes and clients. There are also "messes" known only to a select group of members or clients; these are usually well-furnished apartments managed by a *mamasan* who arranges for pimps to send over prostitutes for the clients who can use the rooms in the apartment. To avoid detection, the messes, vice dens and illegal massage parlours frequently change premises.

In the Philippines, the complexity of the sex sector has been described in terms of the "bought", the "buyer" and the "business". The "bought" are distinguished by the type of commercial sex worker, the location of work (which could even be overseas), the nature and class of clientele and the level of visibility of their operations. The prostitutes could be self-employed (operating independently or within a loose pimp or patronage system); employed as "hospitality women" in bars, nightclubs or massage parlours with definite work rules; enslaved or exploited in brothels where they are guarded and virtually owned by their employers and where they have no choice over customers, numbers served or working hours; or exported by well-organized networks, including crime syndicates, to work willingly or unwillingly as prostitutes in other countries, e.g. in Europe and Japan. The "self-employed" often include street children who sell sexual services as part of a range of income-generating activities to support themselves. The "hospitality women" are the only group officially recognized under labour law as workers; they are also the ones who have to carry valid health cards to indicate that they are "safe" for clients. The "buyers" are not only locals of all classes and occupations but also, and importantly, foreign tourists, foreign military personnel and seamen. The establishment and subsequent closure of American military bases in the Philippines had a major impact on prostitution; thousands worked as hospitality women and later found themselves without their military clients. The "business" covers various types of establishments, including brothels, special tourist agencies, saunas and health clinics, escort services, bars, cabarets and hotels. It also includes independent operators or intermediaries who profit directly or indirectly from commercial sex services. The business interests are not only local; many of the sex establishments in the Philippines were found to have Japanese capital.

In Thailand, the sex establishments from earlier periods, such as prostitutes' houses, have become brothels, and the "opium houses" have become tea rooms which provide sexual services in addition to tea. New forms of packaging commercial sex were copied or adapted from Western countries, with massage parlours, nightclubs, beer bars and dance clubs becoming popular in the 1960s as venues for locals and tourists to obtain sexual services or meet prostitutes. More recently, there has been a proliferation of "indirect" prostitution, with women working as restaurant waitresses, salesgirls in department stores, hairdressers and golf caddies also offering commercial sex. Police raids and fears regarding the spread of HIV/AIDS have resulted in a decline of brothel prostitution and the remodelling of brothel establishments into "restaurants" and "discotheques".

The sex sector has also expanded beyond national boundaries. There has been an increasing incidence of trafficking in women and children for prostitution. Under-age girls from ethnic minorities and from poor neighbouring countries, especially Myanmar, China, Laos and Cambodia, are being brought into Thailand, while Thai women and girls are being taken to Japan and various Western countries. A survey in January 1997 by the Thai Ministry of Public Health estimated that non-Thais accounted for some 16 per cent of the total 64,886 commercial sex workers and that about 90 per cent were Burmese, but warned that these figures could not be confirmed. The survey report also noted that the trend of girls from neighbouring countries being lured into prostitution appeared to be increasing (Bhatiasevi, 1997). Another report (Lintner and Lintner, 1996) estimated that roughly half of the prostitutes trafficked from Myanmar were already HIV-positive. International syndicates bring foreign women from as far away as Latin America for prostitution in Malaysia. A number of Indonesian and Filipino women work as prostitutes in the East Malaysian States of Sabah and Sarawak, and some Thai women are prostitutes in the southern Malaysian State of Johore, where there is a large number of migrant workers. There have also been counter-flows of Southeast Asian women, especially Thais and Filipinos, to Japan, South Africa and European countries for prostitution (Lim and Oishi, 1996). Some 80 per cent of the Asian female migrant workers legally entering Japan in the early 1990s were "entertainers", a commonly used euphemism for prostitutes. Many more were brought into the country illegally. Malaysian women were also reportedly working in Singapore and Hong Kong as prostitutes.

Sex tourism represents a high-profile segment of the sector, with males from Western countries, Japan, and Taiwan, China coming to the Philippines and Thailand on specially organized sex tours. Such tours were organized as part of a package deal involving "interlocking interests between air carriers, tour operators and hotel companies which led to the formation of a new type of conglomerate specializing in the production of packages of services in tourism and trade" (De Dios, 1991, pp. 3-4). In recent years, however, the tours have been discouraged by international campaigns spearheaded by women's groups and are not overtly organized. Cross-border transactions are also significant. Malaysian men cross over to the southern Thai border towns for commercial sex, and both Singaporean and Malaysian men frequent the prostitution complex on the Indonesian island of Batam.

The size and significance of the sex sector

The illegal or underground nature of the sex sector makes it very difficult, if not impossible, to determine its actual size and economic significance. Estimates cited in the subsequent chapters suggest that between 0.25 per cent and 1.5 per cent of the total female population in Indonesia, Malaysia, the Philippines and Thailand are prostitutes and that the sex sector accounts for between 2 per cent and 14 per cent of gross domestic product (GDP).

Estimates made in 1993/94 suggest that there were between 140,000 and 230,000 prostitutes in Indonesia, between 43,000 and 142,000 (most likely closer to the upper limit) in Malaysia, between 100,000 and 600,000 (most likely between 400,000 and 500,000) in the Philippines, and 150,000 to 200,000 at a point of time or 200,000 to 300,000 over a one-year period in Thailand (and perhaps another 100,000 Thai women working as prostitutes in other countries). These prostitutes were mainly, but not only women; there were also male, transvestite and child prostitutes. More recent overall estimates are not available, but limited information on recorded prostitution suggests that there may be some recent changes. In Thailand, for instance, data from an annual survey by the Ministry of Public Health show a decline in the number of sex workers from a record high of about 85,000 in 1990 to 65,000 in 1997, although there has been an increase in the number of commercial sex establishments (see Chapter 5). But the current numbers are still much higher than they were a decade ago.

There were some 50,000 to 75,000 female and male child (below 18 years of age) prostitutes in the Philippines; the estimates for Thailand ranged from 13,000 (by the Ministry of Public Health), through 30,000 to 35,000 (by Guest, 1993; and the National Commission on Women's Affairs, 1995), to 200,000 to 800,000 (by ECPAT, 1993, 1995). In Malaysia, during the period 1986-90, of the 2,626 women and girls taken by the police from brothels, bars, massage parlours and houses of prostitution, 50 per cent were under 18 years of age and the rest between 18 and 21 years (Bruce, 1996, p. 31). In one of the major brothel complexes in Indonesia, about one-tenth of the workers were below 17 years of age, and of those of 17 years and above, almost one-fifth became prostitutes when they were under age 17. A 1994/95 survey of Indonesia's registered prostitutes found that 60 per cent were aged between 15 and 20 years (ECPAT, 1995).

The estimates range so widely that they should obviously be treated with caution. For instance, the figure of 800,000 Thai child prostitutes has been seriously questioned by several sources familiar with the situation in Thailand. For example, Saisuree Chutikul, an expert from the Office of the Permanent Secretary, Prime Minister's Office, pointed out that the figure came from a worker at the Foundation for Children in Thailand who inferred that since the number of children found working in one brothel was 12 and there were about 60,000 brothels in Thailand, the total would be 800,000 (Otaganonta, 1990). A total of 800,000 child prostitutes would make the child prostitution/population ratio 1:144 – a ratio somewhat difficult to believe since the comparable ratio for the Philippines was only about 1:1,118 (Nyland, 1995, p. 547).

Although it is not possible to determine which country has the most accurate estimates, it is worth noting that the estimates do imply that very different proportions of the female population were engaged in prostitution. An estimate of 400,000 to 500,000 prostitutes in the Philippines would mean that the proportion of the total female population who were prostitutes was about six times higher than the proportion among Indonesian women, and double the proportion among Thai women. It is likely that the estimate for the Philippines – and also for Malaysia – (of roughly 1.5 per cent of the total female population) was on the high side, while the estimate for Indonesia (of about 0.25 per cent of the total female population) was too low.

The Coalition against Trafficking in Women (CATW), an international network of feminist organizations and individuals, issued a map for the Fourth World Conference on Women in 1995 with information on countries in the Asia-Pacific Region. If anything, the wide range of figures it quotes confirms the difficulties of estimation and the need for caution. For instance, the estimate of 2.8 million prostitutes in Thailand given by the CATW is outrageously high, since this figure would mean that all women between 15 and 29 years of age living in urban areas were prostitutes (Chapter 5). The CATW's map contains the following eclectic data:

- Australia: Federal police estimate that prostitution grosses A$30 million annually;
- Bangladesh: An estimated 200,000 women have been trafficked to Pakistan over the past ten years, and the trafficking continues at the rate of 200 to 400 women monthly. In 1994, 2,000 women were trafficked for prostitution in six cities in India;
- Hong Kong: Fake contracts for domestic work land women in brothels that employ minders to prevent escapes. There has also been an influx of East European women in high-priced clubs; and Macau has Russian mafia bringing in women;
- India: 2.3 million women in prostitution, of which a quarter are minors. There are more than 1,000 red light districts all over the country, some with caged prostitutes who are mostly minors from Nepal and Bangladesh;
- Indonesia: There were 65,582 registered prostitutes in 1994, but the highest estimate is 500,000 women in prostitution. The estimated financial turnover ranges from US$1.27 billion to US$3.6 billion;
- Japan: The sex industry accounts for about 1 per cent of the gross national product (GNP). Over 150,000 non-Japanese women are in prostitution, more than half are Filipinas and another 40 per cent are Thai women. One "sex zone" in Tokyo, only 0.34 square kilometres, has 3,500 sex facilities. Japanese men constitute the largest number of sex tourists in Asia;
- Republic of Korea: Around the military bases, there are 18,000 registered and 9,000 unregistered prostitutes;
- Malaysia: There are an estimated 142,000 women in prostitution, with between 8,000 and 10,000 in Kuala Lumpur;

- Myanmar: An estimated 20,000 to 30,000 Burmese women work in the sex sector in Thailand. As illegal immigrants in Thailand, prostitutes are arrested, detained and deported back to Myanmar, with some 50 to 70 per cent being HIV positive;
- Nepal: Some 5,000 women are trafficked to India yearly, and about 100,000 Nepalese prostitutes work in India. After India, Hong Kong is supposed to be the biggest market for trafficked Nepalese women;
- Philippines: The estimate is 300,000 women in prostitution and 75,000 prostituted children;
- Taiwan, China: Forty per cent of young prostitutes in the main red light district are aboriginal girls;
- Thailand: The estimates range from 300,000 to 2.8 million, of which a third are minors and children. Thai women are also in prostitution in many countries in Asia and Europe, as well as in Australia and the United States. Prostitutes are used by 4.6 million Thai men, and 500,000 foreign tourists visit prostitutes annually; and
- Viet Nam: Most trafficking is to China and Cambodia and includes children. Prostitution is becoming a feature of the burgeoning tourist industry.

If we include the owners, managers, pimps and other employees of the sex establishments, the related entertainment industry and some segments of the tourism industry, the total numbers earning a living directly or indirectly from prostitution would be several millions. In the entertainment establishments such as massage parlours, for example, the number of support staff, including the cleaners, waitresses, cashiers, parking valets and security guards, exceeds the number of prostitutes. A January 1997 survey by the Ministry of Public Health of Thailand found that out of a total of 104,262 workers in 7,759 establishments where sexual services could be obtained, only 64,886 were sex workers; the remainder were support staff (Bhatiasevi, 1997). The Malaysian study (Chapter 3) lists those with links to the sex sector as including medical practitioners who provide regular health check-ups for the prostitutes; the operators of food stalls in the vicinity of the entertainment establishments; suppliers of cigarettes and liquor, which tend to be consumed in large quantities in the sector; and owners of apartments and buildings used for sexual transactions. If we also consider those who benefit economically from the activities of the sector, such as the families of the sex workers who rely on remittances or the public officials who receive payments or bribes, then the numbers would be even larger.

The economic bases of prostitution

Policy makers have to deal with an industry that is highly organized and increasingly sophisticated and diversified, as well as having close interlinkages with the rest of the national and international economy. The commercial sex sector not only provides substantial income and employment for those directly or indirectly involved in prostitution; it also serves as a mechanism for redistributing incomes (particularly through income remittances from urban to rural areas and from prostitutes working overseas), as a survival mechanism for coping with poverty and as a method of compensating for the lack of social welfare and income maintenance programmes for large segments of the society. It is a significant source of foreign exchange earnings, with links between the growth of prostitution as a highly structured transnational business and the expansion of the tourist industry in these countries, as well as labour exports from these countries.

A substantial amount of money changes hands through the direct and indirect activities of the sex sector, and these activities are often crucial, especially in local economies. In Indonesia, for instance, the financial turnover of the sex sector was estimated at between US$1.2 and 3.3 billion per year, or between 0.8 and 2.4 per cent of the country's GDP. In Thailand, close to US$300 million was transferred annually from urban to rural areas in the form of remittances to rural families by women working in the sex sector in urban areas. This sum was much larger than the budgets of many development programmes funded by the Thai government. A recent study on public policy and the illegal economy in Thailand, conducted by the Chulalongkorn University Political Economy Centre, found that for the period 1993-95, prostitution was the largest of the underground businesses, the others being drug trafficking, arms trading, contraband in diesel oil, trafficking in human labour and gambling (Tunsarawuth, 1996). It estimated that these underground businesses generated an estimated minimum income of at least US$33 to 44 billion a year, representing some 15 to 18 per cent of the country's GDP, and that prostitution accounted for about two-thirds of the total illegal income. Annual income from prostitution was between 450 and 540 billion baht (US$22.5 and 27 billion) or about 10 to 14 per cent of the GDP. The industry showed a tendency to grow rather than contract, mainly because of profitability and ineffective law enforcement. Local taxes from activities related to the sex sector, such as from licences issued to entertainment establishments, assessments levied on apartments and buildings, liquor and cigarette taxes could also be significant.

Recognizing the economic base of prostitution means that the relationship between the growth of the sex sector and economic development cannot be ignored. We need to understand why more and more women, children and men have been drawn into the commercialization of sexual services and why there is a growing demand for such services. While the growth of the sex sector is closely tied to economic progress, modernization and a growing sense of materialism, an important question is whether it is an intentional policy of these countries to promote prostitution as an economic activity. The sale of sexual services is illegal in both Thailand and the Philippines. However, government policies, such as for the promotion of tourism, migration for employment and also the export of female labour as important sources of foreign exchange earnings, may have indirectly encouraged the growth of prostitution and perhaps even trafficking in women. Other economic development policies may also have influenced the proliferation of the sex sector through their impact on, for example, the availability of viable or remunerative employment alternatives for the poorly educated or unskilled, the marginalization of significant elements of the labour force, the increasingly adverse terms of trade between rural and urban areas, growing income inequalities and their cumulative socio-economic consequences, and the strategies adopted by poor families for survival, especially in the absence of social safety nets.

This study attempts to identify those macroeconomic policies that have directly or indirectly influenced the growth and increasing complexity of the sex sector. By highlighting the close interlinkages between the sex sector and the rest of the economy, both nationally and internationally, it helps to define the conflicts and challenges confronting policy makers. It also aims to show that specific policies, legislation, regulations and welfare and health measures are often neglected or difficult to put into effect in targeting the sex sector when they are seen by policy makers to conflict with broader macroeconomic objectives.

The economic bases of prostitution are important because it is not just the individual prostitutes and their families who rely on earnings from the sex sector. There are all the commercial businesses that are directly or indirectly involved in the industry. The economic bases also comprise other powerful interests that control and maintain the structures within the sex sector. The national case studies all emphasize that a critical reason why the sex sector flourishes is because it is protected and supported by corrupt politicians, police, armed forces and civil servants, who receive bribes, demand sexual favours and are themselves customers of the sex establishments, or may even be partners or owners of the establishments. In the official brothel complexes in Indonesia, the local authorities, police and military both regulate and manage these complexes. There is also plenty of evidence of official involvement in trafficking. Burmese child victims speak of how policemen or border guards were involved in their trafficking into Thailand and how they had to entertain policemen or other government officials (Asia Watch and the Women's Rights Project, 1993, p. 47). The report of the United Nations Special Rapporteur on the Sale of Children, Child Prostitution and Child Pornography also noted that "corruption and collusion among various law enforcement authorities are widespread and pervasive" (United Nations, 1994, p. 36).

These economic bases underscore the importance of the commercial sex sector in the economies of Southeast Asian countries, and help to explain why the policy issues cannot be seen only from the perspective of the welfare of individual prostitutes. The highly structured and organized nature of the sector and the vast network of dependencies and powerful vested interests involved indicate the difficulties of regulating or controlling the sector. The various vested interests and dependencies tend to be more deeply entrenched the more complex the organization of the sex sector and the greater the degree of linkage with the rest of the national and international economic system. The economic bases also draw attention to the fact that the nature and pace of development in these countries has influenced both the supply of workers to, and the demand for, the services of the sex sector. With the financial stakes in the sex sector so large, it is easy to understand the view espoused by some, especially those with vested interests, that commercial sex is an economic sector like any other and offers gainful employment for the large numbers involved.

The social bases of prostitution

In addition to economic bases, prostitution also has strong social bases, which have remained largely unchanged over time. The roots of prostitution are to be found in the socio-cultural institutions and traditions that dictate gender relations and the relations between parents and children. As one aspect of unequal gender relations, prostitution will continue so long as the social structures surrounding it and contributing to it prevail. It will persist so long as men are considered naturally sexually active and aggressive, but "respectable" women must preserve their chastity and honour. Prostitution is accepted socially in some areas because it is seen as a "universal and inevitable social evil, necessary to satiate an uncontainable male sexuality. Prostitution is therefore considered society's safety valve against the rape of 'innocent women' and the disintegration of the institution of the family" (D'Cunha, 1992, p. 36). Even women themselves often share this perspective. In Thailand, for example, research conducted by the Foundation for Women found that "many teachers, especially women, believed that prostitution was necessary. They felt that it protects 'good' women against rape because men have another outlet for sexual relief" (Rattanawannathip, 1991, p. 18). The premium placed on virginity and the sense of unworthiness of those who have lost their virginity to lovers or relatives (in the case of incest or rape) led many women in the Philippines to go into prostitution thinking that this is what they deserved. There have also been several instances where the traditionally-defined attributes of femininity – passivity, submissiveness, sentimentality and sexual desirability – which are often associated with Asian women are exploited commercially by the sex sector. Many of the sex tours, for instance, advertised these attributes of the women as the reason why potential clients should choose the South East Asian destinations.

In Southeast Asia, women have traditionally played a major role as family breadwinners (though not necessarily as decision-makers). In recent years, the number of female-headed households in the Association of South East Asian Nations (ASEAN) countries has expanded, and female-maintained households are often among the poorest of the poor. The surveys conducted for this study reveal that many of the women in prostitution are divorcees or single mothers. The economic role of daughters in families has also been changing, as families increasingly rely on income and remittances from their young daughters. For poor rural households in particular, remittances from daughters often represent the main or sole source of support. The obligation placed on children, even under-age ones, to contribute in any way they can to their families and the pressure they face in being responsible for family survival, may push them into prostitution.

In many Southeast Asian countries, children, especially girls, are brought up to feel a sense of duty or moral obligation to earn money to repay the care and protection given them by their parents in raising them: "having entered prostitution against their will, many children none the less felt that they had fulfilled their obligations for the care and protection given them by their parents in raising them – thus gaining merit according to Buddhist principles. Despite the risks of disease and physical abuse, girls who had been sold into prostitution returned home with honour because they had brought money, goods and security to their families" (Belsey, 1996, p. 18). Another factor which increases the demand for child prostitutes is "the preference for female virgins which exists in many cultures. In some countries, sex with virgins or pre-pubescent children is seen as a proof or enhancement of virility, in others it is believed to cure sexually transmitted diseases or to mitigate the effects of age" (ECPAT, 1995).

Policy issues and concerns

Along with these economic and social foundations controlling and maintaining the sex sector, there are important questions related to moral values and human rights, the working conditions of the prostitutes, the commercial sexual exploitation and forced labour of the child victims of prostitution and health concerns. Many of the policy issues and concerns which this study seeks to address, and which are highlighted below, would be of interest to policy makers not only in the four Southeast Asian countries but also in other countries concerned with the problems related to prostitution.

Social mores and the influence of religion

Prostitution tends to thrive in patriarchal societies where there are two systems of morality, one for men and one for women. "Patriarchal society defines a male's honour in terms of his conduct in public life and permits him the freedom to formulate his own rules in matters of sexuality. It allows him access to sexual pleasure in varied forms and with several women" (D'Cunha, 1992, p. 38). Women, on the other hand, are shaped by family, religion and school to be dutiful daughters, virginal girlfriends, devoted wives and sacrificing mothers. Based on these deeply rooted socio-cultural assumptions about the differences in the sexual nature of men and women, prostitution is widely accepted as necessary. However, prejudice against the individual prostitute is nearly universal and few words carry the same amount of contempt and loathing as "whore" and its equivalent in any language (Reanda, 1991, p. 203). Women who break away from the prevailing moral codes are condemned. Consequently, policy makers and legislators often direct their efforts at the individual women prostitutes and focus on their socially "deviant" or "morally reprehensible" behaviour and the need, on the one hand, to separate them from "respectable women" and preserve public morality, and, on the other hand, to "rehabilitate and resocialize" them.

The issue here, though, is whether a narrow perception of prostitution as a distinctive social institution emerging from the contradictions of the moral system, and of prostitutes as "deviants" from traditional codes of sexual conduct, contributes to understanding of the phenomenon or to the formulation of effective policy measures. A moralistic view of prostitution tends to ignore the fact that sanctions or other measures targeted at individual prostitutes will not be effective unless the economic and social bases of prostitution can be dismantled. These foundations endure because they are sustained by underlying social relations and individual, family, private sector and government interests. The artificial isolation of the sex sector from the rest of the economy by the moral and legal systems of the countries (either attaching a social stigma to it, making the sex sector illegal or ignoring its presence in development and social programmes) allows the underlying vested interests to flourish and to perpetuate exploitation of individual prostitutes.

The issues are also complicated by the role of religion. Thailand is strongly Buddhist, the Philippines strongly Catholic, and Indonesia and Malaysia are Muslim countries where there has been a rise in religious fundamentalism. Indonesia is, in fact, the largest Muslim country in the world. An interesting question is whether religion actually has any significant influence in reducing either the supply of or demand for prostitutes. The answer would appear to be no, although all the major religions condemn prostitution and extramarital relations. Individual prostitutes often report that they feel "conscience stricken", but neither religious beliefs nor the religious authorities appear to have prevented the spread of prostitution. It is only Islamic law, the *Shariah*, that specifically punishes extra marital sexual relations and illicit sexual intercourse, including prostitution, and this prohibition is reflected in all legislation applying to Muslims, even when prostitution is legal under criminal law. Religious fundamentalism has tended to motivate stricter implementation of the *Shariah*, and in one state in Malaysia, the law has been revised to punish Muslims involved in prostitution with penalties heavier than those provided for in the country's criminal code. In both Malaysia and Indonesia, the act of prostitution is not illegal under criminal law.

Human rights

In addition to the view that prostitution is morally reprehensible is the concern that prostitution is a human rights violation – that there should be no distinction between "free" and "coerced", "voluntary" and "involuntary" prostitution, since any form of prostitution is a human rights violation, an affront to womanhood that cannot be considered dignified labour (Barry, 1993). Groups such as the CATW see prostitution and trafficking as violating women's human rights and as severe discrimination.

However, proponents of sex workers' rights argue that some adult sex workers make a relatively free decision to go into prostitution and that they should be at liberty to do so and have the right to the type of sexual behaviour they choose. The World Charter for Prostitutes' Rights drafted by the International Committee for Prostitutes' Rights calls for the decriminalization of "all aspects of *adult* prostitution resulting from individual decision" (Pheterson, 1989). Those advocating prostitutes' rights recognize, however, that there are differences between those who choose sex work as an expression of sexual liberation, those who choose such work due to economic pressures and those exposed to overt pressure or coercion from third parties in the form of deception, violence and/or debt bondage. They agree that some sex work contexts are akin to slavery but contend that, as a general principle, individuals should have the right to choose sex work. From the point of view of some groups, then, it is the laws against prostitution that constitute the violation of human rights, rather than prostitution itself. For instance, the World Charter for Prostitutes' Rights calls for the eradication of "laws that can be interpreted to deny freedom of association or freedom to travel to prostitutes. Prostitutes have rights to a private life." It also states that "there should be no law which implies systematic zoning of prostitution. Prostitutes should have the freedom to choose their place of work and residence. It is essential that prostitutes can provide their services under the conditions that are absolutely determined by themselves and no one else."

Early international conventions distinguished between prostitution as a personal choice and slavery-like prostitution due to coercion or traffic in persons. They banned the international traffic in persons but regarded prostitution as a human rights violation only if it involved overt coercion or exploitation. Successive international instruments which embodied this approach, such as the United Nations International Convention for the Suppression of the White Slave Traffic, 1910, and the International Convention for the Suppression of the Traffic of Women and Children, 1921, were increasingly criticized for failing to acknowledge and confront the less visible forms of coercion – economic, cultural, social or psychological – which have pushed women into prostitution. Therefore, there have since been moves for the international community to address all forms of prostitution as a human rights violation. The 1949 Convention for the Suppression of the Traffic in Persons and of the Exploitation of the Prostitution of Others declared, for the first time in an international instrument, prostitution and the traffic in persons to be "incompatible with the dignity and worth of the human person and [to] endanger the welfare of the individual, family and the community" and made no distinction between forced and voluntary prostitution. The Convention views a prostitute as a victim; it does not recognize the right of an individual to choose to work as a prostitute.

Other more recent international instruments also emphasize the human rights dimension. The 1979 Convention on the Elimination of All Forms of Discrimination Against Women directs States Parties to "take all appropriate measures, including legislation, to suppress all forms of traffic in women and exploitation of prostitution of women". The 1989 Convention on the Rights of the Child has several provisions against the commercial sexual exploitation of children. The Platform for Action adopted by the Fourth World Conference on Women in 1995 calls specifically for action to "strengthen the implementation of all relevant human rights instruments in order to combat and eliminate, including through international cooperation, organized and other forms of trafficking in women and children, including trafficking for the purposes of sexual exploitation, pornography, prostitution and sex tourism" (United Nations, 1996, paragraph 230).

Some aspects of the prostitution problem, in particular sex tourism and child prostitution, have become the subject of international concern and action. In the case of children, major international conventions emphasize that "the commercial sexual exploitation of children constitutes a form of coercion and violence against children and amounts to forced labour and a contemporary form of slavery" (World Congress against the Commercial Sexual Exploitation of Children, 1996). The most significant international legal instrument which protects children from commercial sexual exploitation is the 1989 United Nations Convention on the Rights of the Child, which Indonesia, Malaysia, the Philippines and Thailand have all ratified. The United Nations Commission on Human Rights has appointed a Special Rapporteur on the Sale of Children, Child Prostitution and Child Pornography and is considering introducing a Draft Optional Protocol to the Convention on the Rights of the Child, on the Sale of Children, Child Prostitution and Child Pornography. A coalition to End Child Prostitution in Asian Tourism (ECPAT) was established in 1991 in Bangkok and now has more than 250 groups in over 25 countries worldwide, campaigning for action by governments and the international community. The International Labour Organization's International Programme for the Elimination of Child Labour (ILO/IPEC) has launched a global effort against the commercial sexual exploitation of children as an intolerable form of child labour. A World Congress was held in August 1996 in Stockholm to develop a global agenda for action against the commercial sexual exploitation of children. International round-table conferences, held throughout 1997 and early 1998 in Amsterdam, Cartagena (Colombia), Oslo and Kampala brought together high-level government officials, including ministers from many countries, and child labour experts from around the world to identify strategies to eliminate the most intolerable forms of child labour, including the use of children for prostitution and pornography.

Working conditions

One obvious policy concern is the working conditions of commercial sex workers. Anti-prostitution groups base their campaigns partly on the poor working conditions of prostitutes. Other groups argue that, rather than banning prostitution because of poor working conditions, efforts should focus on measures to improve their working conditions. The sex workers' rights movement insists that for those women who have freely chosen this line of work, there should be measures to improve their working conditions and social security benefits. Groups such as Anti-Slavery International and the Network of Sex Works Projects (an international network of organizations that provide legal, social, health and other services to sex workers) have been proposing that prostitution should be considered as work, so that attention can be devoted to ensuring that they are covered by the labour code. They suggest that prostitutes should be treated like other vulnerable workers and express concern that "the designation of prostitution as a special human rights issue emphasizes the distinction between prostitution and other forms of female or low-status labour, however exploitative, and thus reinforces the marginal position of the people involved in prostitution" (Bindman, 1997).

Again, the issues are complicated, partly because the working conditions would depend very much on whether the women are "self-employed", "employed", "enslaved" or "exported", and also on whether their working conditions are evaluated on the basis of moral, social or economic standards. The surveys for this study reveal that the independent streetwalkers or high-income call-girls may set their own terms, choose their hours of work and select their clients. Those employed in sex establishments or other entertainment establishments have specified terms and conditions of work. From an economic perspective, these could be considered reasonably good since the surveys revealed that take-home income tends to be higher than what the women could expect to earn in other occupations open to them. Some establishments even provide accommodation, food, medical services and holidays. Even though prostitutes work long hours, much of the time is spent waiting for customers. Most of the commercial sex workers get to keep only a portion of their earnings, but many tend to view deductions, such as payments to pimps or other intermediaries, as the costs involved in their jobs rather than as real "exploitation".

However, the higher incomes some sex workers earn are supposed to include a premium to make up for the stigma, health risks and other unpleasant aspects of the occupation. A significant proportion of the sex workers claimed that they wanted to leave the occupation if they could. In the experience of most of the women surveyed, prostitution is one of the most alienated forms of labour. Most of the prostitutes interviewed in the Philippines carried out their job "with a heavy heart," "felt forced" or "were conscience-stricken". Far from exercising sexual freedom, the majority of the women have negative self-identities. While some of the freelancers, especially those in the upper income class, may claim to have choice or control over their working conditions, many have no say over the choice of clients, the pace of work, price fixing or forms of sexual activity. Those working in brothels in particular often even have their freedom of physical movement limited. Especially among younger women and children, there is exploitation involved where payments for sexual services are made directly to parents or other relatives, where women and children are subject to debt bondage and have to work off debts for loans given to their families at exorbitant interest rates, or where bribes are paid to corrupt officers.

The important question is whether prostitutes are recognized as workers with rights under standard labour legislation. Where the sex sector is not illegal and prostitution is recognized as a valid occupation, the concern should be to ensure that prostitutes, like other legitimate workers, are entitled to proper working conditions, protection from exploitation and discrimination, and social welfare benefits. Where prostitution is illegal, waitresses, massage parlour attendants, hairdressers and "hospitality women" would be legitimate workers only insofar as they did not sell sexual services, but once such workers crossed the line they would no longer have certain rights, and would be criminals under the law.

Irrespective of the legality of the sex sector, there are some workers who need special protection. For example, those who are illegally recruited or sold to brothels, especially children, tend to be virtual prisoners and slaves subject to abysmal working and living conditions. Child prostitution has been classified by the International Labour Office (1996) as an intolerable form of child labour. Descriptions of conditions in some brothels also clearly depict a form of slavery: "in the brothels, the owners use a combination of threats, force, debt bondage and physical confinement to control the women and girls, force them to work in deplorable abusive conditions, and eliminate any possibility of negotiation or escape" (Asia Watch and the Women's Rights Project, 1993, p. 53). Also, those who are exported as "entertainers" are highly vulnerable to exploitation and abuse; doubly so if they are illegal migrants and if prostitution is illegal in the receiving country. They can expect no assistance from the authorities; instead, they are subject to official harassment, raids and deportation. There are innumerable reports of women entertainers in the clutches of crime syndicates, subject to sexual molestation, rape and battery, virtual imprisonment and even unexplained deaths.

The relative powerlessness of female and, especially, child prostitutes must be considered. These women and children are normally in highly unequal power relations. They are relatively helpless and unable to negotiate or bargain with their parents and other family members, to whom they feel obligated; their employers, who determine the conditions of their employment; their pimps and other intermediaries, who live off their earnings and on whom they rely for putting them in touch with clients and protecting them from harassment; their clients, whom they normally cannot refuse, no matter what their sexual demands; or corrupt police and government officials, to whom they have to pay bribes or offer sexual favours. The nature of their work and their isolation from the rest of "normal" society mean they have little or no recourse to support structures or to the law to redress the unequal power relations.

Demographic dimensions

Prostitution is closely related to both internal and international migration. Prostitutes generally do not engage in the trade in their own home towns or villages. They tend to be procured from rural areas or small towns for the cities or, as young, first-time job-seekers new to urban areas, are vulnerable to being drawn into the sex sector. The expansion of prostitution has been linked to the increasing feminization of migration from rural to urban areas in these countries. For young female school leavers, moving away from home and earning an income for the first time is often accompanied by increased expectations of a more materialistic lifestyle and the opportunities to participate in the nightlife available in an urban setting. But the costs of living such a lifestyle have gone up tremendously and, in the struggle to cope, young women may be tempted to find work in the sex sector, where earnings are generally higher. The need to meet family expectations and to juggle remittances sent home and personal expenses may also draw women into the sector. The reverse flow of remittances from the migrant women and children makes it possible for many poor families in rural areas to survive. As a means of income redistribution and as a survival mechanism for coping with poverty in rural areas, such migration for employment is obviously important.

Another demographic aspect is the international migration of women to work overseas as "entertainers" and "hostesses". These women give up home and families to "earn well, save and give their family a bright future" (Levinson, 1994), but they are highly vulnerable to various forms of exploitation and, because many enter the host country illegally and because prostitution may not be a legal occupation in the host country, are often outside the protection of the law.

There is alarming evidence that cross-border flows for prostitution and the international trafficking in women and children have been growing. The illicit recruitment and sale of women and children across national borders is organized not only by individual agents but also by international underground syndicates operating effective networks with official connections. A report on the trafficking of Burmese women and girls into brothels in Thailand emphasized that there are "well-established networks" and "clear official involvement in virtually every stage of the trafficking process" (Asia Watch and the Women's Rights Project, 1993, p. 47). Under international covenants and anti-trafficking laws, those sold or trafficked into a country should be considered victims exempt from fines or imprisonment and granted safe repatriation back to their countries of origin. However, these women and children are commonly dealt with under the immigration and alien laws of the receiving country, arrested and often imprisoned for long periods without charge or trial and eventually deported.

Health aspects

Control of the sex sector can be traced historically to health-related concerns. Social and legal control of prostitutes has commonly been justified as a public health measure. In Indonesia, Malaysia, the Philippines and Thailand, early attempts to regulate the sex sector were to prevent the potential threat of the spread of sexually transmitted diseases (STDs). With the HIV/AIDS "time bomb", the health concerns have moved to the forefront. Much of the current debate on the sex sector, especially on whether to legalize prostitution, centres on the health concerns.

The basis for these health concerns needs, however, to be questioned. Current laws and programmes usually cover only the prostitutes, on the assumption that they are the source of STDs or HIV/AIDS. While it is true that prostitutes often suffer from STDs and the fact is used to stigmatize them, this may actually be due to inadequate health services or because the prostitutes cannot afford private medical services. Measures are not directed at the clients, yet the chain of transmission from the commercial sex sector to the population at large involves the clients who also have unprotected sex with their spouses or others. The transmission could also be between countries, not only through tourist flows but also through the "commuter-like" flows of prostitutes and clients among the Southeast Asian countries. There are reports of young girls from Myanmar and other neighbouring countries brought into Thailand for prostitution who are sent back to their own countries to die when they are found to have contracted AIDS (Lintner and Lintner, 1996).

The AIDS epidemic appears to have indirectly resulted in a rising demand for ever-younger children because of the belief among clients that they are not likely to be infected by the disease. Yet prostitution results in serious, often life-long, even life-threatening, consequences for children's physical, psychological and social health and development. Moreover, a child who has sexual contact with someone who is HIV positive is more susceptible to infection than an adult. The World Health Organization (WHO) has drawn attention to the public health risks of child prostitution (Belsey, 1996). While there is no clear evidence, the growing involvement of children in commercial sex work could have increased the rate of transmission of HIV/AIDS – because of children's increased biological vulnerability to STDs and their lack of power in negotiating safe sexual behaviour.

Criminal aspects

The nature of the sex sector and the high potential economic gains tend to attract criminal elements, including drug pushers, small-time gangsters, corrupt officials and organized crime syndicates with national and international networks. The most serious aspects are, of course, trafficking in women and children, debt bondage and illegal confinement, forced prostitution, child prostitution and paedophilia, and sexual violence against women and children. It is in relation to these criminal elements that the unequal power relations and the vulnerability of the women and children drawn into the sector give most cause for concern. It is not clear whether criminalization of the sex sector through legislation can effectively control these elements or whether such a move would further marginalize the sector, drive it underground and lead to more rampant abusive practices and greater corruption.

Heightened concern, prompted by major international conferences and media coverage of recent sensational cases of child prostitution, trafficking and abuse, has encouraged countries to impose stronger criminal sanctions, including new or amended national legislation. Legislation has been introduced by a number of Western countries to punish nationals for crimes such as paedophilia committed outside their own countries. Some countries have also enacted specific provisions on child prostitution or on sexual exploitation and abuse which cover prostitution. The major challenge is now one of law enforcement. The national case studies in the subsequent chapters all emphasize that the criminal codes covering offences related to prostitution are often difficult to enforce, especially when some of the criminal elements are the supposed law enforcers themselves.

Legislation

The various problems and concerns raised above lead to the inevitable question of whether the sex sector should be criminalized and totally prohibited, legalized and regulated, or decriminalized. Governments use the instrument of the law as a means to deal with prostitutes and with the sex sector, and it is the legal framework that determines the status of the sex sector and the rights and protection of workers within the sector. The predominant approach to combating child prostitution is to rely on the repressive and deterrent effect of criminal law (ILO, 1996, p. 66).

Legal systems can be analysed in terms of whether they prohibit, regulate or decriminalize prostitution; these systems can be evaluated in terms of their relative effectiveness in dealing with the various problems associated with the sex sector.

The "prohibitionist" or "abolitionist" system views prostitution as immoral, and aims at its eradication by banning the sector and criminalizing the activities of all those involved, i.e. the sex workers, the people procuring for or profiteering from prostitution, and the clients. There is recognition, however, that banning the sector may merely serve to push it underground and further marginalize those most in need of protection from exploitation and abuse. Criminalization may also create opportunities for systematic corruption by public officials, who may use the criminal status of the prostitutes to violate their human rights. Those against criminalization also point out that it would tend to discourage the prostitutes from openly seeking safer sex education and health services, and may enable clients to act irresponsibly with regard to STDs or HIV/AIDS transmission.

The "regulationist" or legislated system provides for the registration and licensing of the sex sector so as to confine prostitutes to brothels in red light districts in order to ensure official control of public order and public health. This system tolerates the existence of prostitution. The act of prostitution is itself not illegal and the prostitutes are not criminalized by virtue of their work. Especially in the face of the HIV/AIDS threat, some groups have called for the provision of legal status to prostitution, through appropriate legislation and regulations covering the sex establishments and registration of prostitutes. They put forward several arguments. First, legislation would recognize an existing social situation and provide a legal framework which allows for regulation of the sector, including directing legal sanctions at profiteering and trafficking rather than at the prostitutes themselves. Secondly, a system of registration of commercial sex establishments and of their workers could help to ensure that all prostitutes undergo regular health checks. If guests were also registered, there would be a way to trace contacts in the event that the prostitute is found to be infected with STDs or HIV. Thirdly, registration may enable better control of the criminal aspects of the sector, including ensuring that a minimum age of prostitutes can be prescribed and that child prostitution and prostitution through coercion can be more effectively controlled. Fourthly, recognition of prostitution as a valid occupation could help protect prostitutes from various forms of exploitation. A legalized system offers a framework for the protection of their rights as workers, including their working conditions. Prostitutes could then come under the country's labour code and be entitled, like other categories of workers, to at least minimum provisions for proper working conditions. Fifthly, legalization would bring prostitution within the taxable sector of the economy. When the commercial sex sector is illegal or underground, much of the income from the lucrative direct and indirect activities is not taxed.

Other groups, however, reject the legalization of adult prostitution on several grounds. They argue that compulsory registration and health checks or segregation in specially designated red light districts discriminates against and stigmatizes the prostitutes. Registration or regulation may not bring everyone in the sex sector under the purview of the law. So long as not all workers are registered, the aim of legalization to prevent the spread of diseases would be defeated. There would be no effective way to regulate health measures or protect unregistered workers, who would be the most vulnerable to exploitation. The belief that compulsory health checks for prostitutes will control the spread of AIDS is fallacious; there are many others in society at risk from the disease. Some women's non-governmental organizations (NGOs) and human rights groups also argue that legal recognition of prostitution violates the human rights of prostitutes by giving official and societal legitimacy to the commoditization of women's bodies and sexuality for sale and profit by the sex industry. In addition, legalization may lead to an increase in both the supply and demand sides of the commercial sex sector, from those who previously refrained because of the illegality of the activity.

More recently, there have been growing calls, particularly from some feminist, civil liberty and prostitutes' rights groups, for the decriminalization of prostitutes. Decriminalization of prostitutes is based on the fundamental idea that prostitutes should not be treated as criminals; instead, their human rights and dignity should be respected, their proper working conditions should be ensured and they should be protected against becoming victims of coercive and exploitative institutions. Those advocating decriminalization stress several important points. First, a clear distinction "between the individual prostitute and decriminalizing her and the institution of prostitution and its decriminalization [should] be made, for while the former is necessary, the latter is unacceptable" (D'Cunha, 1992, p. 43). The distinction is important because decriminalization of the institution of prostitution would mean acceptance or endorsement of the economic and social bases which are rooted in and thrive on the exploitation and abuse of women and which perpetuate the myth that men are naturally promiscuous and have uncontrollable sexual needs that must be satisfied. Decriminalization does not mean that the exploitative vested interests would disappear. Nor will decriminalization necessarily change deeply internalized sexist assumptions about male and female sexual morality. Secondly, decriminalization does not imply doing away with all criminal sanctions against prostitution. While there should be legal reforms to repeal legislation or regulations that allow commercial sex workers to be victimized or that penalize or discriminate against them, criminal sanctions should be tightened and enforced against those trafficking in, exploiting or abusing prostitutes. There also should be penal provisions against corrupt enforcement authorities and against clients of under-age prostitutes. Thirdly, decriminalization as a legal approach to the sex sector can be effective only if supported by a range of other policies and programmes (discussed below).

A major concern is that prostitution laws are discriminatorily enforced against women. Various studies have pointed out that the women prostitutes tend to be overwhelmingly penalized, while the men who derive profit (the organizers of the sex sector) or pleasure (the clients) are often free from penalty. The much larger number of prostitutes arrested and convicted as compared to prostitution racketeers and clients has been interpreted as gender bias against women and class-based discriminatory enforcement against workers and victims. There have also been many reported cases of the police or other enforcement officers overstepping the boundaries of the law, for example, through the practice of entrapment in the course of arresting prostitutes, verbal and physical abuse and the demand for sexual favours.

In the case of children, the legal stance is more clear-cut: the sale and trafficking in children, child prostitution, the sexual exploitation of children, paedophilia and child pornography are all violent crimes against children and are treated as such in both international and national law. Child prostitution is defined as the "act of obtaining, procuring or offering the services of a child or inducing a child to perform sexual acts for any form of compensation or reward" (United Nations Economic and Social Council, 1996, p. 27). The stress of this definition is that child prostitution is not "committed" by the child but by the person engaging or offering the services of a child. The more appropriate terminology is therefore "child victims of prostitution". The definition of a child used here is that of Article 1 of the United Nations Convention on the Rights of the Child: every human being below the age of 18 years unless, under the law applicable to the child, majority is attained earlier. The Convention on the Rights of the Child has achieved almost universal ratification and no State Party has notified a reservation on article 34, the main provision concerned.

However, national laws concerning child prostitution differ significantly with regard to the age limit. The aspects that are criminalized also vary. Normally, one aspect is based on the exploitation of the helplessness of the child to force her or him to engage in sexual activities with or without economic benefit; another aspect relates to the economic benefit derived from the sexual activities of the child. National laws can differ with regard to those who are subject to criminal sanction. More countries are holding parents, guardians or caretakers criminally liable for causing or allowing a child to engage in prostitution. The applicability of criminal law to crimes committed in another country (to deal with the international implications of the sexual exploitation of children) is another point where national laws differ.

Child prostitution as an intolerable form of child labour is also being addressed through various ILO Conventions and Recommendations. The most important standards include the Minimum Age Convention, 1973 (No. 138), the Forced Labour Convention, 1930 (No. 29), and the Abolition of Forced Labour Convention, 1957 (No.105). In 1998, the International Labour Conference will consider a new ILO instrument specifically aimed at preventing and stopping the most intolerable aspects of child labour, namely the employment of children in slave-like and bonded conditions and in dangerous and hazardous work, the exploitation of very young children and the commercial sexual exploitation of children. The consideration of a new Convention is not intended to imply that the existing child labour Conventions would be weakened. Rather, the aim is to complement them but to focus on the most extreme forms of child labour and thereby set the priorities for action at the national and international levels.

Social programmes

While legislation controls and regulates the operation of the sex sector and the protection of commercial sex workers, law enforcement is the major challenge, and any type of legal approach can be effective only if supported by a range of other policies and programmes. These normally deal with health, resocialization and reintegration, legal aid, counselling and crisis intervention, training and assistance for alternative livelihood, education, information and advocacy. These programmes, which are implemented by government and non-governmental organizations at national and international levels, can be distinguished in terms of whether they aim essentially at recovery, reintegration or rehabilitation (for those who are already in the sector, or are victims of trafficking or commercial sexual exploitation), prevention (for those who are in danger or at risk of being drawn into the sector) or development (to improve access of women and children to education, skills training and alternative employment opportunities). They can also be distinguished in terms of whether they address the root causes or merely the mani-festations of prostitution. For efforts to be successful, a combination of these different types of programmes is necessary. Prevention is the key, especially where there are large numbers of women and children at risk of being drawn into the sex sector, because the effects of commercial sexual exploitation tend to last the entire lifetime of a victim. However, the current situation of abused and exploited children and women demands programmes to address their needs, and cannot wait for social and economic change.

The governments in Indonesia, Malaysia, the Philippines and Thailand exercise control over the health of prostitutes through legal regulations, but they also provide health and medical services. The health programmes broadly consist of the provision of information and advice on health risks and preventive measures, health checks and treatment for commercial sex workers, monitoring of their health status and the control and treatment of STDs and HIV/AIDS. The national case studies show, however, that the countries differ greatly in terms of the enforcement of health regu-lations and the types and coverage of the health services provided for prostitutes.

Based on the perception that prostitution is forced or deviant behaviour, the major programmes that are directly targeted at the sex sector focus on the recovery and reintegration of prostitutes into society. They aim to help prostitutes acquire skills, attitudes and values that will encourage them to leave the sex sector and enable them to be reintegrated into the mainstream of society. Programmes nor-mally cover social, psychological, religious, moral and vocational education and training, health education, employment skills and job search techniques. They are normally offered on both a voluntary (for adults who wish to leave the occupation) and mandatory (for minors who are picked up in police raids) basis. The residential or institutional programmes involve stays in rehabilitation centres for fixed periods of time, while the non-residential programmes are offered at the community level. Studies in Thailand and Malaysia show that many commercial sex workers view the "recovery and reintegration" programmes with apprehension because of the fear of being institutionalized for a length of time and the stigma attached to institutionalization.

Assessments of these programmes should focus especially on: (a) the coverage in relation to the number who need assistance or who are in high risk groups; (b) whether they address the root causes or merely the manifestations of prostitution;

(c) who is targeted by the programmes – the prostitutes, their families, law enforcers, government officials and authority figures or the community at large; (d) the impact in terms of actually encouraging or enabling the women and children to take up alternative employment; (e) the advantages and disadvantages of community-based versus institution/centre-based programmes and also of residential versus non-residential programmes; (f) whether the programmes have effective monitoring, follow-up and aftercare measures; and (g) the role of government agencies, NGOs, the private sector and the media in these programmes.

Education, awareness-raising and advocacy programmes are important preventive measures. They can specifically target poor and rural communities and families which send women and children into the sex sector, to inform them of the dangers of commercial sexual exploitation. They can address the commercial sex workers themselves, to inform them of their legal rights, the health and social dangers of their work and the support structures available to them. Basic literacy education can help give commercial sex workers more options, especially if they want to leave the occupation. It can also help them to have easier access to information they need to work in a safer manner. Assertiveness training can help empower sex workers, raise their self-esteem and strengthen their ability to avoid risk behaviour patterns. Awareness-raising programmes can target law enforcers and other government officials, so that they are better informed of the problems of prostitutes, more sensitive to those at risk, and better able to implement legal and other measures effectively. The programmes can also aim to raise awareness at the community or societal level of the economic and social bases of prostitution, including drawing attention to the vested interests involved and the unequal relations between the sexes and between generations. Advocacy efforts, especially when supported by high-profile media publicity at both national and international levels, can be effective in harnessing commitment from governments and the private sector and in galvanizing action to deal with the problems related to prostitution.

In dealing with the child victims of prostitution or children vulnerable to being drawn into the sector, the main aims of social programmes have been to: (a) prevent children from being lured, coerced or trafficked into prostitution; (b) withdraw child victims from commercial sexual exploitation and facilitate their rehabilitation, repatriation and reintegration into society; (c) create public awareness and mobilize public support against all forms of commercial sexual exploitation of children; and (d) create a climate – through education, social mobilization and development activities – that will ensure that parents and others legally responsible for children are able to fulfil their rights, duties and responsibilities to protect children.

In Thailand and the Philippines, where the problem of the child victims of prostitution has been recognized to be serious, concerted strategies and national programmes have been drawn up. Various reviews and programme evaluations suggest that programmes are more likely to be effective when they adopt a multi-pronged approach and target not only children but also their families and communities. Community participation is critical, including through programmes to watch out for children at risk and through the use of para-professionals (teachers, religious leaders, village leaders) who have first-hand knowledge of the community and who are trusted by its members. While programmes aim to work simultaneously with the family and the child at risk or the child victim, it has to be recognized that sometimes families are the cause of the problem and that measures including fostering and adoption may be needed.

There is also an increasing number of programmes at the international level to combat the commercial sexual exploitation of children. In 1992, the United Nations Commission on Human Rights adopted a Programme of Action for the Prevention on the Sale of Children, Child Prostitution and Child Pornography. The Programme's multidisciplinary approach calls for improved law enforcement and cooperation between key organizations. It includes measures for raising consciousness and concern; improving information gathering and monitoring; offering alternative educational programmes for children at risk; assisting in the rehabilitation and reintegration of child victims and their families; improving economic conditions; and imposing punishments on procurers, intermediaries and clients. A Special Rapporteur is appointed to examine the issues and situation worldwide and to provide regular updates to the Commission on Human Rights. Among the United Nations agencies, the ILO plays a key role. Its IPEC has identified commercial sexual exploitation as an intolerable form of forced and hazardous child labour and has initiated a number of activities for its elimination.

NGOs such as ECPAT have developed national and international networks and conducted media campaigns to end child prostitution. The International Catholic Child Bureau (ICCB) has also been active in the fight against child prostitution. Organizations in the tourist industry have taken up action to combat child sex tourism. For instance, the World Tourism Organization passed a resolution on the prevention of organized sex tourism which denounces child sex tourism as a violation of Article 34 of the Convention on the Rights of the Child. The International Union of Food, Agricultural, Hotel, Restaurant, Catering, Tobacco and Allied Workers' Associations also adopted a Resolution on Child Prostitution urging the tourist industry to ensure that it does not facilitate prostitution. Airline companies are also distributing brochures exhorting passengers to protect rather than exploit children in the countries they are visiting. The various non-governmental and private sector initiatives tend to be most effective in contexts of broad political and social support as well as public awareness and concern about the issue of child prostitution.

Organization of the study

This study is largely based on the results of a research project designed by the ILO. It was funded by the Canada-ASEAN Women's Initiative Fund under the ASEAN Regional CIDA Programme and implemented in coordination with the Institute for Population and Social Research of Mahidol University, Thailand. The research, based on a detailed outline and field questionnaire provided by the ILO, was conducted by national consultants in Indonesia, Malaysia, the Philippines and Thailand in 1992/93. The research included small surveys of specific sub-sectors of the sex industry in each country. The surveys comprised standard questionnaires administered to women working in these sub-sectors and unstructured interviews conducted with key informants, including owners or managers of the sex establishments, police, and other government and non-government officials with links to the sector. Interviews were conducted mainly by academics and university students in the different countries; it was only in Malaysia that some of the interviewers were social workers from the Department of Social Welfare. Parts of the national studies have been published for local dissemination and discussion. The findings were also discussed at a regional workshop with policy makers and representatives of non-governmental organizations at the end of 1994. The four country studies have been substantially edited and revised, based on the discussions from the regional workshop and recent and updated information, to provide a comparative overview and to draw policy and programme lessons.

Chapters 2 to 5 present the country studies of prostitution in Indonesia, Malaysia, the Philippines and Thailand. They trace the history and evolution of the commercial sex sector and identify the economic and socio-cultural factors behind the growth of the sector. Each country case study also provides an estimate of the size and significance of the sex sector and a description of the organizational structures of the sector. The descriptions illustrate the wide range and diversity of arrangements, the differences in terms and conditions of service of commercial sex workers, the large number of vested interests involved and the close links between the sector and the rest of the national and international economy. To show how the economic and social bases of prostitution actually operate at the level of the individual prostitutes, the studies also present the results of small surveys conducted among the prostitutes and informants in specific sub-sectors in each country. The country studies also describe the main laws and regulations governing the commercial sex sector and discuss the problems of enforcement. National legislation covering the sector includes criminal law, immigration law, local regulations concerning zoning or soliciting and loitering in the street, ordinances and by-laws for the registration of entertainment establishments and for health control, labour regulations and, in the case of Malaysia and Indonesia, Islamic law, or the *Shariah*. The country studies also describe and assess the effectiveness of the main types of programmes carried out by government and non-governmental organizations and the private sector in dealing with health, recovery and reintegration, legal aid, counselling and crisis intervention, training and assistance for alternative livelihood, education, information and advocacy for those in the commercial sex sector.

Chapter 6 addresses the special problem of the child victims of prostitution. Although not originally part of the research project, it was decided to include the discussion to underscore the importance of the topic. Two perspectives are adopted. On the one hand, child prostitution is described as part of the overall commercial sex sector to draw attention to the fact that, as with adult prostitution, there are strong economic and social bases and vested interests involved. On the other hand, the chapter emphasizes the differences and complexities of the problem of child prostitution as compared to adult prostitution, with the aim of showing why it is necessary to have tougher legislation and additional strategies for dealing with the child victims of prostitution. A section deals specifically with legislation and national and international policies and programmes to end child prostitution.

Given the magnitude and significance of the sex sector and the urgency of many of the related issues, such as the child victims of prostitution and HIV/AIDS, the concluding chapter emphasizes that prostitution cannot be ignored or neglected by policy makers and legislators. Since the sex sector is not likely to decline substantially while the economic and social foundations remain strong, Chapter 7 urges that policy makers and legislators adopt clear and sustainable official positions for dealing with prostitution. It reviews the main issues and concerns that ought to be taken into account in deciding whether to prohibit, legalize and regulate, or decriminalize prostitution, and in deciding on the related question of whether the labour code and social security provisions should be extended to prostitutes as workers. The chapter suggests that it will be easier for policy makers to adopt an official stance if child prostitution and adult prostitution are treated separately. To address both the root causes and consequences of adult and child prostitution, the chapter recommends a multi-pronged approach encompassing a clear legal stance and effective law enforcement, improvements in development planning so that the indirect effects of macroeconomic policies can be taken into account, ameliorative, alleviative and preventive social programmes, and the involvement of all social partners at community, national and international levels.

PROSTITUTION IN INDONESIA 2

Gavin W. Jones, Endang Sulistyaningsih and Terence H. Hull

Historical and social factors behind the development of the sex sector

The commoditization of women in Indonesian history

The origins of modern prostitution in Indonesia can be traced back to the time of the Javanese kingdoms, in which the commoditization of women was an integral part of the feudal system. Although the feudal system did not contain the fully commercialized sex industry which we associate with modern industrial societies, it did provide the foundations for the industry through valuing women as commodities to be exchanged and accumulated in the constant male quest for power and wealth.

When the Javanese-Islamic kingdom of Mataram, located in the southern hinterland of central Java, was divided in 1755, two of the most powerful and lasting Javanese kingdoms were formed. In this period, the kings were considered all-powerful. They owned everything, not only land and property but also the lives of their subjects and in the case of women, this was an attribution which was often taken quite literally. A measure of the king's power was the number of concubines *(selirs)* in the court. Some of the *selirs* were daughters of noblemen given to the king as a token of their loyalty; others were tributes from other kingdoms; and many were lower-class women sold or given over by their families to take minor positions in the royal household. Each of the Javanese courts drew *selirs* from particular regions, which came to be noted for producing beautiful and alluring women. The areas in Java which have communities famous in history as sources of women for the courts are even today noted as sources of urban prostitutes (Koentjoro, 1989, p. 3). Women's status in the Kingdom of Mataram was reflected in their role as the currency of the *upeti* (tribute paid by subjects) and as *selirs* reflecting the power of the king. Although male commoners were permitted by the Muslim religion to take up to four wives, financial constraints prevented most of them from polygamy while their social status prevented them from taking *selirs*.

The treatment of women as commodities was not limited to Java. It was common in other parts of Indonesia and in other Asian countries, where slavery, systems of indenture and lifelong servitude were common feudal forms. In the Indonesian island of Bali, for example, a low-caste widow without strong family supports automatically became the property of the king. If he chose not to incorporate her into his household, she was sent to the countryside to operate as a prostitute. A share of her income was to be regularly returned to the king (*Encyclopaedie van Nederlandsch-Indie,* 1902, p. 342).

* * *

During the Dutch colonial period, the more organized forms of the sex industry greatly expanded. Traditional systems of slavery and concubinage were adapted to the needs and mores of the European communities which were being established in the port areas of Indonesia. The sexual gratification of soldiers, traders and emissaries became one of the key issues in the clash of alien cultures. From the outset, this issue posed many dilemmas for the Indonesians and Europeans alike. On the one hand, the large number of single men brought to Indonesia by the colonial governments and business interests produced a demand for domestic and sexual services, which was readily satisfied by local families with saleable daughters and by women seeking material gains from the foreigners. On the other hand, both the native and colonial communities perceived the dangers of unregulated interracial liaisons. Formal marriage was discouraged or forbidden, and interracial concubinage was frowned upon but tacitly accepted as a necessity. In this context, unstable and inequitable cohabitation and outright commercial relationships were options available to the European men, and they were tolerated by their leaders. This situation put Indonesian women in an invidious situation and subjected them to many disadvantages with regard to the law, community disapprobation, and personal welfare and security.

During the 1600s, the government passed laws forbidding Christian families from employing native women as housekeepers and "forbidding a person from inviting a virtuous woman into fornication", but avoided the question of which women were to be regarded as "virtuous". In 1650, a "house of correction for women" was established to reform prostitutes and protect public order. One hundred and sixteen years later, a regulation in 1766 forbidding prostitutes from entering the wharves "without permission" testified to the failure of the earlier attempts at correction and to the toleration of commercial sex that was prevailing at the time (*Encyclopaedie van Nederlandsch Oost-Indie*, 1919, pp. 511-515).

In 1852, the colonial government introduced a new law which acknowledged the commercial sex industry but which stipulated a series of regulations "to avoid harmful consequences resulting from prostitution". The legal framework that was established at that time remains basically intact to the present day. Today's *"wanita tuna susila"* (women lacking morals) were referred to in the 1852 Act as "public women" who were to be "under the direct and strict supervision of the police". All registered "public women" were required to carry a card and to undergo weekly medical examinations to detect syphilis and other contagious diseases. If they were found to have a disease, they were required to cease their sexual activities immediately and be isolated in an institution. To aid the police in the management of the sex industry, prostitutes were encouraged to operate in brothels. In 1858, another government regulation clarified that the 1852 Act was not to be interpreted as having legitimized brothels as commercial institutions. Rather, they were identified as places where medical consultation could take place "to limit the harmful effects" of prostitution.

Two decades later, the responsibility for supervising brothels was shifted from the central to the regional governments. The 1852 central government regulations were effectively repealed and replaced by local regulations. The regional authorities were most concerned about venereal disease, but the shortage of physicians and the inefficacy of treatment options made it virtually impossible to prevent the spread of disease (*Encyclopaedie van Nederlandsch Oost-Indie*, 1919). Each Residency was required to establish its own detailed regulations to control prostitution. For example, in Surabaya, the Resident established three brothel *kampungs* (hamlets or villages) in an effort to keep venereal disease under control, and prostitutes were not permitted to operate outside these brothel *kampungs*. All prostitutes in these *kampungs* were registered and medical checks were carried out (Ingleson, 1986, pp. 127–128).

According to most accounts, despite these regulations, the extent of prostitution increased dramatically in the nineteenth century, especially after the amendment of the Agrarian Laws in 1870 opened the colonial economy to private capital (Ingleson, 1986). The expansion of plantations, especially in West Java and Sumatra, the growth of the sugar industry in East and Central Java and the building of roads and railways involved considerable migration of male labourers, some of them itinerant. This created a demand for the services of prostitutes. During the construction of the railway linking the major Javanese cities, prostitution flourished to serve the construction workers. Also, at each major town served by the railroads, the arrival of passengers increased the demand for board and lodgings as well as for sexual services. Brothel complexes sprang up close to the railway stations in every city and near the harbour areas as well. Most of these prostitution complexes operate today.

The history of the sex industry in Surabaya is unique. As the second city of Indonesia, and the main focus of trade routes in Eastern Indonesia, Surabaya developed during colonial times as a major port city, naval base, garrison and railway terminus (Kunto, 1993; Dick, 1993). It was notorious around the region in the nineteenth century for extensive prostitution:

Freighters and naval ships entering the outer harbour were quickly surrounded by a flotilla of *prahu* (boats) filled with local prostitutes touting for customers. Until the mid-nineteenth century, prostitutes were allowed on board naval vessels, in the belief that it was better to keep sailors under some sort of supervision than to let them loose on the town. (Ingleson, 1986, p. 126.)

An official history of Surabaya stated that, in 1864, there were 228 prostitutes under the control of 18 brothel owners, but this was undoubtedly an underestimate, reflecting only officially registered sex workers. Prostitution in Surabaya was divided into eight categories: prostitutes based in small cafes near the harbour and in the old port town; street prostitutes from local villages; brothels in the centre of the city owned by the Chinese and Japanese; brothel *kampungs* on the outskirts of the city; discreet services of native female servants; even more discreet services of housebound Dutch women for young, unmarried Dutch men; European prostitution in organized brothels; and homosexual prostitution and pederasty.

The social composition of colonial towns and cities was also conducive to prostitution. There was a high proportion of single males among the civilian and military Dutch population. Half the European men were living with local concubines up till 1890, and thereafter, the decline in acceptability of concubinage appeared to lead to greater recourse to prostitutes (Ingleson, 1986, p. 124). Among the Indonesian urban workforce in the last decades of colonial rule, about 40 per cent were circular migrants, mainly male. Prostitution thrived in this setting. The plantations established in Java and Sumatra after 1870 recruited large numbers of resident labourers. These labourers – and also the Dutch supervisors and managers – in the new cash economy usually visited surrounding villages in search of sexual gratification, and in this way young village girls were drawn into prostitution.

Local government regulations could not keep pace with the rapid growth of the sex industry and the spread of venereal disease. There were three basic medical challenges: first, few of the operating prostitutes were registered, thus they were not examined; second, even if they were registered there were not enough physicians and facilities to examine the large numbers of sex workers on a weekly basis; and third, the government did not provide adequate resources nor institute rational priorities for the detection and treatment of dangerous infectious diseases (Haga, 1901).

In part collapsing under the weight of its own irrelevance, the nineteenth century model of regulation essentially ended in 1910 when routine medical examinations were terminated through a resolution of the Governor-General. The local regulations were effectively swept aside by the new "public morality laws" which were first enacted in the Netherlands in 1910 and extended to the Netherlands Indies in 1913. These new laws declared it a crime to "purposely bring about the fornication of others with a third party and make that his profession or habit". This clearly referred to pimps and procurers, but the laws provided no guidance as to how such charges could be proved or enforced. Thus, in the 1920s and 1930s, Indonesia faced the anomalous situation of having strongly worded laws at the same time as having no effective means of dealing with the rapidly growing number of brothels. For a time, the police could not investigate brothels without the permission of the local government leader (*Encyclopaedie van Nederlandsch Oost-Indie*, 1919, p. 514).

* * *

The commercialization of sex in Indonesia was further entrenched during the Japanese Occupation between 1941 and 1945. Women who were already working as prostitutes were rounded up and, after health checks, some were allocated to brothels to serve the Japanese soldiers while others continued to operate as before. Many adolescents and schoolgirls were also deceived or forced into prostitution. In addition to forcing local and Dutch women into prostitution, the Japanese brought women to Java from Singapore, Malaysia and Hong Kong to serve the officers.

Economic and social change:
The setting for the sex sector

Social change and the development of the sex industry

In the late 1940s, the population of the newly independent Indonesia was concentrated in the island of Java, with the vast majority living in rural areas. The 1950s were characterized by underemployment and poverty. Households in rural areas commonly relied on multiple sources of income. Their survival strategies, especially among the poorest groups, usually involved having members working outside the agricultural sector, at least on a part-time basis. Because of the limited employment opportunities and keen competition in rural areas, many young women from poorer households migrated to the nearest cities or towns. The social values of these migrants tended to change once they arrived in the cities. Village social values, favouring community solidarity, and in some cases dominated by religious beliefs, were often replaced by more individualistic values.

By the late 1960s and 1970s, the flow of migrants from rural areas had an increasing component of women in search of paid employment in the formal sector, especially in and around the largest cities. At the same time, many migrants participated in circular flows, spending periods in the city before returning to their permanent base in the villages. The increasing number of female migrants in the big cities led to intensified competition for employment among women workers and between women and men workers. As most female migrants were young and inexperienced, with low educational attainment and limited skills, their opportunities were restricted to low-status occupations with low remuneration. The most common activities for women migrants were in the informal sector – as traders, unpaid family workers or domestic labour; others became prostitutes.

Another factor responsible for the entry of young women into prostitution in Java in earlier times was undoubtedly the very high rates of divorce. In the 1950s, divorce rates in West Java may have been the highest in the world, with the rates in Central and East Java not much lower (Jones, 1994). Divorce tended to be at very early ages, shortly after a parent-arranged marriage to a man unacceptable to the girl. There were enough cases of divorce where the outcome left the woman in difficult financial and, perhaps, emotional circumstances, to have been an important factor in the availability of young women for prostitution. In recent times, however, divorce rates have fallen to much lower levels (well below the levels in Western countries), and therefore no longer exert the influence they once had.

Since the early 1970s, the structural transformation of the Indonesian economy has been dramatic. The primary sector's share of total employment fell from 74 per cent in 1971 to 50 per cent in 1990. There has been considerable displacement of women from agricultural activities. Many of the displaced women moved to cities where jobs have opened up in manufacturing, clerical work, sales, hotels and restaurants, and domestic service. However, wages in many of these activities are very low, and the possibility of earning five to ten times as much in the sex industry is very tempting. The relative anonymity and freedom from familial and village surveillance while in the city facilitates entry into prostitution.

The sex industry is becoming increasingly complex, consistent with the increasing mobility of the Indonesian population, faster pace of life, rising incomes and challenges to accepted mores. Mobile populations tend to have greater motivation and opportunities for commercial sex. The concentration of stalls where sex can be purchased near railway stations and roadside rest-stops for long-distance truck drivers is testimony to the demand from these sources. A survey of truck drivers on the Surabaya-Denpasar route found that 68 per cent paid for sex at rest-stops (Suarmiartha et al., 1992). Concentrations of sex workers are also found near military bases, timber and mining camps and universities.

The traditional official view of women's roles as good housewife (assisting her husband's career), socializing mother and good citizen is being increasingly challenged by the behaviour of educated youth in the large cities. Since the mid-1980s, the phenomenon of *perek (perempuan eksperimental)*, meaning "experimental or loose" girls, has received considerable media attention. The behaviour of these girls, many of whom are from middle-class backgrounds and still at school, represents a considerable challenge to social norms. It is strongly influenced by materialism and rising expectations fuelled by the media and advertising; it stresses individualism, having sexual relations with whomever they like, whether paid or unpaid, and a parodying of military-bureaucratic discourse in the organization of *perek* groups (Murray, 1993, p. 5). While the term shocked the older generation, it was quickly picked up by workers in the sex industry, especially those who sought clients in coffee houses and bars. To claim to be a *perek* is to claim youth, adventurism and a kind of obscure purity that is missing from the term "prostitute".

Economic development and prostitution

The general development strategies of the Indonesian government have influenced prostitution indirectly through their effects on both the demand for and the supply of commercially provided sexual services. These effects have operated through the impacts of economic development on, for example, levels of purchasing power, inequality of income distribution, job opportunities and the motivation and opportunities for migration. Expansion of education, which has been one of the great achievements of the Indonesian government over the past twenty years, could be expected to lead to a decrease in prostitution, but only if it is matched by appropriate job opportunities for the educated. Another significant achievement of theIndonesian government has been the reduction of the proportion of the population living in poverty. Indonesia entered the decade of the 1970s with 70 million people or 60 per cent of the population living in absolute poverty. By 1993, this had been reduced to 14 per cent of the population, or about 26 million poor people. This is clearly great progress, but 26 million people are still enough to supply vast numbers of prostitutes, if sheer poverty is the major cause of prostitution.

There is a large supply of women for the sex sector partly because the formal sectors of the economy do not pay adequate wages to employees. For example, some of the low-level workers within the textile, garment, tobacco and electronics industries, in which some 90 per cent of the workers are young females, do not earn enough money to cover their own living expenditures, much less allow them to remit funds to their families.[1] Shop assistants and market sellers also receive very low incomes. In all these occupations, low wages provide the incentive for workers to supplement inadequate incomes in other ways if the opportunity presents itself. Thus, some workers enter the sex business in the evening to earn instant money. In Surabaya, even some of the workers living in the prostitution complexes admit that they moonlight as streetwalkers to supplement their incomes as registered prostitutes.

It may be that wide income differentials, as well as poverty *per se*, make for prostitution, providing both customers from the better-off groups and potential prostitutes from the lower-income groups. Indicators such as Gini coefficients show that there has been some narrowing of both personal and regional income disparities. However, at the very top of the income range there has been a great concentration in the hands of a few large conglomerates and rent seekers with strong political connections, which could easily lead to envy and bitterness among many in the community. If it is a sense of relative deprivation rather than absolute poverty that fosters a willingness to put aside moral scruples in order to obtain a better income, then recent developments in Indonesia would not have helped reduce the incentives for women to engage in prostitution.

Another aspect which has received some public attention, but little scientific study, is the use of sexual services as part of an unwritten "rule of the game" in legitimate commercial enterprises. This may range from the overt expectation that a public relations person should be a beautiful young woman with definite sex appeal, to the covert assumption that she should be willing to satisfy the sexual desires of clients to secure or maintain a business contract. The September 1994 issue of the magazine *Popular* lifted the lid on these practices with a story entitled "Sexy Women Smooth the Way in Business", which contained a series of interviews charging that the practice was not only increasingly common but also increasingly elaborate and expensive. Although leading women in the public relations industry condemn the practice, they agree that it does occur and that it presents dilemmas for young women wishing to develop a career in the lucrative public relations industry.

It has also been suggested that prostitution increased in recent years due to economic initiatives by the government:

In the late 60s, the municipality of Jakarta, for example, legalized a brothel complex, called Kramat Tunggak, because it was short of budget for city development programmes. Jakarta politicians also legalized a number of recreation centres (massage parlours, nightclubs, steam baths, bars, a casino) on the pretext that they would boost tourism in the city. Following legalization, they implemented a new policy of taxation on these establishments. These facilities became instant revenue earners for the economically strapped city... Related to boosting tourism, ... sex tourism is one of the services being marketed by the government to attract tourists to come. A great number of new massage parlours, nightclubs, bars, striptease clubs, *karaokes*, hotels, travel agencies have been opened in major cities of Indonesia. The municipality of Jakarta has even planned, for example, to arrange a tour package which includes visits to massage parlours in Jakarta where tourists may obtain standard and "extra" services (Sabaroedin, 1991, pp. 5-6).

Will increasing prosperity as Indonesia achieves economic progress reduce prostitution? The answer to this question rests with the nature of the market for sexual services. On the supply side, in terms of the availability of a pool of young women prepared or forced by economic circumstances to engage in prostitution, the demographic consideration is an important one. Population trends in Indonesia indicate that the increase in the number of women aged 15 to 24 years will be slowing down. After increasing by 23 per cent between 1985 and 1995, the number of women entering this age group over the next 20 years is projected to grow by less than 9 per cent. Educational levels should also be going up, and job prospects should improve as the Indonesian economy continues to grow and diversify. This means, on the one hand, that the "supply" of poorly educated young women should actually decline drastically and, on the other hand, that the pressure on these women to enter prostitution as a means of escaping absolute poverty should lessen. Of course, many women will remain poor, and relatively attractive earnings in many parts of the sex sector will continue to provide a strong incentive to enter prostitution. Although there is certainly a widely recognized tendency for the uneducated or poorly educated to be over-represented among prostitutes, reasonably high levels of education do not prevent women from entering the sex sector, as the experience in more developed countries has shown. The push of absolute poverty may lessen with time, but the frustration with glaring income inequalities may not, and the pull of promises of easy affluence through commercial sex may also grow with economic prosperity.

On the demand side, growing prosperity may increase the capacity of men to buy sexual services and to be more discriminating about the setting in which these services are purchased. Therefore, within the extraordinarily diverse range of sexual service settings in Indonesia, it is likely that the balance will tend to tip towards those in less "basic" settings. However, whether the overall demand for commercial sex will increase or decrease will tend to be strongly influenced by changing social norms and government policy towards the sector. Some important questions would relate, for instance, to the attitudes towards prostitution among the rising middle class in Indonesia; the position adopted by influential women's organizations and the media towards the sex sector; whether religious movements which are strongly opposed to prostitution gain in influence; and how men react to the growing threat of HIV/AIDS. The future of the market for commercial sex in Indonesia therefore remains highly speculative, but the potential role of policy should not be underestimated. In fact, different interest groups have been demanding clearly articulated and sustainable official positions on the issue. But their calls have been contradictory, with moralists calling for closure of the prostitution complexes, and pragmatists calling for more effective regulation and reform.

The organizational structure of the sex sector

A customer seeking commercial sexual services in Indonesia can expect to find them in the following locations or from the following categories of commercial sex workers:

(a) Fixed locations where the sex transaction can be performed:
- brothel complexes *(lokalisasi)*, both official and unofficial;
- massage parlours *(panti pijat)*;
- brothel houses *(rumah bordil, lokalisasi)*, which are generally small units or single dwellings.

(b) Established locations where the initial contact can be made (but the sex act generally takes place elsewhere):
- nightclubs *(klub malam)*;
- salons *(salon kecantikan)*;
- discotheques *(disko)*;
- call-girl establishments, which are generally single dwellings with a supply of prostitutes on the premises or available to be called from nearby and sent to the client's hotel or house;
- lobbies, bars and coffee shops of certain hotels.

(c) Independent operators who can be contacted in various places:
- call-girls *(wanita panggilan)* who cater to the upper-class market;
- streetwalkers *(wanita jalanan)* who cater to the lower to middle-class market;
- *perek* (experimental girls): young women, sometimes students, who go with selected men, usually for pay in cash or kind;
- "ABGs" (precocious teenagers), high school students who selectively pick up males for sex and are often paid in gifts rather than cash.

How the sex industry functions

To understand the operations of the sex sector, it is useful to distinguish between the organized and unorganized activities (Purnomo and Siregar, 1985), although even the organized category is not rigidly structured. Organized establishments have a proprietor or manager and clearly defined work relations with the sex workers. There is frequently the use of intermediaries, such as pimps and *mamasan* or *mami* (female managers), who are paid for putting the sex worker in touch with the client. Included in the organized category are those working in brothel complexes, massage parlours, nightclubs and call-girl establishments. Prostitutes in the organized sector rely on pimps, security guards and other agents to assist them in dealing with clients and to protect them from harassment by the authorities or police.

The official prostitution or brothel complexes *(lokalisasi)* represent a unique aspect of the organizational structure of the sex sector in Indonesia. *Lokalisasi* cater to an almost entirely Indonesian clientele, who tend to be poor to middle class in their circumstances. Though set against the background of government promotion of brothels in the last century, the modern *lokalisasi* were formed in the early 1960s, as one element of promoting social discipline and control. In these complexes, which are found in several cities, a large number of brothels are clustered together along one or a few streets, and control over order and security is maintained by a group of local government, police and military authorities. The official complexes are under the auspices of the *Dinas Sosial*, the Municipal Social Affairs Office, while unofficial complexes often spring up with the tacit approval of local officials but with no formal links to the rehabilitation efforts of the social welfare officers.

In 1961, the city of Surakarta in Central Java declared the village of Silir to be exempt from the 1953 regulation forbidding prostitution. It was thought that by centralizing prostitution in one small area, the city would prevent commercial sex activities from being transacted in main streets, residential areas or in major hotel and tourist areas of the city. Moreover, by giving temporary and grudging recognition to the practice, the government was able to regulate the activities of the pimps and sex workers and to influence the behaviour of clients. The regulations for the adminis-tration of Silir, published in January 1967, provide that newly arrived prostitutes must register with the local government within one day of their arrival and must strictly follow the code of conduct covering the hours of work, health examinations, educa-tional activities and social conduct in the area. Interestingly, the government also called upon clients to "remember that sex workers are normal human beings, the same as you, but who find themselves in a weak social/ economic/moral position" (Soedjono, 1977, p. 191). The Silir complex set the pattern later followed by localized brothel areas in other cities in Indonesia, such as the Kramat Tunggak area in Jakarta which was established in 1970,[2] the Dolly-Jarak Area of Surabaya and the Sunan Kuning complex in Semarang.

In Kramat Tunggak, the intention of "rehabilitating" the sex workers out of prostitution is supposed to be achieved through compulsory education, skills training and mental and social guidance to be carried out by the Panti Rehabilitasi (a programme operated by the Directorate-General for Social Rehabilitation of the National Department for Social Affairs). To enable them to find work after leaving the complex, the women are also supposed to save money in a government bank. Each prostitute in the complex has to pay Rp.3,500 (US$1.75) a month while the brothel proprietor has to pay Rp. 2,000 (US$1) a month for each prostitute under his or her control into a fund to cover the costs of the rehabilitation programme. Those leaving the complex to return to normal life are entitled to receive a payment of Rp.250,000 (US$125) from this fund (Uwiyono et al., 1992, pp. 16, 33-34).

The regulators of the officially sanctioned brothel complexes are the MUSPIDA (*Musyawarah Pimpinan Daerah*, Regional Executive Council), consisting of regional administrators, the local prosecutor, police chief and military commander. Under the structure of localization, this group not only regulates but also participates in the management of prostitution in areas such as Kramat Tunggak and Dolly-Jarak. This is why such areas operate relatively efficiently, with little trouble in the form of brawls, drug use or robberies. The local authority also controls the use of buildings for prostitution, requiring the renewal of the permit every four years and thereby restricting the expansion of the brothel complexes. The regulations in the contem-porary brothel complexes are very specific. As described in the section on legislation below, these regulations include various stipulations for the owner and manager of the brothels, the prostitutes and also the customers.

In the unorganized activities, the prostitutes work on their own to find and contact their clients. Sex workers in this category comprise not only those for whom prostitution is their sole activity, but also those who moonlight in addition to their main occupations as shop assistants, factory workers or students. They make direct deals with the clients, and the price for their service depends normally on how well they are able to bargain. Included in this group are streetwalkers and others who operate clandestinely in public or semi-public places (such as markets, cemeteries or railway marshalling yards), call-girls and women who operate independently out of hotel coffee shops and discos. These sex workers are generally in a very weak position with regard to harassment by their clients, the authorities or the police. On the other hand, they do not have to regularly share their income with intermediaries.

Prostitutes usually group themselves together in clusters, based on their towns or villages of origin. There is limited contact between prostitutes of different clusters. Sex workers in a brothel complex tend to form different groups based on their home region. Such groups represent a very strong influence and important support to the women in the complex. During difficult times these groups look after each other, for instance, in cases of sickness, pregnancy or family crisis. A group may also act as a kind of informal union which can assist in bargaining for better working conditions.

Entry into the sex industry may follow a variety of paths, each having a particular relation with different sub-sectors. At one extreme are the women who weigh the relative returns offered by different types of work, consider the various benefits and drawbacks of selling sexual services to particular types of clients, and then decide that they prefer prostitution to other occupations. This is apparently a rare form of entry into the business. More common are the women who are compelled by circumstances, such as a failed marriage or love affair, a lack of alternative opportunities and ultimately a desperate need to earn income to support themselves, their families and their children (Nitimihardjo et al., 1994, p. 25). Prostitution can offer a relatively good living to unskilled and poorly educated or uneducated women, who represent the bulk of commercial sex workers. There are also young girls or young divorced women who are still sold into prostitution by their families. It is not possible to gauge the proportion of prostitutes who start off in this way, partly because of *post facto* justification of parental behaviour, and partly because the participants often see it as a simple "contract" and do not acknowledge the parallels with slavery or trafficking in women, both of which are clearly against the law. Yet in 1994, decades after the Netherlands Indies ratified the International Convention Against the Traffic in Women and Children, it is still possible to find cases of parents selling 14-year-old daughters into two-year indenture periods in brothels in West Java, for sums of Rp.500,000 (US$250) (based on field observations) or Rp.700,000 to 1.3 million (US$350 to US$650) (*Republika*, 18 October 1994). While there is a range of methods for entering the sector, the cases of "voluntary, deliberate" entry tend to be few, most are semi-voluntary or involuntary recruitment based on the pressure of circumstances or (more rarely) outright force or coercion.

The role of pimps and other agents

The sex sector has its own hierarchical power structure. The *germo* (brothel proprietor) plays an important role in the organized sex sector; he or she is directly responsible for providing the facilities that enable the prostitutes to operate. The *mucikari* (pimp or procurer) is a person who lives off the earnings of a prostitute and in return provides her with services such as protection and contact with customers. But there are many others whose income depends significantly on the sex trade, including taxi drivers, pedicab drivers, room cleaners and launderers in massage parlours, hotel security personnel and *calo* (procurers) who hang around hotels and other places where potential clients are likely to be found. Some pimps run a sex business located outside brothel complexes, providing a house for sex transactions, usually with a stock of prostitutes on hand.

Pimps *(germo or mucikari)* who run private brothels provide facilities and accommodation including rooms and daily meals for the prostitutes, and manage the contacts with clients. The women generally go to the clients' homes or hotel rooms to provide the services. Prostitutes in this category must sometimes accept the pimp's negotiations over price on trust alone. To market their sex workers, pimps distribute photographs and information to taxi drivers or other middlemen. The arrangement with the clients, including the price, is often conducted by phone. In most cases, the prostitutes hand over 50 per cent of the payment to the pimps. When a third-party intermediary, such as a taxi driver or tout, is involved, the prostitute will receive less, because the third party also requires a cut of the earnings, though usually less than one-third.

Germos in the official brothel complexes have the same system of sharing the revenue from sex services. But in the brothel complex, the *germos* provide rooms and other accommodation for the sex services at the complex. They set a fixed price which covers both the sex service and the room rental. *Germos* in the organized sector usually conduct regular meetings with the prostitutes to discuss ways of improving the services and attracting more customers, but these are not regarded as opportunities to discuss the prostitutes' personal interests or problems.

Taxi drivers play an important role in the marketing of sex services by providing information to clients concerning the location, rules of the game, types of services available and price of the prostitute's services. Sometimes, taxi drivers can become mediators between the prostitute and the client. They may help to make telephone calls and, especially in the case of medium- and high-price prostitutes, bring the prostitute directly to the client or bring the client to the location of the prostitute. In short, they not only provide information on the sex sector but also transportation and negotiation services to both parties. In this way, they contribute significantly to the operation and development of the sex sector. In smaller cities, this role is frequently provided by the pedicab drivers.

Regional specialization

Certain areas of Java have a long-standing reputation for supplying large numbers of women as prostitutes, and in at least some cases, the reputation is backed by provincial data and other evidence (Koentjoro, 1989, pp. 2-6). Two well-known sources of prostitutes are Indramayu in West Java (Wibowo et al., 1989; Jones et al., 1994) and Wonogiri in Central Java – which in 1981 was the source of 34 per cent of the prostitutes working in the official prostitution complex of Sunan Kuning in Semarang (Lerman, 1983, p. 262). There are undoubtedly facilitating or "push" factors behind these regional specializations, including low rural incomes, large families, early marriage and high divorce rates, low levels of education and weak adherence to orthodox Islam. But it is not clear that such facilitating factors are more marked in these areas than in many other areas of Java, and they therefore cannot fully explain the specialization.

It is more likely that some of these areas have a long history of making women available for sexual services, such as the role of Indramayu in supplying women to the court of Cirebon. In other cases, adventitious factors may have been responsible for the development of a specialization in prostitution, which then strengthened over time. Papanek (1975, pp. 15-17) explains the strong degree of regional specialization in certain ostensibly easy-entry occupations in Jakarta (including, for example, pedicab driving, scavenging, bus recruiting and kerosene selling) in terms of three related reasons: "the preference given by those already employed, or in a position to give jobs to relatives, friends and others from the same group; the information provided to newcomers by established acquaintances; and the greater ease of allocating work or territories in a group with a common background". These reasons seem to be also relevant with regard to prostitution, but another could certainly be added: the demonstration effect of sex workers returning for visits to their home area flaunting symbols of affluence to show their success in the occupation (Jones et al., 1994).

Regional case studies

To describe prostitution in contemporary Indonesian society, a number of regional case studies were selected. They illustrate the highly stratified nature of the sex industry, and the importance of historical and cultural factors and local regulations in determining the size and structure of the sex sector in each locality. The cases include Surabaya and Bandung as examples of the larger-scale settings, Indramayu as an example of a major source area of sex workers and Batam as a site of explosive growth of prostitution in a tourist and industrial economy. They should not, however, be taken as fully representative because they leave out the ubiquitous small-scale operations in small towns in Java, in mountain or beach resort areas (Sunindyo, 1993) and the roadside beer-halls catering to long-distance truck drivers, all of which are distinctive settings for the commercial sex industry. At the same time, the selected cases reflect the situation of large numbers of sex workers, and in this sense are typical of the Indonesian situation.

Surabaya: Commercial arrangements

Prostitution flourished in Surabaya, Indonesia's second largest city and the capital of East Java, in post-independence times. The Bangunrejo brothel complex, an area close to the harbour, was considered to be the largest brothel complex in Asia in the

1950s. This complex has now become a regular elite residential housing area as a result of the increasing price of land; and the brothels have moved to other areas, such as Jarak and Dolly. Many other areas in Surabaya, especially near the railway station and in the slum areas, such as Kremil, Tandes and Bangunsari, have developed pockets of prostitution catering to lower income groups.

It was difficult to estimate the total number of women in Surabaya who were exclusively engaged in providing commercial sex, partly because of the vastness and variety of the sector, but also because the women had no open organizations, unlike transvestites and homosexual male prostitutes, who had formed groups for advocacy, companionship and representation. Data kept at the *Dinas Sosial* were incomplete and often out of date; and it was also nearly impossible to quantify the size of the informal or freelance sector, which included both "full-time" and "occasional" sex workers. However, to put the size of the industry in some kind of perspective, there were probably no fewer than 10,000 women working in prostitution in the main city area of Surabaya, and if metropolitan Surabaya was included the figure would have reached 20,000[3] in 1993. By way of comparison, the estimated number of male prostitutes was 275, with another 100 or so freelance male sex workers primarily engaged in streetwalking. Many of the male prostitutes offered sexual services to both women and men. There were also about 700 transvestites in Surabaya, nearly all of whom offered commercial sex services.

The largest concentration of female sex workers was in the brothel complexes. In Surabaya, the Jarak complex had approximately 250 brothels of various sizes located in eight streets, with roughly 2,000 sex workers. Dolly had 56 brothels, each with at least 10 women. Tandes had approximately 500 sex workers; while in the ten streets of Bangunrejo there were at least 2,750 prostitutes. Altogether, it is estimated that there were 7,500 prostitutes operating in brothel complexes in Surabaya. There were also smaller numbers of nightclub workers (about 1,000), call-girls (approximately 4,500) and massage parlour workers (approximately 400). The number of female streetwalkers was, however, indeterminate.

The empirical analysis of the characteristics of prostitutes presented here is based on primary data collection from a survey of 52 women workers in the Dolly brothel complex conducted during November and December 1992 (Sulistyaningsih and Swasono, 1993). The analysis also draws on an earlier study of 48 women from the same complex nearly a decade earlier (Purnomo and Siregar, 1985). The original area of Dolly complex was a small street 150 metres long and 5 metres wide which contained a Chinese cemetery. When the area was redeveloped and residential sites were offered, one of the first persons to take up a block was Mrs. Dolly. She established her house for commercial sex activities catering mainly to lower-class men. Others followed the lead of Dolly, and now the sex sector complex reaches up to Jarak, the neighbouring street, and is named after the founder.

Like other brothel complexes in Indonesia, Dolly catered to an almost exclusively Indonesian clientele. Also as in other brothel complexes, the workers were generally young, with less than one-fifth over the age of 27 and about one in ten under 17. These figures indicate that child prostitutes (under 17 years of age)[4] are not uncommon in Dolly, despite the clear contravention of the criminal code. Moreover, when those aged 17 and over were asked at what age they entered the sex sector, 17 per cent replied that they were under 17 years. In other words, more than one-quarter of the prostitutes were under age when they began; 40 per cent were between 18 and 20 years, while just over a fifth were between 21 and 23 years.

All respondents in the survey were born outside Surabaya, with 75 per cent from rural villages in East Java. Most had been in the city for less than three years. Just over half of the women had been married. All of the "ever-married" respondents had one or two children, 70 per cent of whom were living with their grandparents. The poor and disadvantaged background of the prostitutes was evident. Most were from farming households, and their mothers were either paid domestic maids or retail traders. Most of the respondents had not graduated from the six-year primary school and only 8 per cent had gone on to complete the first three years of secondary education. They were distinctly more poorly educated than young women as a whole in the areas from which they originated. Economic factors were cited by more than 46 per cent as the main reason for not continuing their education; most of the others left school because they got married or had to help support the family or failed the examinations.

Most of the respondents in the Dolly complex visited their home village at least once a month because of illness or during their menstrual periods. The main reasons for moving to Surabaya were to find a job (39 per cent) or to join their husbands (31 per cent). One in seven of the women had been specially recruited into prostitution by their current employer or agent. The majority had worked in the sector for less than two years; in fact, 60 per cent of them had worked for one year or less. This response was quite consistent with the finding that for 69 per cent of the women, this was their first job. Immediately before entering prostitution, 15 per cent of the respondents were unemployed (with a waiting period of less than one year), another 42 per cent were in school, 29 per cent were factory production workers or domestic maids and 12 per cent were doing housework. In all cases, prostitution was their only work; none had secondary occupations. Working in the Dolly complex was a sort of training ground for the women before they moved to other brothel complexes or sub-sectors of the sex industry. Most of the massage parlour workers around Surabaya, as a matter of fact, were ex-Dolly prostitutes.

Asked why they entered the commercial sex sector, 29 per cent answered that they had no choice and were coerced into the job. Almost half the respondents gave economic reasons, such as the extreme poverty of their parents (19 per cent) and the need to support young children (17 per cent) or younger siblings (12 per cent). In the Purnomo and Siregar study (1985), economic motives were also dominant, but another 12 per cent gave psychological reasons and 21 per cent said they did not know they were being brought to a place of prostitution. In the present study, the mother, father, spouse or other family members generally did not know of the respondent's occupation. This was also the case in the Purnomo and Siregar study, where 77 per cent of parents had not been told that their daughter was working as a prostitute.

Most of the respondents for various reasons were not comfortable with their work; about 96 per cent of them reported having plans to change their current job. Half of them were trying to save money so that they could stop working in the future; some 23 per cent planned to find another job; and 13 per cent were planning to get married and stop working. These responses indicate that most of the sex workers were eager to move to another occupation as long as the alternative provided sufficient earnings. When asked about their income prospects if they left prostitution, almost four-fifths responded that they were not sure whether their income in the future would be more, the same or less than their current income. As with many questions, their responses seemed remarkably fatalistic.

In general, working conditions in the sex sector were considerably better than those enjoyed by most of the Indonesian labour force at a comparable level. Some 85 per cent of the respondents stated that their employers clearly explained the terms of their employment, including duties of the job, remuneration system, payment for sex service, working hours, location of work and other additional benefits or work facilities. About 58 per cent of them indicated that the expectation that they would have paid sexual transactions with customers was clearly stated and openly understood, but there was no target number of customers to be achieved. Another 15 per cent had expected to have sexual transactions, but this was not clearly stated by employers; rather, they had obtained an understanding of the work from friends or fellow workers. Surprisingly, 27 per cent of the respondents were not told clearly of the employers' expectations, and said that they believed they had a choice whether to accept sexual transactions. (In the Purnomo and Siregar study, 42 per cent of the prostitutes were allowed to refuse particular customers, but over half were not given a "right of refusal".) Most customers in the Dolly brothel complex were local men. In fact, at the end of 1992, the workers in Dolly had signed a written agreement not to accept sexual transactions with foreigners, supposedly to protect themselves from HIV/AIDS.

Almost half of the respondents had between 11 and 20 sexual transactions during the week before the survey, and another 12 per cent had more than 30 sexual transactions. The modal figure of 11 to 20 sexual transactions per week appeared to be consistent with the Purnomo and Siregar study, which found that the minimum number of daily transactions varied between zero and 12, but the modal frequency was between three and five transactions per day.

Normal working hours were from 6 p.m. until midnight with six working days, Wednesday being a holiday. All respondents were entitled to have time off, holidays or leave without pay, including one day off weekly, two weeks annual holiday, sick leave (requiring a doctor's note), 12 months maternity leave and seven days per month menstruation leave. These leave arrangements were quite favourable compared with those in many other sectors of the Indonesian economy.

Working facilities provided by the employer were free accommodation (one room for one or two persons), free meals three times a day, regular medical check-ups (paid for by the workers) and easy loans with low interest and assistance related to the line of work (laundry, security, etc.). The working environment, which was controlled by the police and military, appeared quite safe, with no single case of harassment reported in the Dolly complex during the month of the survey.

Obtaining reliable survey information on income and expenditure was difficult, and responses could have been misleading because of the confidential nature of the information and the inability of the respondents to provide accurate answers. Within this sector, most incomes came to the workers through the pimps or brothel managers, who were directly paid by the clients. There were two main price systems – for short-time and overnight bookings – but there were also other prices for longer-term bookings, such as for taking a prostitute on a trip outside the complex. In the Dolly brothel complex, overnight (after midnight) bookings were charged at three times the short-time rates. In most brothels, the sex worker received half of the fee paid by the client, but the payment was not always immediate. In the Purnomo and Siregar study, almost two-thirds received payment immediately after serving the customer, or later the same night; but in other cases, payment was postponed, and in 29 per cent of cases, payment was once a week or less frequent. This clearly opened up possibilities of the women being cheated by the pimp, or at the very least the pimp having use of her money for a considerable period of time. On the other hand, customers frequently paid a tip directly to the woman, and this was not shared with the pimp or brothel manager.

More than one-third of respondents did not reveal their total earnings. Of those who did, 76 per cent reported that their gross earning the previous month was more than Rp.300,000 (or about US$150), which was much higher than the official salary of middle-level government officials in Indonesia. In fact, 52 per cent of all those who reported their incomes made more than Rp.500,000 (US$250). This finding suggests that the sex industry workers were relatively well-off compared to workers outside the industry with the same level of education and social background.

Although overall earnings were high, expenditures were also quite high, an important expenditure being remittances to relatives on a weekly or monthly basis. The prostitutes also had to give about 30 per cent of their incomes to the manager, and another 30 per cent to the local government for security and for the various classes and activities included as part of their "rehabilitation". In addition, most of the respondents owed money to the person who gave them initial capital for the job, which included clothes and cosmetics, when they first entered the business. The majority (60 per cent) of the prostitutes reported having borrowed money, mostly from the *mamasan* or pimp. The main reason for borrowing money was for supporting family members or paying for medical check-ups. Twenty-three per cent of the respondents had cash savings in a local financial institution, while the remaining 77 per cent saved their money in the form of gold, jewellery, livestock, housing, land and other valuables.

Before the intrusion of the AIDS epidemic into the Dolly complex, approximately 90 per cent of the respondents had already received some kind of information about the possible health danger of the disease. The main sources were the government health officers and the mass media, including television, radio and newspaper. Health information covered HIV/AIDS (44 per cent), prophylactics (44 per cent), sexually transmitted diseases (33 per cent), methods of family planning (27 per cent) and abortion (6 per cent). Seventy-three per cent of the respondents claimed that a condom was always used by their sex partner, while another 23 per cent reported that condoms were only sometimes used, mainly because their clients refused.

For prevention of disease or safety precautions, 85 per cent of the respondents reported that they had monthly medical check-ups arranged by their pimps or managers, by the health authorities or by themselves. The majority went to private doctors or health workers, whom they considered to provide better services than the government doctors, and they consequently had to personally cover the costs. Those interviewed claimed to have good health, 85 per cent reporting they never had any illness related to work. Only a small group of respondents reported job-related health problems, including vaginal infections; but, naturally, it was in the interest of the women to claim to be "clean". The total number of abortions was quite significant, 13 per cent of all respondents having undergone at least one abortion related to the job. The pregnancy risk for this type of occupation was high, and news of pregnancies among prostitutes were major issues and talking points in the complex.

Bandung: Sex establishments in a city environment

Bandung is Indonesia's third largest city, with a 1990 population of over two million. It is situated in the Priangan region of West Java, which is considered to adhere more closely to orthodox Islam than many other parts of Java, although this does not necessarily apply to the city of Bandung, which has long had a cosmopolitan reputation.

Bandung's sex industry was substantial, operating through the same kinds of establishments as in other major cities of Indonesia: brothel complexes, brothel houses and call-girl establishments, traditional massage parlours, pubs, billiard halls, discos and nightclubs. A study (conducted from January to March 1993) found 437 prostitutes working in 94 establishments (*Kompas*, 1993), although it was not clear whether these establishments referred only to officially registered brothels. The study was able to divide the establishments into five categories by location and average gross earnings of the prostitutes, the method being to multiply the average number of days worked per month by the average number of clients per day by the average fee for a short-time transaction (overnight bookings were fairly rare). On the basis of this method of calculation, average monthly earnings were estimated at Rp.200,000 (US$100) for the lowest-class prostitutes, Rp. 500,000 (US$250) for low-class prostitutes, Rp.1 million to Rp.1.5 million (US$500 to 750) for middle-class prostitutes, Rp.2 to 3 million (US$1,000 to 1,500) for high-class prostitutes, and Rp.6 million (US$3,000) for the highest-class prostitutes. The range was striking, with a more than ten-to-one difference in earnings between a high-class and a very low-class prostitute, and a thirty-to-one difference between the very highest and lowest classes. The study stresses that although their incomes were quite good, there was a tendency for the sex workers to borrow money from their pimp when they got into financial difficulties, and hence became bound to continue working for that pimp.

Fieldwork conducted in Bandung by the researchers for the present study revealed that massage parlours (of which there were about 15) employed more sex workers than did call-girl establishments and brothel complexes. Most massage parlours employed about 30 workers each, although some of these workers did not engage in sex with customers. Most of the masseuses did, however, because typically they earned very little from the regular massage. For example, in one establishment, the worker received only Rp.5,000 (US$2.50) from the Rp.40,000 (US$20) charged for body massage as compared to Rp.45,000 (US$22.50) from the Rp.70,000 (US$35) charged for sexual intercourse. Thus, the massage parlours could preserve the pretence of offering only massages, while arranging charges in such a way that the masseuses would almost certainly serve as sex workers. The establishments also made good money from the hourly room charges and the sale of drinks. They would do much less well, however, if they offered only massages, for which the demand was more restricted.

Discotheques were another source of sex services in Bandung, serving as a focus of operation of freelance sex workers, especially on the nights designated as "ladies' nights", on which women were admitted without paying a cover charge. Some discos ran three ladies' nights a week, on nights that would otherwise be quiet. It was very difficult to estimate how many freelance sex workers operated out of discos, especially since an indeterminate proportion of these offered commercial sex only occasionally.

The total number of sex workers in Bandung was clearly much smaller than in Surabaya, despite the fact that Bandung is not a much smaller city than Surabaya. Rough estimates based on the fieldwork suggest that the total number of sex workers in Bandung may have been only about 1,500, although another report (*Kompas*, 1994) put the number at 6,000. The main source of uncertainty concerns the number of freelancers operating out of saloons, discos and bars or through contacts organized by taxi drivers and hotel employees.

Indramayu: A source area for sex workers

It is part of Indonesian folklore that Indramayu is a major source of prostitutes. There is, in fact, a strong basis for this belief: the *kabupaten* (district) of Indramayu has a population of only 1.4 million, or 3 per cent of the total population of West Java and Jakarta combined, yet in a study conducted in the large official prostitution complex of Kramat Tunggak in North Jakarta, officials reported that more than half the prostitutes in the complex originated in Indramayu. Of the prostitutes interviewed, 28 per cent were from Indramayu (Wibowo et al., 1989, p. 5).

Actually, it is not the entire district of Indramayu that is noted for its supply of prostitutes. Of the 19 subdistricts in Indramayu, seven are noted for the supply of prostitutes, and these are close to the main road along the north coast of Java, thus making them readily accessible to Jakarta for those young women who are engaged in prostitution in the national capital, and bringing customers for those engaged in prostitution in the local subdistricts. Many sex workers remain in the area, most of them working out of small restaurants and bars to be found along the main north road.

Indramayu has long been characterized by poverty, low education, parent-arranged marriages at young ages and very high divorce rates. It is not noted for the strength of its adherence to orthodox Islam. It is also accessible enough that women employed in the sex industry in Jakarta can return to Indramayu occasionally without undue difficulty or expense. All these are factors conducive to the entry of young women into prostitution. On the other hand, these factors also characterize other parts of West Java where prostitution is much less in evidence, although divorce rates in Indramayu are certainly higher than anywhere else in Java (Jones, 1994). Therefore, as mentioned earlier, the prominence of prostitution in Indramayu could well reflect elements of historical accident: the development of a specialization which built on itself, just as other villages or districts developed their particular occupational specializations.

A study (Wibowo et al., 1989) which involved interviews with 50 officials and other informants in Indramayu about the reasons for the high rate of prostitution found that poverty was the most frequently mentioned reason (46 per cent), followed by low education (28 per cent) and socio-cultural factors (26 per cent). Low education certainly characterized the 50 prostitutes who were also interviewed in this study: 47 of them had no education or incomplete primary schooling. Broken marriages also characterized these prostitutes: 44 out of the 50 were divorced. The socio-cultural factors mentioned by the community respondents were: (a) the very low age at marriage, to somebody chosen by their parents, and a tolerant attitude towards divorce as a way out of an unsatisfactory marriage (indeed, many parents are proud of a daughter who has been divorced and remarried several times, because it shows her desirability to men); (b) a wasteful way of life and a tendency to demonstrate status by holding expensive ceremonies beyond what people can really afford, thus making for a tolerant attitude towards ways of making money to sustain such expenses, including prostitution; (c) a "couldn't care less" attitude towards neighbours' behaviour, thus people do not feel community or social constraints and even parents frequently do not object to their daughters working as prostitutes; and (d) poorly developed moral standards, allowing gatherings to take place where young people can meet at night free from parental and social control; this freedom can be abused and also used by prostitutes to seek out customers.

A journalist, Her Suganda, writing in *Kompas* on 16 September 1979, noted that women from Gabus Wetan, an area in Indramayu, who entered prostitution were mostly young, divorced, uneducated girls. They worked in cities such as Jakarta, Bandung, Sukabumi and Tanjung Pinang, and typically returned to Gabus Wetan before the Muslim fasting month and went back to the city a week or so after. Enough of them did well, especially by local standards, to attract the envy of other young women. Their clothes and make-up were "flashy" and they adopted urban ways. As they no longer had to work in the ricefields, their skin was relatively fair and much admired by their village friends. Some of them could set up house back in Gabus Wetan complete with colour television and fine furniture. Some of the higher-class prostitutes had built very large houses comparable to the mansions of elite areas in Jakarta, although in general the most impressive houses belonged to the pimps and brothel owners. Sometimes, when the women came back to the area, they brought men with them who had cars and other appurtenances of wealth. Many of them, indeed, continued to practise prostitution while back in Gabus Wetan over the holiday period, and men in cars with Jakarta numberplates were frequent visitors. The demonstration effect on other young women was obvious, and the sex trade is an open secret in the area.

Fieldwork in 1991 and 1994 revealed that these observations continue to hold true. Indeed, a common pattern was for younger women to work for three weeks or so in the city, then return to Indramayu at the time of their menstrual period and engage in prostitution there as well before returning to the city. Their clients in Indramayu may have been local officials or traders or guests they brought back with them from the city. During these monthly visits, they brought money back for their families and gifts for their neighbours. There was still considerable competition among these young women to build houses and acquire land to demonstrate their success. Divorced women continued to be those most likely to engage in prostitution.

Batam: Sex in a growth zone

In recent years, a sex industry has developed on the island of Batam, about 30 kilometres south of Singapore. This is a unique case for Indonesia of a sex industry based mainly on the higher incomes and strong restrictions on prostitution in neighbouring countries, akin to the development of prostitution in Padang Besar and Hat Yai in southern Thailand, mainly to serve visitors from Singapore and Malaysia. The relatively tight control of the sex industry in Singapore and Malaysia provides a ready market and a strong impetus for the development of the sex industry in Batam. Because of much lower income levels in Indonesia, prices of prostitutes in Batam are about one quarter of those in Singapore (*Tempo*, 1993).

Batam has been developed as an industrial and tourist area as part of the growth triangle comprising Singapore, Johore in Malaysia, and Batam and Bintan islands of Indonesia. Batam's population grew from a few thousand 20 years ago to over 100,000 in 1994, and is projected to reach 700,000 in 25 years' time. Part of Batam's growth has been based on recreational facilities for nearby Singapore, including golf courses and high-class hotels. Because of its proximity (a 30-minute ferry ride away), day visits from Singapore are possible. The tourist industry handles some 500,000 visitors a year and is rapidly growing.

On the small nearby island of Babi (Pig Island), a village of prostitutes, consisting of approximately 120 women serving mainly Singaporeans and Malaysians, has developed. On Batam island itself, in 1993 there were 348 prostitutes operating in the official brothel complex area of Bukit Girang (*Tempo*, 1993). Almost all of these women came from Java and North Sumatra, and a large proportion were Sundanese from Indramayu and Cirebon. They lived in a highly controlled, fenced-in community, complete with very rough health facilities and a programme of government-sponsored activities which included sports, literacy classes and religious education. The pimps were the village head and security officers, who appeared to take their roles very seriously; they ran a tight operation, fully sanctioned by the government (Hull, n.d.).

Outside the fence, Hull found a different situation: about 350 prostitutes lived with their pimps or de facto partners and children in a ramshackle settlement with little official support or approval. This group included a few hundred who were formerly on a neighbouring island in an official brothel complex, which had been demolished to make way for new developments. Having nowhere else to go, they migrated to Batam. These newcomers did not receive the health checks or religious education of the "official" brothel group. They were representative of the large number of sex workers on Batam who did not work in official establishments, and who were unofficially said to number 1,800, or about five times the number of registered sex workers inside the complex.

In town, and especially in the small centre of Nagoya, the sex industry was totally different in character. Sex workers operated in massage parlours, discotheques, nightclubs and bars: more than 300 in the Golden Million nightclub, *karaoke*, massage and restaurant complex alone, and another 300 in the Golden Star area (*Tempo*, 1993). These women were largely of Chinese descent, and their clientele mainly Singaporean and Chinese-Indonesian. The charge for an overnight booking of hostesses from the Golden Million was Rp.150,000 (US$75), much cheaper than the cost of a similar service in Singapore. It would have provided a good income for the women, except that the charges were paid direct to the management, which subtracted laundry costs, food, medicine, beauty parlour costs and various fines before handing over the money (*Tempo*, 1993).

The total number of women working in the nightclub-massage-discotheque sector in Nagoya was difficult to estimate, but some local officials put the figure at 1,000 in 1992. Thus, in all, the sex industry in Batam probably employed between 2,000 and 3,000 women or around one-tenth of the women of childbearing age on the island at the time. The rapidly growing and largely migrant population created a frontier atmosphere promoting a highly differentiated sex industry, supported by the purchasing power and appetites of the rapidly growing number of unattached workers and tourists on the island. The threat of the spread of HIV/AIDS in such a situation has obviously been very real. Government officials felt that a major cause of prostitution in Batam was the low level of wages of the female industrial workers. In 1992, the office of the Minister of State for the Role of Women received a report from the Ministry of Social Affairs that some factory workers were engaging in "double occupations". To solve the problem, the Ministry of Manpower, the State Ministry for the Role of Women and the Batam Authority conducted meetings with the Batam business community to persuade them to improve the welfare (including board and lodgings) of their women employees, in order to reduce the "side effect" of women working in undesirable occupations. However, given the clear market for sex workers on the island, it seemed likely that most of those working in the sex industry had come to Batam from other parts of Indonesia specifically for that purpose.

The scope and significance of the sex sector in the national economy

Poverty has never prevented men from frequenting prostitutes, whose fees are geared to the purchasing power of their customers. But the increasing purchasing power of Indonesian consumers has made commercial sex services accessible to a growing number of potential customers. Increased purchasing power and the growing complexity of the Indonesian economy have also resulted in a diversification of the forms of prostitution.

Unfortunately, no accurate statistics are available on the number of prostitutes in Indonesia, mainly because prostitution exists in various forms. Some observers have made rough estimates. For example, Murray (1993, p. 2) estimates that there are about 500,000 sex workers in Indonesia, though no basis is given for this figure. Recent official data have been published annually by the Ministry of Social Affairs. The women recorded in these registrations are those in official *lokalisasi* and other brothel complexes routinely monitored by the Ministry and by the police. The national numbers of registered prostitutes fluctuate substantially, as shown in table 2.1.

These data do not, however, tell us how many women are working outside brothel complexes in massage parlours, bars or high-income range call-girl establishments. They also do not include independent sex workers, for example, streetwalkers or women who occasionally pick up clients in hotels, bars and discotheques and who are not necessarily regular sex workers, but who may sell sexual services if they are attracted to the man or are in need of extra money. There is no available government estimate of the number of unregistered sex workers. Thus, the numbers in table 2.1 represent only a portion, and a fairly formally defined portion, of the commercial sex sector in Indonesia.

The registered establishments are required to report quarterly on the number of sex workers employed, including their demographic characteristics (age, place of origin, family background), and to provide photographs for the confidential records of the Ministry of Social Affairs. The data are used by the Ministry for preparing routine government budget proposals for action programmes for the resocialization of prostitutes through *Panti Rehabilitasi Wanita* (Women's Rehabilitation Centres) programmes and non-*Panti* programmes, and also by the Ministry of Health for designing health programmes.

The breakdown by province of the data in table 2.1 indicates that most of the registered prostitutes were concentrated in Java (a somewhat higher percentage than Java's share of Indonesia's total population); the highest numbers (averaged over the three years from 1992/93 to 1994/95) were in East Java, Jakarta, Central Java and South Sumatra, though West Java and East Kalimantan also have large numbers registered. These figures are related to the high levels of rural-urban migration of women in Java and the lack of alternative job opportunities for unskilled workers in large urban areas, except for low-prestige and low-paying domestic services. The sharp drop in numbers in some provinces and the sharp rise in others over the interval of four years raise some questions about the volatility of

Table 2.1. Number of registered prostitutes, Indonesia, 1984/85–1994/95

Year	Sex workers
1984/85	48 057
1985/86	56 541
1986/87	59 290
1987/88	56 524
1988/89	62 660
1989/90	64 447
1990/91	49 619
1991/92	52 389
1992/93	47 454
1993/94	65 059
1994/95	71 281

Source: Department of Social Affairs Reports

employment in official brothel complexes and about the accuracy of the data collection process.

Data from various non-official sources about employment in official and unofficial brothel complexes in the 1980s and 1990s are quite comparable to the official numbers for the provinces in which they are located. What is important, however, is that the recorded numbers seriously underestimate the total number of female commercial sex workers. The non-official sources of data are mainly from investigative reporting, particularly at times of strong police action (raids) against prostitution. The fact that the numbers are consistent across sources may indicate more about how reporters operate than any serious verification of estimates.

The estimate, therefore, is that the number of prostitutes is somewhere between 140,000 and 230,000 (see table 2.2). The lower figure is based on the assumption that the officially registered prostitutes in 1993 (as shown in table 2.1) are mainly concentrated in the middle-range sector and to some extent in the lower-range sector, as well as that they must be multiplied by two to take account of all other forms of prostitution in those sectors not covered in the official estimates. The official figures barely include any prostitutes in the high-range sector, who are assumed to number 10,000, or less than one-tenth of the number in the low- and middle-range sectors combined. The high estimate assumes a greater undercount in the official figures and a substantially larger number of women operating in the high-range sector.

If the number of sex workers in each category (low, middle and high range) is multiplied by the number of transactions per month, then an estimate is obtained of the total number of commercial sex transactions per month. This number is 5.4 million in the low estimate and 8.6 million in the high estimate. If it is assumed that the average user of sex services has two transactions per month, this implies that each month, between 2.7 million and 4.3 million men are frequenting prostitutes. If all these men are Indonesians, they would constitute about 5 to 8 per cent of

Table 2.2. Alternative calculations of financial turnover of the Indonesian sex sector

	Low range	Middle range	High range	Total
Low estimate				
Number of workers	70 000	60 000	10 000	140 000
Clients per month (average)	40	40	20	
Net income per client (average) (Rp.)	5 000	30 000	100 000	
Average monthly income (Rp.)	200 000	1 200 000	2 000 000	
Income of all workers (Rp. million) per month	14 000	72 000	20 000	106 000
Multiplication factor (turnover)	2	2	2	2
Total turnover (Rp. million) per month	28 000	144 000	40 000	212 000
US$ equivalent per month				$106 million
US$ per year				$1.18 billion
High estimate				
Number of workers	100 000	100 000	30 000	230 000
Clients per month (average)	40	40	20	
Net income per client (average) (Rp.)	5 000	30 000	100 000	
Average monthly income (Rp.)	200 000	1 200 000	2 000 000	
Income of all workers (Rp. million) per month	20 000	120 000	60 000	200 000
Multiplication factor (turnover)	3	3	3	3
Total turnover (Rp. million) per month	60 000	360 000	180 000	600 000
US$ equivalent per month				$300 million
US$ per year				$3.3 billion

Indonesian males aged 15 to 64 years. This highlights an important, if obvious, point: the Indonesian sex industry is large because of the large number of males seeking to purchase sexual services, but at the same time it involves only a minority of Indonesian men.

Earnings in the sex sector

Studies on prostitution in Indonesia are consistent in showing relatively high earnings compared with earnings in other occupations in which women with low levels of education are likely to find work (Papanek, 1975; Krisna, 1979; Lerman, 1983; Purnomo and Siregar, 1985; *Sinar*, 1993). Indeed, at the upper end of the range, freelancers operating out of bars, discos and *karaokes* in cities such as Jakarta, Surabaya and Bandung may be making Rp.3 million to 5 million a month (US$1,500 to 2,500), and top-class call-girls even more. This is much higher than what is earned by middle-level civil servants and other occupations requiring a high level of education. The earnings recorded in many studies on Indonesian prostitutes are high enough to be very tempting. On the other hand, there is sharp social disapproval and strong religious condemnation of prostitution, so part of the earnings might be regarded as a "premium" required to overcome the stigma associated with the occupation and for other unpleasant aspects of the work, including the dangers of HIV/AIDS and other serious diseases.

It is likely, though, that many of the available studies overstate the average earnings of women who engage in prostitution, because they tend to focus on brothel complexes, and when they deal with the informal parts of the sex sector, they tend to concentrate on the upper end of the market, for example, those who work the bars, hotel coffee shops and discos in cities such as Jakarta and Medan, who can make very good money.

Data from a wide range of sources on prices of sex services and earnings of sex workers in different parts of the sex industry and for different time periods were compiled for this study. When these data were cross-checked against prices prevailing in the different sub-markets in 1994, a reasonably clear picture emerged of prices paid by customers for four categories of sex industry activities: the low-range end, the middle range, the upper range and the top end of the market.

The low-range segment includes the brothel complexes serving the low end of the market. Short-time prices here can be as low as Rp.3,000 (US$1.50) but the average is about Rp.5,000 (US$2.50). The facilities in these brothels are indeed very basic. The average-price brothel complexes, including some in Surabaya and Semarang, should probably also be included in the low-price end of the market. These were charging around Rp.10,000 (US$5) in 1994. In the unorganized sector, prices are very low for the streetwalkers and others who operate in slum areas, markets, cemeteries, along the edge of railway lines and other areas where there is more difficulty and sometimes danger in contacting them. Earnings of those in the unorganized sector are almost certainly lower, on average, than those in the organized sector (Lerman, 1983, p. 255), though apparently not lower than those in the low-range end of the organized sector. For example, streetwalkers in Surabaya and Yogyakarta in 1992 were charging between Rp.5,000 and 10,000 (US$2.50 and 5.00).

The middle-range segment of the sex market comprises the higher-price brothel complexes, including Dolly in Surabaya, Saritem in Bandung and Kramat Tuggak in Jakarta, where some brothels were charging Rp.25,000 or 30,000 (US$12.50 or US$15) per transaction in 1994. Higher up the market range, massage parlours in Surabaya charged between Rp.30,000 and 60,000 (US$15 and 30). In Jakarta and Bandung the cost was Rp.70,000 (US$35) inclusive of sexual service and room charge or Rp.50,000 (US$25) for sex plus Rp.15,000 to 20,000 (US$7.50 to 10.00) for the room (which is often charged separately to preserve a pretence of a legitimate massage). The price may double if the woman is taken out for an overnight booking. Some of the women who are picked up in bars or discotheques or brought to hotel rooms also charged around Rp.30,000 to 50,000 (US$15 to 25).

Throughout Indonesia, customers in the high-range segment mostly use nightclubs or call-girl establishments for initial contact or they use call-girls known exclusively to a restricted clientele. For each transaction, they typically pay Rp.100,000 to 300,000 (US$50 to 150), which is doubled for an all-night booking (*Matra*, 1993). Similar prices can be found in a few very high-priced massage parlours. In most sex establishments, prices vary according to the age and physical attractiveness of the workers. Most establishments have their "prima donnas" for whom the going rate is higher than for other workers. Thus, in one disco in Medan the normal price of Rp.50,000 to 100,000 (US$25 to 50) was raised to Rp.200,000 (US$100) for two young women "moonlighting" from their status as kept women of businessmen (*Matra*, 1994).

In the highest-range segment at the very top of the market, certain screen actresses and models charge millions of rupiah (*Matra*, 1993, p. 64). Until his arrest in August 1994, the so-called "super pimp", Hartono Setyawan, ran a organized network of high-end establishments covering Jakarta, Bandung, Surabaya, Semarang and Bali (*Sinar*, 1994). The call-girls could be moved from place to place, depending on demand. Charges were Rp.700,000 (US$350) for a three-hour session or Rp.1.5 million (US$750) for all night; payment could be made by cash or credit card, with the billing slip being filled in to appear as if the client had visited an expensive restaurant. The very large incomes of some Indonesians and the tendency to engage in conspicuous consumption mean that there will always be a market, albeit limited, for sex services at such inflated prices.

The actual earnings of sex workers depend on the proportion of the charge paid by customers that they are able to keep for themselves. This varies considerably between different parts of the sex industry. In brothel complexes, the worker typically receives half the fee charged, but less if an intermediary is involved in bringing the client. In some high-price massage parlours, the worker keeps the entire fee (apart from tips she gives to waiters and to the *mamasan*), as the establishment makes its money from the hire of rooms and sale of drinks. In call-girl establishments operating from private houses, typically the worker keeps half, but less in some high-price establishments, or if a third party is involved in bringing the client. Streetwalkers and freelancers operating out of hotel coffee shops, lobbies and discos may be able to keep all of the fee charged, but in many cases they have to make payments to pimps, taxi or pedicab drivers, hotel security staff, officials and others. Finally, the group of *perek* described earlier commonly accept gifts rather than monetary payments because they do not consider themselves to be prostitutes.

On the whole, the income of prostitutes appears better, sometimes much better, than what they would be able to earn in any other occupation potentially open to them. In addition, despite the obvious disincentives against entering this occupation, some aspects of the working conditions are quite good. For example, most workers who live in brothel complexes and massage parlours are given free accommodation, and free meals are usually supplied to workers in brothel complexes. Menstruation leave is also given, and usually the chance to return to their place of origin for a few days is given as well if it is not too far away. Although hours "on call" can be long, much of the time is spent with friends, talking, watching television, playing cards and seeking other ways to fight off boredom.

It is difficult to give even a rough estimate of the economic significance of the sex industry and the amount of money that changes hands over the course of a year through its activities. What is certain is that prostitution plays a significant role in the Indonesian economy and is a substantial contributor to government revenue, particularly at the local level. For example, it has been estimated that in the Harmoni-Kota area of Jakarta, as much as Rp.1 billion related to sex services changes hands in one night (*Sinar*, 1993). Even if we halve this figure because it appears to relate to busy nights, the implication is that in this area of Jakarta alone, there is an annual turnover of some US$91 million from activities related to the sale of sex. In Surabaya, rough estimates based on the number of establishments, daily sexual transactions per establishment and price per transaction suggest an annual turnover of some Rp.380 million (US$69 million) in the middle- and upper-range sex industry. The annual turnover of the five call-girl establishments operated by a well-known pimp, Hartono Setyawan, was estimated to range between Rp.600 million and 1 billion – US$3.6 million to 6 million (*Sinar*, 1994, p. 17).

Estimation of the total turnover of the sex sector is a problem because of uncertainty regarding the total number of prostitutes, their average net earnings and the income earned by others as a result of their activities. Sabaroedin (1991, p. 16) used the Department of Social Affairs figure of a total of 62,660 prostitutes and 6,368 pimps, each assumed to earn on average US$5.13 a day, to arrive at an estimate of total annual personal earnings of US$129,251,478. This is, of course, a very rough notion of the economic significance of the sex industry.

Table 2.2 offers alternative calculations of the financial turnover of the industry, assuming that the number of prostitutes, as estimated above, is between 140,000 and 230,000. Average net monthly earnings are estimated to be Rp.200,000 (US$93) in the low-range sector, Rp.1.2 million (US$558) in the middle-range sector and Rp.2 million (US$930) in the high-range sector. The average net earnings for all workers in the sex sector, according to this set of assumptions, are Rp.757,000 (US$378.50) a month. This is very far below the earnings of the high-range sex workers, and well below the earnings of middle-range sex workers, but it is assumed that the majority of Indonesian prostitutes fall in the low-range category, where earnings are much more modest. The reason for the relatively small difference in average monthly net incomes in the middle-range sector and the high-range sector is the assumption that fewer transactions take place per sex worker per month in the high-range sector. Income earned by others as a result of activities of prostitutes is assumed to be equal to the net earnings of the sex workers themselves for the low estimate and double the net earnings of the sex workers for the high estimate. This refers to the earnings of pimps, brothel owners, proprietors and other workers in massage parlours, bars and so forth, where sex services are the main focus of the enterprise; payments to police and security workers, to enable the prostitution to continue; and payments to touts, taxi and pedicab drivers, who put clients in contact with sex workers or with the brothels in which some of them work. But it does not cover the earnings of food, drink and cigarette sellers who tend to congregate in such areas. Although these goods are sold in large quantities near these establishments, vendors presumably would continue to make some kind of living elsewhere without the sex industry.

On the basis of these assumptions (and an exchange rate of Rp. 2,150 to US$1), the estimate of the financial turnover of the sex industry in Indonesia (without taking into account the contributions of male prostitutes and transvestites) ranges from US$1,180 million in the low estimate to US$3,300 million in the high estimate, or between 0.8 and 2.4 per cent of Indonesia's GDP.

Legislation covering the sex sector

The attitude of the Indonesian government to prostitution appears to have changed little since colonial times: it is largely determined by health and public order rather than moral considerations. Today, there is no law in Indonesia that prohibits the sale of sexual services as such. Even the terminology used to describe the women in the laws and regulations reveals much about official attitudes. Framers of the regulations avoid the term *pelacur*, or prostitute, because it is considered to be pejorative. Instead they have promoted the term *wanita tuna susila* (WTS) which is literally translated as a "woman lacking in morals", in a concept parallel to other terms such as *tuna netra* for blind people (lacking sight) or *tuna wisma* for the homeless. This wording indicates an unfortunate lack, rather than an overt behaviour for which they can be blamed as individuals. In this sense, the terminology used in Indonesia is non-condemnatory. However, a double standard is revealed by the lack of a term to indicate that the customers of WTS are also lacking in morals. A number of women's groups in Indonesia, like their western counterparts, object to the use of terms like WTS or *pelacur*, preferring to talk of "commercial sex workers" *(pekerja seks)*. However, this terminology is rejected by government officials, particularly those involved in the collection of labour force statistics, on the grounds that it implies the acceptance of prostitution as a valid category of employment, an option they would like to avoid.

The criminal law does prohibit those who help and facilitate illegal sexual activities, as defined in articles 296, 297 and 506 of the Criminal Code (*Kitab Undang-Undang Hukum Pidana*, the KUHP). The KUHP also prohibits the trading of women and under-age boys. The relevant articles are as follows:

Article 296: "Those whose actions or attitudes intentionally lead to or facilitate illegal sexual activities with other people will be given a penalty of one year and four months imprisonment or a fine of Rp.15,000 (US$7)."

Article 297: "Trade in women or in under-age males will incur a maximum penalty of six years imprisonment."

[The definition of "under-age" for the purpose of the KUHP is under 21 years of age if single, but a woman is no longer under-age if she is under 21 but is currently or has ever been married (Soesilo, 1960, p. 169). In other articles of the KUHP, under-age females are defined as being under 15 years of age, and for other purposes, such as being a prostitute in a brothel complex, the legal age is given as 17 or 18 years.]

Article 506: "Whoever as a *mucikari* (pimp) derives profit from the prostitution of women, will incur a maximum penalty of three months imprisonment."

This last article prohibits and punishes the intermediary who intentionally organizes and facilitates sexual activities, such as pimps (the *germo* or *mucikari*), *mamasans* and owners of call-girl establishments, but does not classify the commercial sex act itself as criminal. Prostitution *per se* is not an illegal activity under the KUHP. Reports in the Jakarta newspaper *Sinar* (1994) comment on the difficulties of prosecuting pimps under the KUHP.[5] Some State Prosecutors have attempted to mount a prosecution under article 333, charging that a pimp has "deprived a woman of her freedom", but given the fact that women are seldom actually incarcerated in brothels, such prosecutions are also difficult to sustain.

In theory, other articles of the Criminal Code could be applied to prostitutes who knowingly sell services to married men. For example, articles 284-288, which are based on Islamic law, specify a number of conditions under which *zinah* (adultery) is illegal and punishable by up to nine months in prison. Again, these articles are difficult to enforce because the charge of *zinah* can only be made against a married person, and normally it would be difficult to prove that the prostitute knew the client was married. It also requires a formal complaint from the client's wife and evidence of a breakdown of the marriage as a result of the adultery. Given the clandestine nature of many commercial sex transactions, and the tacit acceptance by many women of the perceived "misdemeanours" of their husbands, the adultery provisions of the Criminal Code are almost never invoked to prosecute prostitutes.

In Indonesian society, "law" extends beyond the legislative provisions of the government and includes both religious laws and customary regulations. While these generally are not open to prosecution in state courts, they do shape community norms and attitudes, and modify the way civil laws are carried out in practice. The apparent official acceptance of commercialized sex is belied by fairly general social condemnation of what is regarded as immorality. A majority of Indonesian politicians consider the subject taboo and generally avoid public discussion. Many religious moralists point out that while the criminal law may not forbid prostitution, the religious law does, and this law provides a stronger basis for community attitudes and actions than does the Criminal Code, which is a legacy of the colonial period.

The analysis of Mu'thi (1965, pp. 13-16) is instructive in pointing out the difference between the meaning of *zinah* in the KUHP and in Islamic law. In the former, only a married person can commit adultery, because the purpose of the law was to support monogamous relationships rather than to pass judgements on premarital sexual behaviour. In Islamic law, all sexual relations outside of a marital union are regarded as adulterous. This means that a polygamous man is not committing adultery by having sexual relations with more than one legal wife, but both men and women can only have sexual relations with their legal spouse. The implication, according to Mu'thi, is that a female sex worker cannot be prosecuted for adultery under the KUHP so long as she is not married, but her actions would still be condemned as sin under religious law. Mu'thi's analysis leads him to question the moral basis for the KUHP, which he says is a Western product of limited relevance to the Indonesian people, the majority of whom follow Islam. "What's strange", he says, "is the KUHP article 296", where the *germo* can be prosecuted, but the person who has sexual relations for money is free from restraint, except under the most unusual of circumstances relating to sex with a mentally incompetent or under-age client.

Nonetheless, the criminal law remains the only consistent basis for regulation of the sex sector in secular nations such as Indonesia. Since prohibition of the direct commercial sale of sexual services does not exist in national law, the regulation of the sex sector tends to be based on provincial or subdistrict government regulations as well as the actions and pressures of various social groups in support of or in opposition to the sector. The local government regulations vary from region to region.

Streetwalkers are prohibited under numerous and varied regional regulations. These regulations prohibit soliciting and loitering in the street because this hinders the creation and maintenance of "clean" cities, and streetwalkers are perceived as an affront to the community. When they are caught in a raid by the authorities, the streetwalkers might be sent to a "rehabilitation centre for immoral women" for specified periods to be rehabilitated into "normal" citizens. In most regions, such rehabilitation programmes take one year. The legal basis for their incarceration is the public order provision of the law, rather than a specific prohibition of the sale of sexual services. The local government rehabilitation centres are often under-funded and, at times, are essential extensions of the *lokalisasi* (complex or localization) system of official brothels. The central government Department of Social Affairs also runs 22 rehabilitation centres nationwide.

The lower the level of government administration, the more regulations tend to be in force, as it is at the local level that officials deal with the daily reality of prostitution. Existing regulations, such as prohibition of soliciting, migration regulations and the requirement for citizens to report changes of residence to the local administration, can be and are all used to control prostitutes. These local regulations can be considered a *de facto* reflection of the unstated central government policy. In a nutshell, these regulations target the streetwalkers for making the city "unclean", but generally leave untouched both the clients and prostitutes who work behind closed doors in approved areas. The pressure on streetwalkers thus drives lower-income women workers into brothel complexes, where they are controlled by pimps, procurers and the local government and police, but generally tolerated by the society.

Official prostitution complexes

Indonesia is the only one among the four countries with a form of quasi-legalized prostitution in official brothel complexes. The quasi-legalization of prostitution is based on the reasonable assumption that prostitution cannot be stamped out, and that it needs to be controlled in the interests of public safety and order. It is also argued that health and regulatory and rehabilitation services can be better supplied if prostitution is localized as much as possible. "There are, however, elements of hypocrisy in the system when many of the areas set aside for the localization of prostitution are justified on the grounds that they are being set up for the 'rehabilitation' of prostitutes, but where strong incentives exist for the continued growth of the activity."

(Jones et al., 1995, p. 18.) The local authorities, police and military are in the somewhat inconsistent position of being both regulators and managers of these complexes.

The brothels in the official prostitution complexes are subject to very strict rules and regulations, which are basically aimed at maintaining order as well as protecting both sex workers and customers from any violence or disruptions. The regulators are the Regional Executive Council or MUSPIDA, consisting of regional administrators and the local prosecutor, police chief and military commander. The regulations are very specific. The owners of all establishments in the official brothel complexes are required to report and to register with the local regional authority all prostitutes working for them. Enforcement of such regulations is supposed to tightly control the movement of prostitutes both within and outside the complexes. The brothels may open daily for business from 6 p.m. to 1 a.m.; the owners must maintain all "business" facilities, including toilets and rooms; they must encourage prostitutes to have medical check-ups and routine injections given by health personnel from the local authority. The regulations also stipulate that the establishments can only employ prostitutes who have legal identity (residential) cards, and they are prohibited from employing an under-age girl or a married woman as a prostitute. The brothels are also prohibited from selling alcoholic drinks and accepting overnight guests (unless they have a special permit).

Many obligations are imposed on the prostitutes. In addition to legal citizenship, the prostitute is supposed to have regular injections of antibiotics as a preventive measure against venereal disease and to avoid conflict with customers. There is also a regulation which prohibits the prostitute from changing her pimp or brothel without a special permit, or from staying outside the brothel complex. In addition, new prostitutes are required to report their presence in the *lokalisasi* to the local authority. This regulation promotes, but does not necessarily ensure, tight control over the movement of prostitutes, both between brothels and inter-regionally.[6] In theory, the sex workers are supposed to be working in the complexes only temporarily while undergoing rehabilitation and resocialization; therefore they are only permitted to stay in the complex for a maximum of five years or until reaching the age of 35.[7] The minimum age to enter the complex is 17 years.

The customers of the *lokalisasi* are also subject to special regulations; for example, they are not allowed to be drunk in the brothel complex, or to carry weapons, or to stay the night without authorization from the local security officer.

The regulations for the official brothel complexes sit uneasily with other laws and with social realities in Indonesia on four counts, which can be expressed in terms of questions:

- Has the establishment of *lokalisasi* succeeded in reducing or eliminating prostitution in other areas?
- Have the programmes succeeded in rehabilitating prostitutes?
- Is the official role given to the *mucikari* (pimps) in these complexes consistent with the article of the KUHP penalizing those who profit from the prostitution of women?

- Is there consistency in the role of the state as both the regulator and manager of brothels?

On the first question, the answer in brief is that, although the regulations setting up the complexes mentioned specific areas from which prostitutes were to be moved and where the practice was to be subsequently disallowed, prostitution in a variety of forms has continued to flourish in areas outside the official complexes. On the second question, there appears to be general agreement that the programmes have succeeded to only a very limited extent in "returning prostitutes to the community" in the sense of ceasing the practise of prostitution. This is not surprising given the better earnings available from prostitution than in alternative occupations open to poorly educated women. On the third question, the officially approved pimps find it not only profitable to run a brothel in the *lokalisasi*,[8] but are also safe from prosecution. On the fourth question, local government authorities gain substantial revenue from the prostitution complexes. Although the stated aim is to rehabilitate the prostitutes, were this to be successfully achieved, the lucrative source of revenue would dry up. One sociologist in Indonesia, Hotman Siahaan, notes that the profits derived from *lokalisasi* are not treated as official state income, because to do so would open the transactions to investigations by the legislative branch, and this would expose the contradictory nature of the arrangement (*Sinar*, 1994, p. 23).

Social programmes affecting the sex sector

As far as official government attitudes towards the commercial sex sector are concerned, there do not appear to be recent signs of change. At the central government level, the Department of Health acknowledges the existence of prostitution and carries out health programmes to prevent sexually transmitted diseases, while the Department of Social Affairs accepts quasi-legalization and official brothel complexes in order to mount "rehabilitation" programmes. The Department of Manpower, however, does not recognize prostitution as an occupation, and thus essentially excludes prostitutes from possible protection through labour laws and regulations. The Department of Women's Affairs continues to promote marital fidelity and to oppose prostitution. At the local government level, there is tacit recognition of the commercial sex sector, as demonstrated by the collection of various taxes and fees. In Indonesia's Sixth Five-Year Plan (1994-1999), there is very little mention of prostitution either in terms of programmes of control or as a source of government revenues. What little there is follows the bureaucratic structure of the Department of Social Affairs in categorizing prostitutes with former jail inmates, the homeless and beggars as *tuna sosial* – those needing assistance to be converted into useful and productive members of society. Although the Sixth Five-Year Plan comes nearly a decade after the advent of HIV/AIDS in Indonesia, it makes no mention of the threat of the disease to those who practise risky sexual behaviour, including unprotected commercial sex.

Health programmes

Historically, many of the legal initiatives to control prostitution were based on concern over the spread of venereal disease. Rates of syphilis and other sexually transmitted diseases were very high, and medical treatments were difficult and often unsuccessful. In the middle of the nineteenth century, efforts were made to conduct physical examinations of registered prostitutes, but these were of doubtful impact. In 1874, the government codified the policy of isolating or quarantining prostitutes found to have venereal diseases in "sick women houses" which were overseen by medical personnel. Any woman unlucky enough to be put in such a facility was given two sets of clothes and some basic toiletries, and then condemned to wait until she could demonstrate good health and be released. By the 1900s, commentators noted that the system was doing little to prevent the spread of illness, less to cure sufferers, and called for its abolition. Routine health checks were abandoned in 1911, but sex workers and the military remained the focus of efforts to fight sexually transmitted diseases (STDs).

With the advent of antibiotics in the 1940s, the vision of conquering venereal disease loomed large in the thinking of policy makers. This was manifest in the Indonesian attempt to institute a system of Regular Mass Treatment (RMT) as early as 1957 to provide commercial sex workers with regular doses of antibiotics as a means of combating venereal disease, especially syphilis (Soewarso, 1988). The programme relied on the compliance of the sex workers as well as the cooperation of the local leaders and pimps, to gather the prostitutes working in the official brothel complexes in a convenient location for a weekly health check and injection. The programme had various shortcomings, including creating the public impression that regular injections were a guarantee of health and that the prostitutes were "clean", when in fact the injections were ineffective against a wide variety of STDs, in particular HIV/AIDS.

In 1987, the centrally funded RMT programme was discontinued due to funding constraints. Although the Department of Health encouraged local government health units to continue the activity with other funding, the coverage has since declined significantly, with some areas completely stopping public-funded examinations and treatment, while other areas have reduced services to minimal levels. In many of the official complexes and private brothels, women are encouraged or required to seek health checks through private physicians, and if they are found to have a sexually transmitted illness, they are expelled from the brothels and then left to their own devices to obtain and pay for treatment. Some brothel owners contract private physicians to provide medical care for the workers. However, it is not known how many of the workers in the sex industry comply with the health requirements, since statistics on examinations carried out by the public sector services are neither consolidated centrally nor published, and no attempt is made to collect any statistics on services provided by private medical practitioners.

The quality of services, whether provided by local health officers or private physicians, is thought to be generally poor, due both to the lack of systematic application of standards of care and to failure to ensure compliance with treatment regimes. There are no national standards or comprehensive training programmes for doctors and other health workers dealing with the sex sector. Health checks are rarely more than cursory, and one disposable needle is routinely used for up to six different women, sometimes with no pretence of even rinsing the device between injections. "Preventive measures which rely on education of the community are hampered by lack of appropriate and thorough training materials. The national offices of the Health Department do not compile statistics on the number of women covered by local programmes of regular mass treatment or routinely treated by private physicians, so it is impossible to plan or monitor the needs for needles, medicines and diagnostic materials" (Jones et al., 1995, p. 23). In response to the growing threat of HIV/AIDS, the government has developed some elements of a strategy to conduct surveillance, provide clinical management of detected cases and prevent transmission. Publicity and community involvement in the HIV/AIDS campaign has so far been limited.

What impact the HIV/AIDS threat will have on the sex industry is not clear. In 1991, soon after two prostitutes in the Dolly complex were found to be HIV-positive, the Health Department planned to collect 400 blood samples as part of their surveillance programme. Instead, 785 women stepped forward to have their blood tested, declaring that if the government was not able to pay for all the tests under the scheme funded by the World Health Organization, they would personally pay for the extra tests. They wanted to demonstrate that the AIDS threat had been overcome in Dolly and attract back their clientele who had been frightened off. At the same time, prostitutes in Kramat Tunggak staged a dance where 15,000 condoms were distributed, and throughout Indonesia pimps and sex workers made special efforts to fill in medical records and have check-ups. It seemed obvious, though, that these efforts represented attempts to win back business rather than serious changes in behaviour related to the risk of HIV infection.

Social rehabilitation programmes

Indonesia has two types of rehabilitation centres for female prostitutes. The first type is the official brothel complex which is operated by the local authorities under the auspices of the *Dinas Sosial*, the Municipal Social Welfare Office. The stated objective of the authorities is to concentrate the sector in specific locations, so that they are better able to exercise control and to institute programmes to rehabilitate the prostitutes. The idea is that the women are only operating in the complex temporarily while they undergo rehabilitation and resocialization. They are expected to pay fees for the locally run rehabilitation activities, which normally consist of training classes located in the official brothel complex or in a special location (a room or a house) provided by the community close to the complex. Lectures on ethics and religion are given, but the women remain active prostitutes throughout the period of "rehabilitation". The impact of these courses on their resolve to give up prostitution is therefore questionable. Official statements claim success in terms of the number of women who leave the complexes supposedly also leaving prostitution: from 1972 to March 1993, the "rehabilitation centre" at Kramat Tunggak sent 11,624 prostitutes "back to normal life", 2,795 of them into marriages, 6,229 to their families and another 1,420 to jobs. An average of 600 prostitutes leave the area every year, according to a 1993 report in the *Jakarta Post*. However, it has been found that most of the women either re-register under a different name or move to other complexes (Murray, 1991, p. 106). The general assessment is that the localization programme has succeeded only to a very limited extent in getting prostitutes to leave the practise altogether.

It is only the second type of programme operated by the Directorate-General for Social Rehabilitation of the National Department for Social Affairs in Indonesia that can be considered as having the serious objectives of retraining the prostitutes for work in other sectors of the economy, as well as encouraging them to leave commercial sex work permanently. With central government funding, the Department operates 22 women's rehabilitation centres nationwide. In 1994, the Directorate estimated that there were over 65,000 registered prostitutes in Indonesia, but targeted "rehabilitation" of only 940, at a cost of Rp.417 million (US$194,000) or just US$200 per "graduate" of the programme or under US$3 per registered prostitute.

In principle, the rehabilitation programmes are open to women who want to leave the sex industry but who lack the skills or confidence to do so. In fact, many of the women in the centres were rounded up in police raids on illegal brothel complexes or hotels, and were strongly "encouraged" to join the programme. The criteria for entering the programme are that the women must be active sex workers below the age of 35 years, must be healthy (except for venereal disease, which can be treated in the centre), must be of sound mind, and must voluntarily agree to live in a dormitory and complete the programme. The rehabilitation programme, which is of six or 12 months' duration, includes basic elementary skills such as reading and writing, lectures on social norms and values, religious education and basic skills or trades such as hairdressing, sewing, home-based work and secretarial work. The women are given lectures to help them develop self-confidence and commitment to leave the sex industry. They are also provided assistance in resocialization and job placement. After completion of the programme, their recovery and reintegration is monitored and evaluated for a period of two years. The Department of Social Affairs also arranges special non-residential rehabilitation programmes for pimps and transvestites, using facilities and trainers attached to local government agencies, but there are no published data on participation in these programmes.

Preventive programmes

There have also been some programmes aimed at "preventing" vulnerable women and children from being drawn into the sex sector. The main prevention efforts have been distinguished in terms of primary and secondary prevention, and prevention of relapses. Primary prevention efforts focus on those who are vulnerable but are not yet prostitutes. The target groups have been identified as housewives with low incomes, widows who have to support their families, and young women between 17 and 35 years of age. Such primary prevention normally involves raising general awareness of the dangers of prostitution, and inculcating moral and social values. Secondary prevention efforts are directed at slum areas, industrial areas, port areas and poor villages where women may already be engaged in prostitution. "The goal of these activities is to prevent these groups from continuing their negative behaviour, by giving them counselling to develop alternative activities" (ESCAP, 1991). Prevention of relapse efforts are directed at those who have been rehabilitated (former prostitutes), their families and their neighbourhood to ensure that these women do not go back to prostitution.

To carry out these various types of prevention efforts at the national level, the Indonesian Ministry of Social Affairs has integrated programmes with a number of other agencies, namely, the Ministries of Home Affairs, Health, Religious Affairs, Education and the Minister of State for the Role of Women. The regional offices of the Ministry of Social Affairs implements programmes for the local community assisted by an inter-agency coordination team, under the governor at the provincial level and under the municipality mayor at the local level. At the village level, preventive programmes are implemented as part of the village social institutions programme, under the guidance of the district chief and social worker. The prevention programmes normally comprise mental and spiritual guidance, vocational training, enhancement of women's social skills to improve communications and relationships, family welfare counselling, and savings and loan cooperatives.

Notes

[1] World Bank surveys show that women are paid far less than men in the same age group and educational category, confirming the findings of an ILO study (White, 1990) in Indonesia that women workers in manufacturing are plagued by very low wages, long hours and related health and nutritional problems.

[2] Murray (1991, p. 106) describes Kramat Tunggak thus: it is a self contained place with streets lined with bars and mobile vendors of drinks, snacks and meals. At night, there is a party atmosphere with people drinking and dancing to disco music, and bands playing on open stages for *jaipongan* dancing in the streets. The rooms used by the women are behind the bars and are rented on a daily basis. Although Kramat Tunggak is rowdy, crimes and drugs are strictly controlled by the pimps and their security guards.

[3] Estimate provided by the Surya AIDS Hotline Service, when discussing the scope of heterosexual prostitution with the authors for the case study.

[4] There appears to be some confusion over what exactly constitutes the minimum age for a prostitute in a brothel complex. Sometimes it is suggested that an under-age person is one who has no KTP (*Kartu Tanda Penduduk* or Residential Registration Identification Card) because the KTP is usually given to a person who has already reached 17 years of age. But this does not provide a clear definition since married women who are under 17 can legally obtain a KTP, and false identification cards are commonplace in the social circles around a *lokalisasi*.

[5] In one case, the well-known "super pimp" Hartono Setyawan operated high-range call-girl services in Surabaya and Jakarta. He was charged in 1986 under Article 297, but the prosecution was unable to prove that he had indeed trafficked in under-age girls. When he was brought to the court again under Article 506, which is taken as a misdemeanor, the judgement was that while the accused could not be proved to have "traded in women", or "operated a house of ill-repute", he was guilty of "deriving profits from prostitution" and was sentenced to eight months' imprisonment. On appeal, the Jakarta High Court reduced the sentence to a two-year probationary period. After the appeal was handed down, the press reported that Hartono's brothel in central Jakarta was still in business, with a clientele of foreigners and rich Indonesians, including high government officials; the reports referred to him as being "immune to prosecution".

[6] The data on the number of prostitutes maintained by the Subdistrict Social Affairs Office are based in part on this compulsory reporting regulation.

The sex sector

[7] The reality is generally very different. The minimum stay regulation is often overcome by prostitutes registering under another name when the five-year limit has been reached. Although official statements boast of the number of women who leave the complexes and supposedly also leave prostitution, other reports claim that most of those who leave the complex simply move to other complexes in other cities.

[8] They could earn a net income of Rp.100,000 to 250,000 (US$50 to 125) per night, both from the rental of rooms and from the sale of beer and non-alcoholic drinks. Pimps also say that a major advantage of working in the *lokalisasi* is that the atmosphere is safe and they do not suffer threats or the exaction of heavy random payments from authorities, which they would if operating in the general community. Higher incomes could be found in the non-official brothels, but these are subject to potential official harassment and possible prosecution.

PROSTITUTION IN MALAYSIA 3

Shyamala Nagaraj and Siti Rohani Yahya

Historical and social factors behind the development of the sex sector

This chapter deals with prostitution in Peninsular Malaysia. The sex sector in East Malaysia, which is in the northern part of the island of Borneo, is not described. About 82 per cent of the total population of Malaysia is on the Peninsula, which adjoins Thailand. The multi-ethnic character of the population has influenced the development of the sex sector. The dominant ethnic group of Malays are Muslims, with Islam the official religion of the country and Islamic law punishing both prostitutes and their clients. The Chinese (who account for about a quarter of the population) are mainly Buddhists, Confucianists or Taoists, and the Indians (who comprise about 7 per cent of the population) are mostly Hindu or Christian. The non-Muslim religions also abhor prostitution as a profession for women, but couch the rules for men within the broader context of adultery. There has been a rise in religious fundamentalism, especially among the Muslims but also among the other religious groups, and, correspondingly, increasing calls for stricter legal control of prostitution.

A disparate sex ratio: The setting for the sex sector in the past

With the Malay Peninsula located strategically along the trade route that linked the Far East to Africa, a sex sector must have been fairly important historically. By the time the great trading empire that was Malacca was founded around 1400 AD, Peninsular Malaya was already "for hundreds of years part of a complex trading network that stretched from Africa to China" (Andaya and Andaya, 1982, p. 10). Given the long sea journeys undertaken by men, a sex sector, perhaps small, must have existed in a demand-driven environment.

This inference is stronger in the case of the trading port of Malacca. In the sixteenth century it was "admirably equipped to handle the physical needs of traders" (Andaya and Andaya, 1982, p. 42). There were traders from eastern and western India, coastal

67

Myanmar, Java and China, who numbered about 100,000 by the beginning of the sixteenth century. Given such large numbers and the fact that these traders were far from home, one can speculate that the sex sector must have been fairly active at that time. The existence of prostitutes servicing the needs of seafaring people was first referred to in the *Hikayat Abdullah* (the Story of Abdullah), the autobiography of a noted and well-travelled teacher, Abdullah bin Abdul Kadir Munshi, who observed in 1838 a number of "loose women" approaching the traders' boats at the coast during the early hours of dawn (Hill, 1955).

There is better documentation of the growth of the sex sector during the nineteenth century, when along with increasing numbers of male labourers recruited to work in the plantations (mostly Indians) and in the mines of Perak and Selangor (mostly Chinese) came a thriving trade in sex workers, with attendant health and security problems. Purcell (1948, pp. 175-6) divides the development of the sex sector into three main periods:

- 1718-1927: brothels were allowed to operate freely and Chinese girls who wished to work as prostitutes could freely enter the country;
- 1927-1930: brothels were still allowed to operate, but no avowed prostitute could enter the country; and
- 1930 onwards: brothels could no longer operate legally.

The increasing numbers of male migrant workers had long-lasting effects on the demographic composition of the population. During the nineteenth century, economic opportunities in the tin mines, the sugar, pepper, gambier and rubber plantations and the ports brought waves of immigrants from China and India into the Malay Peninsula. In the early years, workers were brought in especially for the sugar plantations under an indentured system that provided little room for wife and family. Most of these workers were males, and women were often recruited to serve them as sex workers.

In 1839, there were about 400 Chinese workers in the whole state of Perak. By 1862, the number had increased to between 20,000 and 25,000 in the Larut district alone (Joginder, 1964, p. 225). The number of Chinese migrants to Singapore (a base for subsequent transfer to Malaya) rose from under 80,000 in the 1870s to more than 230,000 in the 1880s (Lee, 1978, p. 86). Since primarily males were recruited, there was such a shortage of women that at one time the ratio of men to women in the Larut mines was five-to-one (Purcell, 1948, p. 174). This imbalance was attributed partly to the influence of religion and national sentiment, which favoured the retention of women in China, and also to the fact that a Chinese labourer under the *singkheh* (or indenture) system was in no position to support a wife if he had arrived with her in Malaya. The situation was not very different for the large number of Indian labourers. In the 1870s, there were about 30,000 Indians in the country, a figure which rose to 75,000 by the late 1880s (Arasaratnam, 1979, p.28). The sex ratio was worse for the Indians than the Chinese; in 1891 there were 18 Indian women to every 1,000 men in Malaya and Singapore. Towards the latter part of the nineteenth century, the *kangany* system, where an immigrant worker himself returned to India to recruit and bring back to Malaya a group of workers, led to more balanced sex ratios.

The early economics of the sex sector

A consequence of the shortage of women was the growth of traffic in and the exploitation of women and girls for the purpose of prostitution. Labourers who had no opportunity to get married, due to financial constraints and the difficult lifestyle, provided a ready pool of clients for the sex sector. The potential demand led to an active trade in the recruitment of young girls from Hong Kong and China, and, to a much smaller extent, from India, to force them into prostitution.[1]

Warren (1993) argues that the trade in sex workers from the Far East through Singapore contributed greatly to the development of Singapore's economy in the nineteenth century. Singapore, serving as a transit centre, brought in sex workers from China and Japan and moved them on to centres in Malaya, Thailand, India, Burma and Indonesia. The demand for sex workers was particularly high in the tin-mining state of Perak, and also in the state of Johore with its rubber plantations and proximity to Singapore. Girls were also sent to Taiping, Klang, Kuala Lumpur and even Sandakan in East Malaysia. The traffic in girls was facilitated by the inadequate legal and administrative control over the movement of persons out of China. The trade was extremely lucrative; there was a high turnover of girls in Singapore "to licensed brothels that served the mass of labourers and tradespeople" and to meet the "demand from the wealthy and better-off artisans" (Warren, 1993, p. 71).

The largest group of women supplied by traffickers to brothels in Singapore was Chinese, but there were also Japanese, European, Malay and Thai women. The Chinese commercial sex workers serviced mainly Chinese men. Hong Kong served as the clearing house, where the business of procuring girls was separated from that of shipping them to various destinations in Southeast Asia. Both patriarchy and poverty were to blame for the common practice of Chinese parents selling their young daughters. The traffickers who purchased girls in China were usually elderly women. The traffic inevitably led to much abuse: lures and tricks were used to deceive reluctant parents, and kidnapping was common. Girls were deceived into thinking that they were coming for education or respectable work. In contrast, some of the Japanese women brought in were aware of their jobs. Some brothels advertised European women who catered almost exclusively to the large number of British men, many of whom were in the colony without their families. The Japanese women, on the other hand, entertained clients of various nationalities.

Secret societies played an important role in the sex trade by providing protection to brothels. There are references to the sex sector and its linkages to Chinese secret societies in the early nineteenth century (Andaya and Andaya, 1982, p. 142; Warren, 1993, p. 7). These references note that prostitution, gambling and the control of coolie labour were the primary economic activities of the secret societies. Secret societies fought over rights to operate prostitution dens and to import women from China.

In the brothels, there were three types of sex workers. Those "sold" were purchased by female brothel keepers[2] and belonged to the house. They were provided with their daily necessities and all their earnings went to the brothel keeper. Those "pawned" or "hired" to a brothel worked for some years, usually six, to pay off the debts of their parents or guardians. After this period, the women were theoretically free, but many continued to work or were sold to another house. The "voluntary" sex workers received food and rented a room in the brothel, paying half their earnings to the keeper. In the early part of the century, the sector was extremely profitable. A sex worker could be sold in Singapore for three to eight times as much as she cost in China, depending on "virginity, age, beauty and origin" (Warren, 1993, pp. 59-63).

Early regulation of the sex sector

The British authorities found it difficult to suppress the traffic in sex workers but considered it unfeasible to declare brothels illegal (Warren, 1993, p. 100). At the same time, the potential threat of the spread of sexually transmitted diseases (STDs) made some form of control imperative. Legislation was introduced in 1870, under the Contagious Diseases Ordinance, to register and inspect brothels as well as to provide for medical inspection and detention of diseased sex workers. With the implementation of this regulation, each brothel maintained an official list stating the number of sex workers allowed (which was a function of the size of the brothel building), their names, ages and nationalities. Workers also had a protection ticket, as part of a system that was supposed to inform them that they could turn to colonial officials in the event of ill treatment. The Act was repealed in 1887 in response to mounting public pressure in Victorian England against state regulation and legitimization of prostitution. Its replacement, the Women and Girls Protection Ordinance of 1888, continued to require registration of brothels and inmates, but was no longer concerned with medical inspection. This led to a venereal disease pandemic in the late nineteenth century and the early part of the twentieth century (Warren, 1993).

Legislation to control traffic in sex workers was first introduced in 1882, when the Penal Code was amended to extend protection to women of any age forced into a life of prostitution. The Chinese Protectorate in Singapore then turned away any woman or girl under the age of 20 years coming into the country for prostitution. The Women and Girls Protection Ordinance of 1888 was amended several times in the Straits Settlements,[3] but none of these acts abolished or prevented exploitation of the sex workers.

While the Straits Settlements (Malacca, Singapore and Penang) were controlled by British law, the remaining Malay states had their own independent laws governing the sex sector. To trace the early regulation, we can describe the legislation of one state, Perak, which was a tin-rich state that encouraged the immigration of Chinese men to work in the tin mines. As most of the immigrant miners were either single or had left their families in China, brothels sprang up to service them, and women were brought into the state to work as prostitutes in these brothels. Early legislation relating to the sex sector in Perak was in the form of Orders in Council, aimed at regulating the management of brothels and at controlling health problems and the use of young girls as prostitutes.[4]

By recognizing the existence of brothels, the early registration rendered the sex sector legal. This policy was, however, changed with the introduction of the Women and Girls Protection Order No. 1 of 1895. After Perak joined the states of Pahang,

Selangor and Negri Sembilan to form the Federated Malay States (FMS), the FMS passed the Women and Girls Protection Enactment No. 7 of 1902 which repealed the Women and Girls Protection Order of 1895. The enactment of 1902 was replaced by enactments of the same name in 1914 and in 1931. These latter enactments were intended to protect women and girls, particularly those of a young age and those forced into the business, and to suppress brothels "in certain cases". They created offences similar to those that exist in present-day legislation, such as procuring, trafficking, detention in a brothel against the will of an individual and having carnal relations with those under 15 years of age. The Protector appointed under the enactments could remove the women and girls to places of safety.

A form of protection that was available under the 1902 and 1914 enactments was the "protection ticket", which the Protector could give to any prostitute found in a brothel. The ticket was in Chinese and English and stated that "whenever a prostitute has any grievance, she may come to the Protectorate, District Office or Police Office and complain. Anyone daring to prevent her will be arrested and punished. These tickets are always to be kept by you on the person." Prostitutes issued with these tickets could not be removed from the brothel or be allowed to quit the brothel until the brothel keeper had taken her to inform the Protector. The keeper of the brothel was also required to ensure that the ticket was carefully preserved, and, if lost, was replaced. The brothel keeper was also required to take inmates to the Protector if they wished to complain of ill usage or any breach of the enactment. All provisions carried sanctions in the form of fines or imprisonment.

This form of protection for the prostitutes was possible, as operating a brothel was then not an offence. The suppression of brothels "in certain cases" referred to the power given to the Protector or Magistrate to issue a summons to the keeper of a brothel, requiring discontinuation of use of the premises for such a purpose. The closing down of brothels was done in stages. It was only in the 1931 enactment that there was total suppression of brothels by criminalizing their operations and all related activities. As a consequence, the protection ticket ceased to be a form of protection for prostitutes.

The decline of the open sex sector

The disparate sex ratio among the Chinese continued to deteriorate through the nineteenth century so that by 1901 in the FMS, there were less than 10 Chinese females to every 100 males (Purcell, 1948, p. 174). The problem of prostitution and trafficking in women and girls continued. The severity of the spread of venereal disease eventually led the British government to adopt stronger measures. The first step was taken in 1927, when commercial sex workers were banned from entering Singapore. Subsequently, the Women and Girls Ordinance was amended to compel closure of brothels. With the reduction in supply, the traffic began to diminish. Prostitution was relegated to the "unseen" sectors of society, hiding behind "restaurants, boarding-houses, massage parlours and dance academies" (Warren, 1993, p. 176).

The sex ratio began to improve in the twentieth century. With the conditions for a settled existence for the Chinese population constantly improving, the new colonies became more attractive to young Chinese women. Another factor promoting family life was the increase in the number of schools at the beginning of the twentieth century. Migration laws also changed the pattern of migration. In 1922, the Indian government made it mandatory that there should be two females for every three males emigrating to Malaya; while the passing of the Aliens Ordinance in 1933 in Malaya restricted the entry of males but encouraged that of females.

By the late 1930s, when the Indian government banned emigration of unskilled labour to Malaya, and the British colonial government in Malaya banned entry of Chinese women, immigration ceased to be an important factor determining population growth. During the Second World War, the Japanese occupation of the ports in South China forced a more permanent settlement of the Chinese population in Malaya, which then experienced an improvement in the sex ratio to 815 females to 1,000 males by the 1947 census. In contrast, the Indian community took longer to settle down, so that the sex ratio was more unbalanced.

Economic development:
The setting for the sex sector

Malaya gained independence from the British in 1957 and in the four decades since, there have been significant gains in per capita income, reductions in poverty, growth of urban population and shifts in employment away from agriculture to the urban industrial and service sectors. Despite almost a doubling in the population size between 1970 and 1992, the country's economic growth has been phenomenal; per capita gross domestic product increased in monetary terms almost eight times. Malaysia has certainly been one of the most successful developing countries in the world in recent times. But the pace and nature of socio-economic development has influenced both the supply of workers to and the demand for the services of the sex sector. In the context of the economic progress that the country has been enjoying, it has not been growing poverty but substantial income differentials that account for the expansion of the sex industry.

Income growth has not been evenly distributed in the economy. Between 1980 and 1985, wages grew rapidly, especially in manufacturing, increasing the differential between the agricultural and non-agricultural sectors. Although the recession of the late 1980s slowed down the increase of manufacturing wages, the gap remains significant. At the same time, the differential between the corporate and non-corporate sectors is large. On the demand side, increasing incomes have made it possible for a larger number of men to seek the services of sex workers as part of the recreation associated with a modern urban lifestyle. A large pool of single men, unmarried or living apart from their spouses, in the urban areas is a ready source of demand. Economic growth and the subsequent increase in the number of businesses has influenced the sex sector through increased business patronage. It is a relatively common practice for businesses to entertain their clients by paying for various services from the sex sector as part of their business entertainment expenses. Another source of demand from locals could be from the armed forces, especially from young recruits on their weekends off, and those on assignment in particular locations away from home and family. The size of the armed forces and the number of their bases around the country has increased since Independence.[5]

Yet another source of demand is from the growing number of international migrant workers in the country. Rapid and sustained economic growth and burgeoning employment opportunities in Malaysia have led to a situation where labour is scarce, particularly in unskilled and semi-skilled jobs. The shortage has been critical in the construction, manufacturing, services and plantation sectors. By 1994, it was estimated that there were over 1 million foreign workers, many of whom were illegal and in the country without their families (World Bank, 1995; Lim, 1996). They come mainly from neighbouring Indonesia, the Philippines, Bangladesh, India and Pakistan. There is also a smaller but growing community of expatriates at top levels of management. Living in Malaysia, often without their families, but used to the comforts of home, many expatriates have live-in girlfriends, who are generally well-educated. These "girlfriends" are often free to entertain other men in the apartment when the expatriates travel, which they frequently do.

However, tourism appears to have had relatively little impact on the growth of the sex sector in Malaysia, as compared to its influence in neighbouring countries such as Thailand and the Philippines. Tourists do form part of the demand, but, to date, their role has been minimal. Perhaps the location of a far more varied and well-known sex sector in neighbouring Thailand could help to explain this factor.

On the supply side, growing income differentials and increasing materialism, coupled with the increasing cost of living a conspicuous urban lifestyle, appear to provide the motivation for young women to seek higher incomes through prostitution, despite strong social norms that frown upon the profession. The growth of the sex sector has been occurring in the context of shifts in the employment pattern away from agriculture to the urbanized manufacturing and service sectors. With the opening up of large-scale employment opportunities in export processing zones, many young women and girls, especially Malay women and girls, migrate from rural areas to take up these jobs. They live away from the direct control of their families and are exposed to modern urban lifestyles. For the young female migrant worker, earning an income for the first time is often accompanied by increased expectations of a more materialistic lifestyle and the opportunities to participate in the nightlife available in an urban setting. The need to financially support family back home, in conjunction with increased personal expenses, may make the earnings available in the sex sector tempting.

During the recession in the first half of the 1980s, more than half of the workers retrenched were from manufacturing, particularly electronics and garments factories, which were major employers of women in unskilled jobs (Rohana, 1985). Furthermore, clerical work, another feminized category, had the highest number of registered unemployed between 1983 and mid-1988 (Hugo et al., 1989, pp. 367-369). Since the recession of the 1980s, many factories have moved towards the use of contract workers to avoid the rigidities and compulsory benefits to workers imposed by permanent employment structures. Thus, there is added insecurity in employment, and those unable to easily find new jobs may be tempted to enter the sex sector. This may be the case especially among retrenched workers who are indispensable income earners for their families. What started as a response by the women to opportunities for wage employment in factories became, in many cases, increasing responsibility for the livelihood and support of their families in rural areas. Because the retrenched workers were mostly unskilled and women, and as the unemployment rates for women were generally higher than for men, especially in urban areas, many women had to wait up to a year to secure another job, often with lower pay. In such circumstances, the attractions of entering the sex sector would have tended to be high.

In the 1980s, many rural Indians also left the plantations for urban employment. Like their Malay counterparts, the young Indian female migrants have been exposed to new lifestyles and pressures, and have also assumed greater responsibility for the support of their families. Unlike the Malays, however, the Indian women tend to move with their families out of the plantations rather than on their own. With the escalating costs of living in the urban areas, they have clearly been under growing pressure to contribute to family income in whatever way they can.

Among the Chinese, who were mainly concentrated in the commercial and urban sectors, the mean income level was 70 per cent higher than that of the Malays, and 33 per cent higher than that of the Indians.[6] But Chinese and Indian youths between the ages of 16 and 19 were more likely not to be in school than Malay youths (Fong, 1984, p. 115). A study of squatters in the Federal capital of Kuala Lumpur found that as the tertiary sector of the urban economy grew, more Chinese squatters were employed in petty trading and services "as masseurs, prostitutes, hawkers and casual labourers ... because other jobs are hard to find" (Chan, 1983).

In the urban areas, life can be difficult, especially for the migrants and the poor (see, for example, Azizah et al., 1987), with wages often not matching the rising costs of living and the pressures of supporting households of as many as six members (Husna and Nurizan, 1987, p. 233). Today, although the incidence of absolute poverty has been reduced to 7.5 per cent,[7] relative poverty and the demonstration effect of conspicuous consumption remain serious problems for all ethnic groups. The large number of squatters and poor urban families can be a source of sex workers. Families struggling in the urban environment can easily find the sex sector an attractive source of income. Young women and girls in the lower income groups can then afford the lifestyle of their middle- or higher-income friends. Families may be tempted to use one of their daughters to earn enough to pay monthly bills. Young men may find it easy to act as pimps or procurers for sex workers.

The organizational structure of the sex sector

The types of establishments in the sex sector

Almost every Malaysian town has a red-light district. In Alor Star in the north, streetwalkers are found in Lorong Patani. In Bukit Mertajam, Jalan Menglarang is well known for its bars and hotels. In Penang, the red-light areas are along Lorong Gaharu, Jalan Perlis, Jalan Irving and Jalan Melaka. Johore Bahru reportedly offers a variety of services in Jalan Meldrum, Jalan Maju and the Lien Hoe Complex (Yeow, 1992).[8] In Kuala Lumpur, bars and hotels may be found in the Chow Kit area. Jalan Bukit Bintang, with its Sun Complex, a large apartment block, provides meeting places for more up-market engagements. Several other apartment complexes are also well known for providing the right "sex work environment". One regular client declared that "every condominium has at least one apartment that is used for this activity". A social worker declared every hotel to be a brothel. No doubt generalizations, these statements nevertheless indicate the widespread nature of the sex sector.

The sex sector currently appears to comprise mainly locations that facilitate access to sex workers. The management and operation of the establishments within the sector tend to be related to the type of services provided. To access the services of a commercial sex worker, a client could use establishments involved in the recreation business (e.g., entertainment and fitness establishments, or beauty and hairdressing salons) where these workers may be found; visit the establishments where the sex workers' services are advertised directly (such as brothels); or, in the case of regular clients, select girls in messes through pimps or *mamasans*.

There are, for example, the "papaya and grape" lounges where commercial sex workers can be seen and touched (Yeow, 1992, p. 193). For example, in Johore Bahru a man can have a nude woman sit on his lap at RM$10 (US$4) a touch. In other lounges, women in flimsy negligées entertain men and are available for night bookings. There are variations in the kind of services provided; for example, in the *korek* (dig) lounges, "touching" can be quite extensive and intimate, but does not include sexual relations. These kinds of lounges are more common in smaller towns where the entertainment sector may not be large enough to allow for the discreet operations of guest relations officers (GROs). The establishments usually pay the sex workers RM$30 (US$12) a night and commission on drinks. Under the current strict enforcement of legislation to suppress "places of assignation", these establishments no longer operate openly.

In the larger towns and cities, *karaoke* lounges, coffee houses, nightclubs and supper clubs employ young girls as GROs. The establishments pay the GROs a daily wage plus a commission on drinks, and the women can choose to be available for night bookings. Some lounges employ GROs for a fixed salary. Freelancers not directly employed at these establishments can also use the venues to source clients. These establishments provide an access route to sex services for those clients who want such services, and for those women who provide them. What happens outside the establishment is not supposed to be the concern of the establishment. The prostitute-client engagement can occur anywhere, such as in a hotel room or in an apartment rented for the purpose. The sex workers available through such channels tend to be more expensive.

Massage parlours offer massages and commercial sex. Women wearing nothing except perhaps a towel perform massages for men. Masturbation is charged additionally, and the workers may choose to be available for sex on night bookings. There are licensed massage parlours which have to follow strict rules for operation, such as having swing doors for the cubicles, but even in these places privacy in the cubicles is ensured.

Small, seedy hotels and houses in certain locations function as brothels where prostitutes can be selected by clients. These hotels, which are often conveniently located near bus routes, tend to serve the lower-income clients. They provide rooms with the bare minimum, a bed and a basin. The sex workers who operate in such cheap hotels are normally freelance, and they can come into the hotel to be selected by clients from a front room. It is not unusual to find women in their forties; some are even in their sixties. In these places, the prostitutes charge RM$15 to 20 (US$6 to 8), RM$5 (US$2) of which goes to the establishment. Brothels are similar in intent, only the location is more pleasant and there is some pre-selection of workers who join the establishment. Compared to those operating in the cheap hotels, the brothel women are more expensive. The location of the brothels tends to be normally in the centre of an entertainment district, usually easily accessible to taxi services and eating places, and not far from bus routes.

The "mess" is usually a well-furnished apartment in a large apartment block where there is only a *mamasan* (female manager) to run the day-to-day operations. Access to a mess is through introduction by other regular clients or known inter-mediaries, an apparently tight-knit community that keeps its operations as discreet as possible. The women obtained in this manner normally command high rates. The client selects a woman through photographs or allows the *mamasan* to recommend one according to his requirements. The *mamasan* calls several pimps and arranges for an appropriate prostitute to be sent over. If the client is dissatisfied, he only pays the return cab-fare of the sex worker. Pimps who continually fail to deliver suitable women are dropped from the *mamasan's* list of numbers.

The business orientation of the establishments in the sex sector is geared to meet demand within the constraints imposed by legislation and its enforcement. The types of organizational structures within the establishments are quite varied. The most organized are the brothels where a *mamasan* manages the sex workers and the pimp or procurer sources the clients. The pimp can play different roles. He can be just a procurer waiting outside the premises for clients, who gets paid for each client he brings to the establishment. He can also wait with women in his car, and both manage them and find clients for them. The cars are normally provided by a syndicate that handles a large number of prostitutes. There are also *mamasans* managing vice dens playing both roles. Then there are the apartment blocks where rooms may be rented. Young men wait around the base of the apartment blocks ready to rent out the rooms. With their mobile phones, they are able to determine if rooms are available.

Since legislation by town and city councils prohibits the use of premises for prostitution, most legal establishments tend to observe the rules and to keep the business of commercial sex independent from their operations. The legal establishments thus try to ensure that young girls and foreigners do not use their premises regularly to pick up customers. But given the demand for young girls and the profits to be made from that sub-sector, it is likely that illegal establishments form the majority of places used to source and service clients. Raids by the police to close down these illegal establishments are quite frequent, spurred in part by public concern over the number of teenage girls entering the sex sector.[9] Instead of reducing the size of the sector, the official crackdown appears to have served to make the sector more innovative, especially in using modern technology (such as mobile phones), managing the operations and making locations more mobile. Raids have considerably reduced the visibility of the sector in most towns.

With the increasing frequency of police raids, the sector has become more discreet. There is no doubt that the hand-held mobile phone has transformed the sector in many ways. It has coincided with self-employment in the sector, another response to the stricter legal enforcement against establishments. There is now increasing use of legal frontline establishments, such as nightclubs, *karaoke* bars and the like, to advertise, without solicitation, of course, the services of the sex workers. There has also been a shift, presumably in response to the preferences of clients, to lounges and pubs in the entertainment world. Taxi drivers have become significant links between the commercial sex workers and the clients.

Police raids have also meant that the messes, vice dens and illegal massage parlours have to be constantly on the move. This implies financial outlay each time new premises are set up; thus law enforcement has probably had some impact on weeding out the less efficient or less lucrative establishments. It is unclear to what extent organizations involved in other vice trades are linked to the sector. Profitable establishments, such as prostitution dens, would continue to require protection services – not necessarily from the police (Mak, 1981, pp. 82 and 115) – to ensure that the prostitute-client engagement can take place in a pleasant environment. Crime syndicates or secret societies are probably more important at the higher level of operations, that is, in the management and provision of capital and infrastructure for the sector.

The types of commercial sex workers

Abdul Hadi (1987), using the means of procuring clients as a basis, identifies six main types of workers in the Malaysian sex sector: the market prostitute (at the lowest rung of the earnings ladder); the streetwalker who advertises her services discreetly since solicitation is an offence (and who could be a low-, medium- or high-income worker); the employed commercial sex worker (one who is an employee rather than operating independently); the massage parlour, bar or nightclub workers; the freelancers; and the special workers (social escorts).

Truong (1985), on the other hand, uses the mode of employment as a basis for classification and distinguishes those working in the primitive labour market (women who solicit in the street any time it is opportune), those in the enterprise labour market (women working in massage parlours and establishments) and those in self-employment (such as call-girls and social escorts).

One reasonable classification is based on their employment status: primary or secondary. Those who have no alternative full-time employment come under the first category. In each of these groups, workers may be part-time (occasional) or full-time sex workers. A second form of classification is their pick-up mode. It is possible to differentiate between those who are selected by clients viewing a group of women, those who are picked up along the streets, those who are picked up at entertainment or health centres, and those selected through intermediaries such as pimps or procurers. Finally, although earnings are an imperfect classification, they do help to differentiate between groups of commercial sex workers, as shown in table 3.1.

Freelancers are all those who do not use the services of any establishment or intermediary to advertise their services. Consequently, this definition covers a wide range of workers, who have three pick-up modes. There are the streetwalkers who usually hang around back lanes and dark corners waiting for clients to approach them. Once the negotiation is completed, both parties will proceed to the nearest cheap hotel. Primary freelancers may work the streets or the bars and nightclubs. Some may have a "sugar daddy" (someone with whom they have a special relationship or understanding and who contributes substantially to their upkeep, including providing them with accommodation or presents). Earnings can be fairly high. Then there are the secondary freelancers, whose rates range from average to high. They may be in a white-collar job by day and choose to work as commercial sex workers at night, meeting potential clients in bars, nightclubs, discos and the like. This category also includes women who move from Peninsular to East Malaysia, to service business clients for about six months. These are usually women intending to earn money for a specific goal or purpose; their rates can be quite high and their services can extend beyond sexual relations to companionship.

The other market prostitutes (*pelacur pasar*) comprise the older sex workers who no longer command high value in the other sub-sectors (Abdul Hadi, 1975) and others who are still young but lack market information or market access (in terms of dressing or having the right contacts to meet clients). They operate in the cheaper areas of town. They get RM$10-20 (US$4-8) per client. A portion of their pay goes to the hotels used. Those who work in brothels can also be placed in this category, although their earnings are higher. These workers may get about RM$70 (US$28) per client. However, entry into the brothels is via a *mamasan* or a pimp who selects the workers usually after a "body check". For these workers, prostitution is their sole means of earning income.

Transvestites and transsexuals form a special category because they cater primarily to homosexual clients. They are usually found in a part of town where there are cheap hotels that they are able to use for their services. Their charges usually begin at RM$30 (US$12). Most members of this group regard commercial sex as their primary means of earning income, since they are generally disavowed by the rest of society. Homosexuality is an offence and thus this group of sex workers, compared to many of their female counterparts, are more likely to be subject to harassment by the authorities.

Mess workers wait at a central location to be called upon for a sexual transaction by the *mamasan* at a mess. In several parts of town, cars driven by pimps park and wait. Around them are many food stalls. The pimps have with them in the car about five to six women and a mobile phone. There are also houses or apartments where

Table 3.1. Types of commercial sex workers in the Malaysian sex sector

Work status	Type of sex worker	Pick-up mode	Typical age range	Earnings level per client
Primary	Market prostitutes	streets	older	low, about RM$15
		cheap hotels	older	low
		brothels	average (early to mid 20s)	average, about RM$70 net
	Transvestites/ transsexuals	streets, cheap hotels	varied	low to average
	Freelancers	streets, bars and nightclubs	varied, mostly younger	average to high
	Mess workers	through *mamasans* and pimps	varied, mostly younger	average to high
Secondary	Guest relations officers (GROs)	bars and nightclubs	younger	average to high
	Freelancers	bars and nightclubs	varied	average to high
	Social escorts	through intermediaries	varied	high
	Male escorts	through intermediaries	varied	high

a larger group of women wait, also managed by a pimp. The pimps may also have contacts with taxi drivers, who are usually the source of tourist clients. In this case, the location for the service would be hotels. Rates vary, but a client could pay for the woman of his choice to be with him for eight hours for about RM$350 (US$140). The operations now are very low-key, the women do not hang around either in hotels or on streets, making detection by the police difficult or possible only after lengthy observation.

GROs are employed by lounges, bars and similar establishments to provide company to men. Many are teenagers and those in their early twenties. The types of arrangements vary. In some establishments, the women are provided with a fixed salary – about RM$540 (US$216) a month – a clothing allowance, medical expenses and leave. They get a commission on drinks. In addition, they receive RM$20 (US$8) for each hour's booking by men.[10] In other establishments, women are employed on a "when you turn up for work" basis, receiving about RM$30 (US$12) a night plus commission on drinks. Sexual relations are not part of the formal employment arrangement: the woman or girl concerned decides. Thus, prostitution is a secondary activity and the amount charged per client can vary greatly. Many of these women also have a "sugar daddy", and they continue to work as GROs but engage in sexual relations with just one person. In fact, their employment profile as a sex worker is not very different from that of the primary freelancer; they differ only in that prostitution is a secondary activity.

The call-girl or social escort may be a secretary or clerk by day. Before the police crackdowns, there were a number of social escort companies openly advertising their services. Now these services have become discreet, working through intermediaries. The social escorts are among those who command high rates.

Finally, a brief word about male commercial sex workers. Such prostitutes are available and are usually patronized by wealthy women; rates are said to be high and the locations are in exclusive, well-furnished apartment blocks. However, it is believed that the numbers involved are extremely small.

The foreign connections

A number of foreigners work in the Malaysian sex sector. Table 3.2 shows arrests of suspected foreign sex workers. Since numbers are necessarily based on the frequency of police raids, detailed patterns cannot be discerned, but a broad picture emerges. Indonesian and, to a lesser extent, Filipino women work as prostitutes in the East Malaysian States of Sabah and Sarawak. Many Thai women also work in the southern State of Johore, where there is a large number of migrant workers and which is close to the Singapore market. Some of the foreign women, including some from as far away as South America, claim to have been forced into prostitution.[11] Others are brought into the country by underground syndicates. These women are sometimes supplied with false identity cards[12] to avoid detection during raids, and perhaps to dupe local clients who are now wary of Thai girls, in view of the negative publicity about AIDS in Thailand.[13]

Malaysian women also work in overseas sex sectors. In Singapore, they account for the majority of registered prostitutes (Ong, 1993, p. 269). In the early part of the century, Peninsular Malaysia received prostitutes from other countries through Singapore. Today, it often plays the reverse role. Thai and Filipino sex workers destined for foreign destinations are moved through Malaysia on to Singapore[14] (although it is unclear whether Singapore is the final destination) and to Japan,[15] sometimes after receiving training.[16] However, recent strict enforcement at immigration checkpoints seems to have had a dampening effect on the flows.

Malaysian sex workers also operate, mostly illegally, in places such as Hong Kong. Newspaper reports claim that a syndicate had been able to get under-age girls passports without the knowledge of their parents, to work in places such as Canada and Taiwan, China;[17] and that there were at least 100 Malaysian males in Japan forced into the sex trade.[18] There have also been newspaper reports of Malaysian women being arrested for prostitution or working as commercial sex workers in Japan, Taiwan (China), Hong Kong and Australia, and even in Indonesia and Thailand.[19] These women remit money back to their families, many of whom are unaware of the true source.

On the demand side, the sector of greatest concern to Malaysia is the one in southern Thailand, which is visited by many Malaysian tourists for the purpose of sex. Hong (1983) noted that, in 1981, one out of every four tourists to Thailand was a Malaysian. Recently there has been greater awareness of the increase in STDs

Table 3.2. Number of suspected foreign sex workers in Malaysia between 1989 and mid-1992

	Kuala Lumpur	Sabah	Sarawak	Johore	Other states	Total
Thais	260	51	134	1 785	686	2 916
Filipinos	111	706	553	24	13	1 407
Indonesians	217	2 197	194	95	71	2 774
Others	69	2	11	8	21	111
Total	657	2 956	892	1 912	791	7 208

among Kelantanese (from one of the states bordering Thailand), and this has been accompanied by stricter enforcement by the immigration authorities. Southern Thailand is still an attractive destination for Malaysian tourists, but now a number of Thai women also operate in Malaysia.

A survey of commercial sex workers

A survey was conducted of a small number of commercial sex workers, most of whom were working within the group of relatively high income earners in the sector. It was not feasible to interview the women in the bars or nightclubs, mainly because the frequency of preventive checks by the police has made the sector even more invisible and wary of strangers. The information is mainly from those under 21 years of age rescued under the Women and Girls Protection Act, and it was complemented by some interviews with older women picked up during preventive checks by the authorities. The interviews were conducted by specially trained police officers, social workers and the researchers. Table 3.3 shows the information base. Contrary to expectations, most of those interviewed, including those in their place of work, were willing respondents. Although the information is from too small a number of women and girls for drawing inferences, the survey (38 respondents) and individual case studies (six) do provide primary information to clarify some assumptions about the sector.

Demographic characteristics

The youngest respondent was 16, the oldest 37; and two-thirds were between 18 and 24 years of age (see table 3.4). Despite the small sample, the diversity of backgrounds of the workers was quite apparent. Twenty-seven were Chinese, a third were Malays and the remaining two were Kadazan and Iban. The Malays were all Muslims; the others were mainly Buddhists or Christians. The women and girls originated from all over the country, indicating that the sex workers normally do not operate in their place of origin.

A little more than half of them had come to the city about two years prior to their "rescue" by the authorities. Eighty per cent came to find work; only one had been

Table 3.3. The information base

Women and girls interviewed by the police — Johore	5
Women and girls interviewed by the police — Penang	5
Women and girls interviewed by the police — Kuala Lumpur	10
Women and girls from rehabilitation homes	14
Guest relations officers interviewed in nightclubs	4
Case studies using information from the Department of Social Welfare	6
Total	44

Table 3.4. Characteristics of the survey respondents and case studies

Characteristics	Number (total 44)	Percentage
Between ages 18 to 24 years	29	66
From the capital city	16	36
From other urban areas	22	50
With primary education	18	41
Ethnically Chinese	27	60
With no religion	1	2
Ever married	9	20
Have children	5	11
Have children under ten years of age	4	9
Live with their parents	4	9
Have siblings	35	80

recruited by an employer and brought specifically for the purpose of sex work. Just under half of the women had only primary education; the median number of years in school was seven. Compared to the much higher national enrolment rates, it was apparent that these women were less educated on average compared to the general population of their age. About a third reported that they left school because of financial difficulties, another third that they were disinterested, and some because they had failed the examinations.

Two women were currently married (one was earning to support her husband's first wife and her children and to pay for a lawyer, while the husband was in jail!), four divorced and three separated. Three had a single child each under 10 years of age, and one had two children, who were cared for either by the grandparents or a maid. One woman had three children, all over 10 years of age and living with her.

Almost 80 per cent of the respondents had parents who were still living, but only four lived with them. Living with parents did not seem to be a deterrent to sex work. One 15-year-old living with her mother in the infamous Sun Complex in Kuala

Lumpur reported being asked by her mother to do sex work once a week (for RM$150 or US$60 a client) to pay the rent. In terms of the occupation of the parents, over 60 per cent of the mothers were in low-level jobs and only one was a professional. Two fathers were professionals, about 20 per cent were in home-based industries and 14 per cent were retired. The commercial sex workers tended to come from large families; more than 45 per cent were from families with seven or more children.

Two interviewees lived at their place of work, one having to pay rent. About a third stayed in rented rooms, another third in rented houses or apartments, and the rest in their own or relatives' accommodation. Rent paid ranged from RM$30 to RM$1,000 (US$12-400), but half the respondents paid less than RM$300 (US$120) per month. Three of those interviewed were living with their boyfriends, 12 with relatives, and seven with friends or co-workers.

To summarize, the Malaysian female commercial sex worker is likely to come from a large family, to have dropped out of school and to be living away from the family. If ever married, she is also likely to be a single parent.

Employment characteristics

About half those interviewed became prostitutes through friends who "showed the way to earn money easily". Often it was a girlfriend who, with her expensive clothes and accessories, was a walking advertisement for the potential earning power in the sex sector. Nineteen women became sex workers of their own accord; for example, one was previously working in a legal massage parlour in a hotel. In other cases it was the boyfriend or the pimp who persuaded her to help him or herself financially.[20] One was forced by her boyfriend, one "sold" by her husband and one forced by her mother.

Eighty-six per cent had been working for a year or less at the job and had been working in just one establishment; one woman had been working for three years and was over 30 years of age (the rest did not disclose the duration of their work in the sector). These findings are not surprising since many of those interviewed had been rescued under the Women and Girls Protection Act, and therefore were mostly young and relatively new in the job. For 23 women, or just over half of those interviewed, prostitution was not their first job; among these, almost 90 per cent had worked previously for less than a year, mainly in hairdressing salons or as factory workers, sales assistants or maids. A few respondents said they had been unemployed for up to two years before getting a job, but most had been on the job market barely a few months. Although about 80 per cent came from families with siblings, only seven (18 per cent) worked to support the family. The majority of respondents said that they were working in the sex sector to support themselves, while another 25 per cent said that it was for the high income. One woman said she liked the work in the sex sector.

Seventy-two per cent of the respondents had experienced sex outside this line of work. Almost half the women said their parents did not know about their type of work; only one woman's parents knew and approved. Of the 14 women who had a husband or boyfriend, 11 said they were unaware of the type of work they were doing. Most of those interviewed claimed they had no other economic activity, although one was studying, one learning to be a beautician, one was doing make-up for others and one worked in a hairdressing salon. Half of those interviewed considered themselves to be full-time sex workers; a quarter were part-time; and the others worked when they felt like it.

Thirty-four out of the 38 interviewees reported that they intended to change jobs. The four who did not want to change jobs were young, between 16 and 23 years, and two out of the four were in rehabilitation homes. Every other interviewee who planned to change jobs claimed to want to go into clerical work, while one preferred to return to school. About 45 per cent of the others hoped to invest in their own tailoring shop, hairdressing salon or some other business. Six expected to earn more, four less, if they changed occupations.

Conditions of employment

Only one of those interviewed was a full-time GRO with specified duties, leave and other benefits of employment. All the others were working either as part-time GROs or operating from a brothel. Twenty-seven out of the 38 interviewees responding said they had been informed about their work, by either the manager, employer, pimp or *mamasan*, or by co-workers. Almost all of them were informed about the duties, payment scheme and hours of work. More than half the women admitted that sexual transactions were clearly stated as part of their job. However, only one woman had a target number of clients specified, but nothing was done if she did not meet the target.

The number of sexual transactions in the last week of employment before the interview ranged from 0 to 60; the median being 11. Some of the GROs were selective about their clients, but their rates were high. Seventeen women catered only to local clients; 19 to both locals and foreigners. One worker only entertained foreigners, but, contrary to expectations, she was an average earner, charging RM$70 (US$28) per client, and had earned RM$3,500 (US$1,400) the previous month.

As part of the terms of their employment, five women were provided with accommodation, ten with transport and seven with meals. Only two women received some sort of medical benefits. Three felt that they could get a loan easily, while nine felt that they could get assistance from their employer, pimp or *mamasan* if, for example, they were arrested. All of them said that they were not harassed by the police.

Incomes and expenditures

Average charges reported for sexual services per hour were RM$121 (US$48), while average charges per client were slightly higher at RM$124 (US$50). Table 3.5 shows the charges per transaction by the location of meeting clients. The rates were highest for those patronizing the messes (the average being RM$158 or US$63 per hour). Mess workers and freelancers also earned more in another sense; they had no monetary costs for each sexual transaction. Their clients paid for all drinks, meals, transport and for the room. In terms of the number of sexual transactions the

Table 3.5. Charges and number of sexual transactions per week

Location	Mean age of sex worker	Charges per sexual transaction				Number of sexual transactions per week			
		Rate	Range RM$	Number who responded	Average RM$	Range	Number who responded	Average	Adjusted average
Mess	19	hourly	59-200	6	158	0-20	9	13	14
		per client	110	1	110				
Freelancers	22	hourly	40-120	6	82	0-20	10	9	13
		per client	100-170	3	130				
Through pimps	24	hourly	120	1	120	6-25	3	14	16
		per client	100	1	100				
Brothels	25	hourly	50-200	2	125	8-60	8	16	17
		per client	50-170	3	123				
At home	15	per client	150	1	150	1	1	1	1

Note: The "adjusted average" is the average number of transactions per week adjusted for the "normal number" as stated by the respondent.

previous week, those working in messes or as freelancers reported a slightly lower number than the other types of sex workers. Adjusting for those who said that they did not have the usual number of transactions in the previous week increased the mean levels for all categories.

Table 3.6 shows that the range of incomes earned was very wide, from RM$100 to RM$28,000 (US$40 to 11,200) per month, with an average of about RM$5,000 (US$2,000), mostly from payment for sex, although earnings from tips were important for those who received them. Six women reported that they earned tips between RM$20 and 200 (US$8-80) per client.

Not many of the respondents could explain their expenditure pattern. The younger women found their income-earning capacity exhilarating; they received cash and they spent it on nice clothes, shoes, cosmetics and jewellery. This was not surprising, given their age and the amount of cash they had at their disposal. When they needed to send money home, they spent less. Most were careful about the amount they sent home, so as to avoid casting any suspicion on their main activity. The older women were, as would be expected, more cautious and better able to explain the way they used their earnings.

The main item of expenditure was clothes; the average proportion spent on clothes was highest for those working in messes (16 per cent), followed by the freelancers (13 per cent), while the rest spent about 9 per cent of their total income on clothes. Savings were the next most important expenditure, followed by remittances home. But not all respondents sent money home. Of those interviewed, 50 per cent sent money home to support children, siblings or other family members. Twenty-eight held their savings in cash, two in the form of gold or jewellery, and one in several bank accounts. Five claimed they had no savings. Two admitted borrowing from their pimps, but provided no further information.

Table 3.6. Average earnings and expenditure per month

Category	Number of responses	Range RM$	Average RM$
Sources of income			
Fees for sex	33	10-18 000	4 374
Commission	6	200-12 000	3 783
Payment to pimps	20	0-500	72
Net income	33	100-28 000	4 860
Selected items of expenditure			
Clothes	30	25-8 000	845
Savings	18	100-4 000	1 644
Remittances	8	0-1 000	448
Food	30	60-2 000	367
Accommodation	23	50-600	240
Cosmetics	21	20-1 000	240
Leisure activities	9	50-500	159
Transport	15	4-300	126
Alcohol	2	100-150	125
Cigarettes	16	10-300	91

Health and medical attention

Over 90 per cent of the women interviewed had received some information on the health risks related their work; however, a fifth found the information inadequate. The main source of information (for about a third of the respondents) was others in the same line of work; the rest obtained information from government clinics or health officers, the *mamasan*, pimp or employer. A few picked up the information from the mass media.

Half of the respondents had received information on contraception and abortion, 37 per cent on prophylactics, 80 per cent on HIV/AIDS and 31 per cent on STDs. That the AIDS awareness campaign in the country has been relatively effective can be inferred from the fact that more women had received such information than the number who knew about contraception. Most of them knew about HIV/AIDS from the mass media. No one knew of any co-workers with AIDS. Most of the women still did not know exactly what the AIDS disease was and seemed to believe that as long as they went for their regular medical check-ups, they would be fine. More than three-quarters of the women reported taking the necessary precautions to avoid pregnancy. More than 60 per cent said they always made the customer use a condom. Eleven of the women said their establishments provided the condoms, and another 12 reported that while their establishments did not provide condoms, they encouraged their use. Of those not taking precautions, the main reason given was that the customers refused to use the condom, while three women did not insist because they thought they were in no danger of infection.

Twenty-four (63 per cent) of the women went for a medical check-up between two and four times a month; one went eight times per month while the high-earning GRO claimed that she went after each sexual transaction (but she had only a few transactions a month). Almost all the women went for check-ups on their own accord, all to private clinics. In fact, the women frequented specific clinics where the doctors knew about their line of work and did all the necessary checks. Correspondingly, most women also paid their own medical expenses. Five women reported having contracted sexually transmitted diseases two or three times, and had to pay for the medication themselves. Six out of 36 who responded had undergone abortions.

The scope and significance of the sex sector in the national economy

The number of sex workers

It is difficult, if not impossible to determine the number of prostitutes in Malaysia. Abdul Hadi (1980) recommends two formulae to estimate the number of prostitutes. According to his own derivation, the number of all prostitutes in Peninsular Malaysia was around 0.237 per cent of the population. Currently, in a total population of about 18 million, this works out to be about 43,000 prostitutes. His second formula was that of Kinsey et al. (1953), who estimated that in an American city of 100,000 people, 3,190 prostitute-client encounters occur per week. If this formula is applied to Kuala Lumpur (current population of about 1 million), then there are 31,900 prostitute-client encounters per week. Assuming that a prostitute entertains on average two clients a night, this works out to 15,950 prostitutes in Kuala Lumpur. A similar calculation for the entire urban population implies a workforce of about 142,000 prostitutes in the country.

The range is therefore wide. For example, these estimates imply a range from 3,000 to 16,000 for the city of Kuala Lumpur, which in 1992 had 597 licensed bars, coffee houses, discos and massage parlours. If each establishment has about ten sex workers plying their services each night, there would already be about 6,000 workers.[21] This does not include seedy hotels or illegal establishments. The cheap hotels tend to have about 30 girls working per night, and brothels may be even larger establishments. In fact, if the latter form the majority in the sector, then the data suggest that the upper value of 16,000 may even be conservative for the city.

Another way to gauge the number of workers is from potential demand. While the high-income segment of the sex sector caters primarily to locals, and while foreign tourists do not represent a significant share of the market, the migrant workers currently in the country without their families account for a growing share of the demand in the low- and middle-income segments. The severe labour shortages in the country have led to the import of over 1 million migrant workers. Assuming that about a quarter of the migrant workers are female, and that the proportion of sex workers is about 3 per cent of the male migrant workforce, there would be about 22,500 sex workers servicing the migrant workers alone.

Considering all this information, it is likely that the number of prostitutes in the country falls in the upper region of the estimated range from 43,000 to 142,000. And what about the pimps, procurers and *mamasans*? Again, estimates are difficult to come by, since not all sex workers operate through pimps or procurers. Some pimps only manage two to three prostitutes; others many more. If about a quarter of the sex sector comprises freelancers, and each pimp handles about seven women on average, then the sector could be providing employment to between 5,000 and 20,000 men. The number of *mamasans* is even harder to estimate, but is probably at least as many as the number of establishments in the business. A conservative range for total employment in the sex sector would then be from 50,000 to 160,000. The lower limit of the range is not very different from the number of persons employed in mining and quarrying in the country in 1992, while the upper limit is just slightly less than the total number of administrative and managerial workers.

If we include those employed in the related service sectors, then the number of employed persons dependent on the sex sector for their livelihood is indeed significantly large. The sex sector uses the entertainment sector as its access channel. Thus, the workers in the hotels, lounges and nightclubs are indirectly dependent on them. The staff manning and maintaining the apartments that serve as the place of business for commercial sex workers directly depend on these women for their livelihood. These include cleaners, security guards, apartment owners and so on. Then there are the food stalls and *the tarik* (tea) stalls which operate throughout the night in the vicinity of the sex sector establishments. There are also the medical practitioners who provide regular medical check-ups and perform abortions.

Although the service sector, which covers hotels and restaurants, utilities, wholesale and retail trade and other services, had about a 5 per cent share of total employment over the past few years, the numbers employed in the sector grew from 1.34 million to 1.84 million between 1986 to 1992. The actual numbers employed in the entertainment and fitness industries are not available, but are large enough to suggest that their services and links to the sex sector are not insignificant. Expanding further, cigarette and alcohol consumption are essential activities in the entertainment world. Though not completely dependent on the sex sector, traders in these goods certainly benefit from it. In an even broader sense, the local authorities also benefit from the taxes collected from liquor sales and from the licences issued to entertainment centres and from assessments levied on apartments. For example, in 1992, the Kuala Lumpur City Hall earned about RM$18 million from federal taxes, about 90 per cent of which came from entertainment and liquor licences.[22]

Earnings in the sex sector

The significance of the sex sector can also be gauged from the earnings, which are indeed very attractive. In manufacturing, for instance, average wages per annum in 1990 were RM$7,131 (US$2,852) for skilled workers, RM$4,279 (US$1,711) for unskilled workers and RM$2,596 (US$1,038) for part-time general workers (Malaysia Department of Statistics, 1990). In comparison, the part-time sex worker

Table 3.7. Changes in rates for sexual transactions over time

Source of information	Earnings
Ruslan (1966)	Streetwalkers, RM$320 monthly
Zakaria (1976)	Bar prostitutes in Penang, RM$700-1 000 monthly
Phang (1979)	Girls in rehabilitation centres, RM$1 400-1 600 monthly
New Straits Times, 27 Sep. 1983	High RM$150-200 per client, middle RM$50-100, low RM$10-20
Her World, June 1987	Average income RM$8 000 per month; or RM$300-500 per regular client; RM$1 000 per day for a millionaire client
Survey for this study, 1992	Girls in rehabilitation centres, RM$4 837 monthly; freelancers over 21 years of age, RM$2 839 monthly

Note: The rate of exchange at the time of the survey was approximately RM$2.5 per US$.

in the cheapest of hotels who receives RM$10 (US$4) per client, sees about ten clients a day, and works only once a week for about 12 hours, can earn RM$5,200 (US$2,080) per annum. One such sex worker observed that with this job, "I can earn enough to look after my two young children. It is so difficult to get someone to look after them when you work elsewhere. Here, I only come when I need the money and it is easy to find a babysitter just for a day". Another said, "My brother's children need money for school expenses. My brother cannot afford it, so my mother asked me to earn some money this way and bring it home tonight". In another case, a man (a clerical worker) and his wife go once a month to the Jalan Bukit Bintang area to find potential clients. The client and woman book into one of the cheap hotels or apartment rooms nearby. The presence of the husband ensures safety for the woman; and her earnings for one night's work are supposed to be enough to pay for the monthly rent and utility bills.

Earnings of the sex worker are affected by age, nationality, personal characteristics, market of operations and, of course, by the number of clients serviced. The rate chargeable normally declines with age; young girls who have not yet reached puberty and virgins fetch a premium. There is also the effect of novelty of nationality; a foreigner from an "exotic origin" can command a higher rate over a local of the same age. In terms of personal characteristics, the sex worker who can carry herself well, dress well and who has the right contacts is able to operate in the high-income sub-sector. The number of customers serviced also varies; those operating in the low-income sub-sector tend to service many more clients than those in the high-income sub-sector.

Table 3.7 gives an indication of the trends in earnings in the sex sector over time. The streetwalker or freelancer earns about eight times more today than she would have 25 years ago. The sex workers who were interviewed in the rehabilitation centre, i.e. the younger girls, earned about three times more than young girls earned over ten years ago. The rates do not seem to have changed much between the mid-1980s and today. But comparing differentials in earnings shows a different picture. For example, the average monthly wage for unskilled work in the manufacturing sector was about

RM$100 (US$40) in 1969 and about RM$450 (US$180) in 1989; this meant that the relative differential in earnings between sex work and unskilled work in manufacturing had increased from about three times in 1969 to about six times in 1989. Thus, it is not just that earnings in the sex sector are higher relative to earnings in other types of unskilled employment; the fact that the differentials have widened over time may explain the sustained growth in the supply of workers to the sex sector.

Legislation covering the sex sector

Malaysian society takes the position that prostitution is deviant behaviour. All religions practised in the country view prostitution negatively and argue for its legal control. The Malaysian legal system, on the other hand, is based on the British system, a legacy of colonial days. The legal system reflects what can be described as a tolerationist view (D'Cunha, 1992, p. 34), which does not prohibit prostitution *per se*, but seeks to abolish trafficking in women and children, brothel keeping and pimping. While civil law does not make prostitution illegal, it does forbid sodomy, which affects some sex workers. The legal system also comprises the *Shariah*, or Islamic law, which expressly forbids prostitution, sodomy and illicit sex.

The law and the prostitute

Both the Penal Code and specific acts cover offences related to the commercial sex sector. The main law in force today is the Women and Girls Protection Act, 1973, Act 106. The Act is currently being reviewed with the aim of introducing amendments to increase punishments, make it easier to obtain convictions, and extend protection to pregnant unmarried women and girls presently not covered by the Act. Provisions in the Act declare in no uncertain terms that activities of the sex sector are prohibited and punishable offences. Relevant sections aim at procurers and those who operate brothels, by dealing with the selling, hiring, procuring and detaining of women and children for the purposes of prostitution, including acting as an intermediary, advertising and bringing women into Malaysia for this purpose. Under the Act, it is a punishable offence to traffic in women and girls, whether or not it is for the purpose of prostitution, to live on the earnings of the prostitution of another person, or to have carnal knowledge of a female below 16 years of age.

Under the Women and Girls Protection Act, the sex worker herself does not commit any offence by earning income as a prostitute. She only commits an offence if she is found soliciting in a public place. Upon conviction, she may be sentenced to imprisonment for a term not exceeding six months, to a fine not exceeding RM$1,000 (US$400), or to both. A prosecution under this Act can, however, be instituted only with the consent of the Protector.

Prostitutes coming into Malaysia from other countries are, however, categorized under immigration law as prohibited immigrants. The Immigration Act, 1959/63, Act 155, provides that prostitutes and all persons living on the earnings of prostitutes are prohibited immigrants. Under section 31, if a person arriving in Malaysia is found to be a prohibited immigrant, he or she can be detained at an immigration centre and subsequently sent back to his or her country of origin. At the time of entry, it may not be possible to establish that a foreigner is a sex worker or procurer, particularly if he or she poses as a tourist. However, should the foreigner be caught by the police in an anti-vice raid, the provisions of the Act will be used to deport the person.

A Malaysian sex worker found soliciting may also be prosecuted under the Minor Offences Act, 1955 (Revised 1987), Act 336. The penalty under this Act is lighter than that under the Women and Girls Protection Act, and the police are not required to seek the consent of the Protector. The Minor Offences Act does not specifically mention soliciting, but sex workers have been placed together with beggars and unlicensed hawkers in section 27, which is entitled "Idle and Disorderly Persons". It provides that "every prostitute behaving in a disorderly or indecent manner in or near any public road or in any place of public resort shall be deemed to be an idle and disorderly person and shall be liable to a fine not exceeding RM$100 (US$40) or to imprisonment for a term not exceeding one month". If the sex worker is a Muslim, she can be prosecuted under Islamic law.

Although the Women and Girls Protection Act creates many offences for those involved in the sex sector, it is not always possible to secure a conviction due to the lack of evidence that is admissible according to the laws of evidence and criminal procedure. The Malaysian police, therefore, sometimes resort to other legislation in order to curb the activities of the sector. One such law is the Prevention of Crimes Act, 1959 (Revised 1983), Act 297, which aims at more effective prevention of crime as well as at the control of criminals, members of secret societies and other undesirable persons. The Act allows the arrest without warrant of any such person and – after the appropriate inquiry – registration, which would have the effect of placing the person under police supervision for five years. The person may also be subjected to other restrictions in terms of place of residence and confinement within doors between specified hours of the night. The Prevention of Crimes Act is usually used against procurers and others in the sex sector only if violence is involved.

A more frequently invoked law is the Restricted Residence Act, 1933 (Revised 1989), Act 377. Under this Act, the Justice Minister can order a procurer to reside within a specified area for a fixed term and to be under police supervision for up to five years. The idea is that if the person is confined to a particular area, he or she will not be able to direct illegal operations and may instead settle into a legitimate business. While these restrictions may have been effective in the past, today's sophisticated telecommunications technology make it necessary to have more than a restricted residence order to stop the activities of a well-connected procurer.

There are also other provisions in the Malaysian Penal Code that address carnal intercourse against the "order of nature". Section 377A declares "sexual connection by the introduction of the penis into the anus or mouth of the other person" an offence punishable with imprisonment for up to 20 years and whipping. The provision is intended for general application and could apply to a male-female relationship whether in the sex sector or otherwise. Its main targets, however, are homosexuals. It is used against the sex sector where the workers are transsexuals or transvestites.

The law and sex establishments

The Women and Girls Protection Act, 1973, provides for the suppression of places of assignation (section 20) and brothels (section 21). A place of assignation is defined in the Act as "any place where communication is established with any female person either directly or through an intermediary for purpose of prostitution". Section 20 mentions associations, clubs or places of public resort. A place of public resort is any place to which the public has access, such as bars and massage parlours.

In addition, city or municipal regulations or by-laws also determine whether establishments can be used as a place of assignation, if not for actually dispensing sexual services. In the capital city of Kuala Lumpur, for instance, a licence is required under the Massage Establishments (Federal Territory) By-laws, 1980 (which were amended in 1991), to operate a massage establishment. The licence is revocable if the licensee contravenes any by-law or breaches any condition of the licence. A relevant prohibition provides that "no licensee shall employ in his massage establishment any person whom he knows or has reason to believe to be a prostitute or a person of bad character". This regulation is supposed to prevent the massage parlour from being used as a place of assignation. Other regulations aim to ensure that sexual activities cannot take place in the massage parlour, by requiring that all treatment rooms be fitted with swing doors which cannot be locked, and by prohibiting "massage" activities in any room that is locked. The regulations also require the licensee to ensure that all masseurs and masseuses undergo an annual medical examination. If the employees are also sex workers, then this regulation is supposed to help control health problems.

The Boarding Houses Rules, 1929, provide that prostitutes or known bad characters shall not be allowed to occupy the premises or to meet or assemble there. The keepers of boarding houses who allow prostitutes into their premises may also be prosecuted under the Minor Offences Act, 1955, which provides that the keeper of any hotel, boarding house, public house, common lodging house, eating house, coffee shop or other place of public entertainment or resort who permits prostitutes to meet or remain there for the purpose of soliciting or misbehaving therein shall be liable to a fine. To ensure that the keeper does not avoid liability by claiming that the act or omission was committed by his employee, the Act provides that he will be so liable if the servant or agent was employed in his business. Likewise, the servant or agent will be liable.

Islamic law and prostitution

The *Shariah*, which applies only to Muslims in Malaysia, prohibits extramarital sexual relations and illicit sexual intercourse, including prostitution, which are offences punishable as crimes. There are two main types of offences: *zinah,* which covers not only adultery but also sexual intercourse between unmarried persons; and the less serious offence of *khalwat,* which refers to close proximity in incriminating circumstances of a man and a woman who are not married to each other.

Islamic law has had a growing impact because of rising religious fundamentalism. Before 1980, enactments applying to Muslims in all Malaysian states contained similar provisions criminalizing any action that could lead to illicit sexual intercourse. Although the enactments did not specifically mention prostitution, they would have applied to such situations. Since the 1980s, various states in Malaysia have moved towards separate legislation for the different areas covered by Muslim law. In the states of Kelantan, Kedah and Melaka, the *Shariah* Criminal Code has been passed to deal with all offences over which the *Shariah* Courts have jurisdiction, including those relating to illicit sexual intercourse and prostitution. However, the Muslim Law Enactments of the other states provide only for illicit intercourse and *khalwat,* without spelling out prostitution as a separate offence. The fact that the woman is a prostitute appears to be a factor for enhancing her sentence, even for the lesser offence of *khalwat.*[23]

There are now provisions in the new *Shariah* Criminal Code in Malaysia that refer directly to the sex sector. For example, in the Malaysian state of Kelantan, the *Shariah* Criminal Code Enactment No. 2 of 1985 makes specific reference to prostitution. It makes it an offence for women to be prostitutes and, unlike provisions of the Women and Girls Protection Act, imposes punishment on the sex worker who takes on the role voluntarily. The sentence that can be imposed is a prison term and a fine, which is much heavier than that for soliciting under the Women and Girls Protection Act or the Minor Offences Act. The heavy punishment reflects how severely Islam views prostitution. Another section of the Kelantan *Shariah* Code is directed at persons who force members of their family into prostitution, including men who force their wives into prostitution or allow them to be prostitutes, and parents or guardians who force their children into the profession.

These sections of the Kelantan *Shariah* Code are difficult to cite because they require evidence of prostitution; in most cases, the accused are charged under the section which deals with *khalwat.* The offence carries a fine of RM$2,000 (US$800) and imprisonment of up to a year for a male offender, and a fine of RM$1,000 (US$400) and imprisonment of up to six months for a female offender. In other Malaysian states, the Islamic law treats the male as the principal offender and the woman as the abettor, but the punishments are the same for both. The Kelantan *Shariah* Criminal Code also makes it an offence for any person to act as a procurer, for any male to wear female attire and pose as a woman in a public place, and for two males to engage in the sexual act.

Development and social programmes affecting the sex sector[24]

The five-year development plans

Concerns specific to the sex sector in the country's various five-year development plans are addressed through allocations to welfare needs and internal security (i.e. the police). The Malaysian government has provided for protection homes or institutions for the care, protection and rehabilitation of young girls and women "exposed to moral danger" since the First Malaysia Plan 1956-60. The protection homes and rehabilitation programmes are under the responsibility of the Department of Social Welfare. The approach in the Plans has been to treat sex workers, especially the young and under-age, as one of the vulnerable or disadvantaged groups in society, and the approach has clearly been a welfare-oriented one. The Royal Malaysia Police is the only arm of the government that has direct dealings with the sex sector; the Anti-Vice Divisions in the different states are responsible for monitoring prostitution, drugs, gambling and secret societies. Under the Women and Girls Protection Act, they are mandated to carry out frequent preventive checks to pick up under-age girls and foreigners suspected of being prostitutes.[25]

More recent development plans emphasize the need for close liaison between the Department of Social Welfare, the police and the courts to provide effective rehabilitation services, especially for juveniles. They also specifically acknowledge the role of welfare organizations and community services, thereby effectively drawing the boundaries of involvement of the government in the success of such programmes.

Beyond the ties with the Department of Social Welfare and the police via the Women and Girls Protection Act, Malaysia's development plans do not directly address the needs of the sex sector, nor do they recognize prostitution as an economic sector. This is in part a reflection of the way in which the sector is dealt with both publicly and by the government. The National Policy for Women, which was adopted in late 1989 and incorporated in the Sixth Malaysia Plan 1991-95, also makes no specific reference to women in prostitution.

Rehabilitation programmes

In Malaysia, the "rehabilitation" and training programmes run by the Department of Social Welfare are closely linked to police enforcement of the Women and Girls Protection Act. The Act empowers the Department to provide shelter and protection to under-age women or girls (below 21 years) who have fallen victim to vice or who are exposed to the danger of moral degradation, and to women of any age who voluntarily seek protection from threats or intimidation to undertake prostitution or immoral activities. The Department works closely with the police and the courts. When someone is referred to the Department, it holds an inquiry and prepares a social background report that is submitted to the court to determine whether any warrant or order should be made in the interest of the person. The report is also used in planning the supervision or rehabilitation programme for the woman or girl in the event that she is ordered to be placed under the supervision of a welfare officer or if she is sent to a protection centre.

The Malaysian Department of Social Welfare provides rehabilitation services in the form of five protection centres that have been set up in different parts of the country, and through field supervision and aftercare for those who leave the centres. Admission of women and girls in urgent need of protection to a centre is sanctioned by a court order or by the Protector. Committal to a centre is for a statutory period of three years, but the institutional form of rehabilitation is seen as a last resort. The Department feels that the best form of rehabilitation is to place the women and girls, especially first-time offenders, in the community under the care of a social welfare officer for a period not exceeding three years.

At the protection centres, training programmes have been expanded from character-building and behaviour modification to include skills training, value orientation and the development of personal resilience in order to withstand challenges and temptations. The aim of these centres is to assist the women and girls exposed to moral danger to acquire skills, desirable attitudes and values that conform to prevailing social norms, so that they can be reintegrated into the mainstream of society. Health education on HIV/AIDS is emphasized in the hope that it may discourage the women from re-entering the sex sector when they leave the centres. For those who have been released from the centres, aftercare supervision is provided by a social welfare officer in the community for a period of one year.

Several studies (Zainah, 1975; Haslani, 1988; Abdul Hadi, 1990) have examined the work of the rehabilitation centres in Malaysia. A major finding was that, despite the many activities and programmes to ameliorate the forced or compulsory nature of their stay, many of the girls felt imprisoned. Thus, whether or not a woman or girl is successfully rehabilitated depends very much on whether she herself is prepared to be rehabilitated.

The programmes in the rehabilitation centres appear to be geared to making the girls into good housewives. Some of the skills taught could, of course, help them to find employment: cooking, sewing and handicraft-making. However, given that many of the girls had the opportunity to earn far more in prostitution, it is difficult to see how they would be willing to work long and tedious hours to earn far less when they are released. Perhaps a more relevant curriculum may help. Staff of the protection centres have noted that the educational level of those entering the centres has been rising, a likely effect of the increase in the number of years of free schooling in the country. It may therefore be useful to offer courses in simple book-keeping, dealing with government departments relating to the establishment of businesses, various modes of saving and the like. Such topics are part of the living skills courses currently taught to lower secondary school students, and given that many of the women and girls at the centres are drop-outs at the lower secondary level, such knowledge may prove useful. The survey for this study showed that many of the women and girls have sufficient savings and interest to begin small enterprises.

Health programmes

The existence of the "underground" sex sector means that there is no effective way to check the health of sex workers, and therefore no means of controlling the spread of disease. Only indirect forms of control currently exist. For example, the licensing regulations of massage establishments require workers to undergo annual medical examinations. Also, sex workers detained in a place of refuge may be required to undergo a medical examination.

95

If a sex worker has had a medical test that reveals an infectious disease covered by the Prevention and Control of Infectious Diseases Act, 1988, Act 342, it may be possible to exercise some form of control on the spread of the disease by the person. The diseases subject to control under the Act are gonococcal infections, syphilis and HIV/AIDS. The Act provides for mandatory reporting of HIV/AIDS infection; it requires any person having knowledge of infection or the death of a person caused by the disease to notify the District Health Officer, government facility, police station or village head. A medical practitioner with such knowledge has to inform the Medical Officer of Health. Persons in charge of boarding houses also have a duty to report if a person in their boarding house has the disease or has died of the disease.

The Ministry of Public Health has tended to keep its distance from the sex sector, perhaps as a reflection of the country's Islamic values and relatively conservative public policies, as well as the underground nature of the sector. It does not have any programme that directly targets the sex sector, but between 1985 and 1990 it carried out surveys among sex workers and, since 1989, it has administered HIV/AIDS tests for all suspected prostitutes picked up in police raids. The Ministry has also mounted a campaign through the media – aimed at the general public – to advocate a "healthy lifestyle" and safe sex, and to raise awareness of the ease of transmission of HIV/AIDS through irresponsible sexual behaviour, including through commercial sex.

Women's NGOs in Malaysia have been increasingly concerned about the sex sector's impact on the growing threat of HIV/AIDS. The National Council of Women's Organizations (NCWO), which is an umbrella organization with over 60 affiliates, holds public forums to discuss prostitution and missing girls, and has planned a comprehensive programme specifically targeting the sex sector,[26] including counselling, outreach work, training, the provision of a resource centre, and the distribution of a kit providing information on issues relating to girls missing from home, who often end up in prostitution. Another NGO, the Pink Triangle, offers free and confidential counselling on sexuality and AIDS, HIV testing, support services for those affected by the disease and awareness-raising programmes among the gay community and injecting drug users. It has enlisted the cooperation of the private sector, such as business chain-stores, to help spread information about safe sex. It also has an outreach programme to deal directly with the sex sector. The groups initially targeted by the Pink Triangle were the transvestites and transsexuals, but the NGO soon realized that it had to also reach women prostitutes. Although the Pink Triangle has become an important NGO in the campaign against HIV/AIDS, it has been finding it increasingly hard to reach out to and gain the confidence of sex workers, because of the increasing number of preventive raids by the police and the closing down of seedy hotels, which has had the effect of dispersing those who usually work in these places. Ikhlas is a special interest group within the Pink Triangle, which works with the prostitutes in the Chow Kit area of the capital, Kuala Lumpur, where it has an office. The group holds peer-group workshops for the prostitutes to help empower them, so that they can understand their rights, especially with regard to police raids. It encourages the prostitutes to save for their future, and it also provides counselling services and general health education, especially with regard to the use of condoms.

Education, awareness-raising and advocacy programmes

The Malaysian Ministry of Education does not deal directly with the sex sector, but it is concerned with using the educational system to inculcate in young minds sound social values and good health practices. For example, HIV/AIDS awareness is introduced to students as early as their second-to-last year of primary school. The family health education programme also seeks to provide current information on human sexuality in its biological, psychological, socio-cultural and moral dimensions. In secondary school, the students are taught about the effects of high-risk lifestyles on health, the signs and symptoms of diseases that may arise from these lifestyles, and measures to prevent their occurrence. They are also given information on reproduction and infectious diseases, including STDs. Islamic education in lower secondary school emphasizes what is illicit and the consequences visited upon those who engage in illicit activities. In upper secondary school, Muslim students are taught about the blessings of marriage as ordained by *Allah* and how important it is to produce a clean new generation, to nurture love, prevent illicit deeds and promote spiritual ties.

In Malaysia, other "preventive" programmes have been described as including: (a) hostels for factory women and girls, provided jointly by the Social Welfare Department and private employers "to help sort out the accommodation problems of these girls, who in addition have to adapt and cope with changes in lifestyle and living which might cause them to fall prey to would-be recruiters of prostitutes"; (b) a "big sister programme" whereby older girls with longer service in employment in factories and other work areas act as a source of help and referral for whatever problems may be encountered by girls new to an urban environment and in first-time employment; (c) a "happy family campaign" which was conducted over a one-year period and which aimed at strengthening the family unit and fostering better relationships among family members so as to reduce the likelihood of young girls with family problems being drawn into prostitution; (d) financial assistance and protection for vulnerable women, such as widows, divorcees and other destitute women, so that they do not resort to prostitution out of desperation; (e) careful approval of procedures for the adoption of children, so as to ensure that they are not adopted to be brought up for the purpose of prostitution; (g) education and awareness given to the public and community through the press and television as part of the HIV/AIDS prevention programme, urging avoidance of sex with prostitutes; (h) frequent checks and close supervision of places of entertainment to monitor the working conditions of the workers; and (i) provision of temporary accommodation for battered wives, so that these women are not so desperate as to be vulnerable to negative influences (Chong, 1991).

The NGO Tenaganita works on empowerment with commercial sex workers as one of the groups of vulnerable women workers (others are plantation workers, industrial workers and migrant workers). It has an outreach programme to empower the prostitutes to avoid further marginalization and dehumanization. Legal literacy sessions and health-awareness talks are frequently held. Legal representation and health referral services are also available. There is a halfway house for health recovery, reorientation and development of alternative work, promoted through counselling, learning to live positively, family reunification, job placement and income-generating programmes. The approach of the NGO is that it is only through care and concern for the sex worker, rather than through condemnation or criminalization, that changes will occur. The sex worker ultimately makes her own decision on whether to return to the sector. The organization operates on the premise that its programmes will assist the sex worker to make the correct decisions that will empower and protect her.[27]

Notes

[1] Arasaratnam (1979, p. 13) writes of the abuses of young women recruited through Madras for the purpose of prostitution in the new labour settlements.

[2] The Cantonese female brothel keeper was known as *kwai-po* and the Japanese female brothel keeper as *mamasan*. The latter term is still in common use today.

[3] Women and Girls Protection Enactment, Cap. 33 of the Straits Settlements; Women and Girls Protection Enactment, 1914; Women and Girls Protection Enactment, Cap. 156, 1931; Women and Girls Protection Enactment, No. 2, 1941. More recent changes are incorporated in the Women and Girls Protection Enactment/Ordinance (Rules), 1971, and the Women and Girls Protection Act, 1973. The latter is the most important piece of legislation used to control the sex sector today.

[4] Examples of the Perak Orders in Council affecting the sex sector include: No. 2 of 1887: Inmates of Brothels; No. 2 of 1888: Registration of Prostitutes; No. 29 of 1889: Removal of Prostitutes from Brothels; No. 8 of 1890: Declaration as to the Age of Prostitutes; No. 5 of 1892: Abolition of Brothel Registration Fees; No. 9 of 1893: Management of Brothels; and No. 21 of 1893: Registration of Brothels, Amendment.

[5] *Asian Defence*, January 1995, reported that the Malaysian army had 105,500 personnel, the navy 11,000 and the air force 13,000. The armed forces accounted for about 15 per cent of government workers.

[6] *Sixth Malaysia Plan 1991-1995*, p. 11.

[7] *Second Outline Perspective Plan*, p. 109.

[8] Publication of the book quoted here produced a public outcry and prompted a series of police raids. Many of these services have presumably moved to other locations.

[9] The Minister for National Unity and Social Development stated that 1,146 teenagers were reported missing in 1991 (*New Straits Times*, 17 July 1992). It is believed that many of those missing enter the vice trade.

[10] *Malay Mail*, 19 July 1993, p. 5.

[11] For example, the *Berita Harian*, 4 May 1989, reported that three women from India had been lured to Malaysia by a businessman through Singapore. They charged RM$150 per client and worked only in hotels.

[12] *New Straits Times*, 14 September 1989.

[13] The *Utusan Malaysia*, 19 September 1989, reported that Thai prostitutes were moving to Malaysia since demand from Malaysians for their services in southern Thailand had declined because of the fear of AIDS.

[14] The *New Straits Times*, 19 June 1993, reported that Singapore turned away hundreds of Thai women arriving by buses at the Johore Bahru immigration checkpoint.

[15] The *Berita Harian*, 27 October 1991, reported that the police had uncovered a syndicate with five local agents involved in sending Thai girls to Japan for the purpose of prostitution.

[16] The *Star*, 27 October 1990, reported that the police had uncovered a training scheme in Malaysia for Thai women who were to be sent to Singapore and Japan to work as prostitutes.

[17] The *Malay Mail*, 8 June 1992. The Immigration Department requires those under 18 to submit letters of consent from their parents or legal guardians when applying for a passport.

[18] *Sunday Star*, 14 March 1993.

[19] *New Straits Times*, 24 June and 14 September 1991; the *Star*, 18 August 1990 and 5 January 1991.

20 The *Sunday Star*, 26 July 1992, carried an interview with a girl who was almost persuaded to join the profession when she faced financial difficulties. She spoke of meeting with smartly-dressed persons (the *mamasan* and a pimp) who treated her well, explained the nature of the job and indicated the likely earnings. She decided not to accept it. Another newspaper report (*Metro*, 21 December 1992) reported that teenage schoolchildren were being recruited by syndicates to persuade their female classmates to enter the profession locally or overseas.

[21] A recent move by the Kuala Lumpur City Hall to require establishments to register all GROs, in an attempt to discourage under-age girls from working in the sector, resulted in 1,776 girls, all 18 years of age and over, being registered by about 70 per cent of establishments (*Malay Mail*, 15 October 1994). If the unregistered under-age girls and the massage parlour girls are also included, then the figure of 6,000 is not unreasonable.

[22] Computed from Kuala Lumpur City Hall Licensing Department records. Entertainment taxes formed the bigger proportion (87 per cent), although they included taxes for all public performances, such as plays and musicals.

[23] In the case of Rusidah bte Abdul Ghani versus *Pendakwa Jabatan Agama Islam* (the religious prosecutor), the accused pleaded guilty to a charge of committing *khalwat* under the Selangor Administration of Muslim Law Enactment, 1952. The prosecutor urged the court to impose a heavy sentence on the grounds that the accused was a prostitute. The accused pleaded that she had ceased to be a prostitute and was looking after her children. The trial judge accepted the prosecutor's arguments and sentenced the woman to a monetary fine and two months imprisonment, because "the court took a severe view of the work as a prostitute, as it is forbidden by the law and condemned by *Allah*, and also lowers the standing of the Muslims among the non-Muslims, and is contrary to the customs of the Malays."

[24] Information on the social programmes was obtained from two primary sources: information supplied by representatives of government agencies on the research panel for this study, and presentations by representatives of government and non-governmental organizations at the Workshop on the Sex Sector and Development in Malaysia: Implications for the Future, Kuala Lumpur, June 1994.

[25] More than 13,000 preventive checks were carried out in 1990, 67 per cent more than in 1989. But the percentage of under-age and foreign women caught per preventive check has decreased dramatically from 33 per cent in 1989, to 24 per cent in 1990, 17 per cent in 1991 and 13 per cent in 1992 (statistics provided by the Criminal Investigation Department). These figures do not, however, suggest a declining sector. The efficacy of the preventive checks has been reduced in the face of technological advances in communications. For example, when the police mount a preventive check, even in nondescript vehicles, they are tracked and watched by operators, and messages are relayed ahead by mobile telephones to those in the locations targeted by the police.

[26] As reported in the *New Straits Times*, 16 July 1993.

[27] Information provided by the NGO at the Workshop on the Sex Sector and Development in Malaysia: Implications for the Future, Kuala Lumpur, June 1994. See Nagaraj (1994).

PROSTITUTION IN THE PHILIPPINES 4

Rene E. Ofreneo and Rosalinda Pineda Ofreneo

Historical and social factors behind the development of the sex sector

Spanish times

There is no record of prostitution in the pre-Spanish Philippines, when women enjoyed relative equality with men. Women could inherit property, manage farms, enjoy sexual freedom, choose their marriage partners, obtain divorce and perform the important role of a *babaylan* (a combination of healer, spiritual leader and cultural transmitter).

When the Spaniards came in the sixteenth century, they imposed Catholicism, introduced feudal agriculture, persecuted the *babaylans* and cultivated a patriarchal culture where women had to subordinate themselves to father, husband and priest. Their world was confined to kitchen, children and church, and their sexuality was controlled through a virginity cult and other aspects of a strict moral code, which prescribed rules of conduct that emphasized modesty and chastity. Ironically, it was during this period that prostitution evolved and spread. The rape of native women by the Spaniards, which was not uncommon at the time, created a reserve of "fallen" women who became available to service not only the homesick Spanish troops and dignitaries, but also the friars. There were accounts of institutions that sheltered young girls from the supposed sinful, which also housed "lewd" or "worthless" women in separate quarters (Anonuevo, 1987, p. 65).

By the nineteenth century, prostitution was an occupation for women in Manila. The colonial authorities tolerated it, but also regulated it in the interest of curbing the spread of venereal disease, especially syphilis, which broke out in epidemic proportions in the mid-1890s. Regulation was also intended to respect public morals, which meant that prostitution had to exist only in the shadows. "This was evident not only in the interdiction imposed on the public solicitation of clients but also in the insistence that prostitution houses should not be located in places where there was much human traffic. The Reglamento also forbade the prostitution houses from revealing their real purpose through billboards." (Camagay, 1988, p. 255.) But the regulation and control of prostitution by the Spanish authorities was neither systematic nor consistent. While one Spanish Governor-General mounted a campaign to suppress prostitution, the civil Governor of Manila was in cahoots with the brothel owners (Dery, 1991, p. 480), and brothel operators refused to register or pay the high licence fees.

Puta or *prostituta* (prostitute), *mujer libre* or *mujer pública* (free or public woman), *dama de noche* (woman of the night), *mujerzuela* (cheap woman), *vagabunda* (vagabond), *ramera* (whore), *indocumentada* (undocumented woman, meaning one who had no residence certificate) and *kalapating mababa ang lipad* (a dove who flies low) were names given to the sex workers of the period. The women came from very different backgrounds. Records of apprehended prostitutes at that time showed that they had other occupations, such as dressmakers, laundrywomen, cigarette makers, vendors or domestic helpers. They had turned to the flesh trade mainly for economic reasons. Especially during the last decades of Spanish rule, rural poverty and displacement that were related to the spread of cash cropping led to migration to urban centres, where the competition for jobs was very stiff. The legalization of gambling was also an aggravating factor, as men who lost heavily often forced their wives or kin to prostitute themselves. Because the Spanish friars had no wives and the Chinese migrants did not bring their wives, they became favoured clients of the prostitutes (Dery, 1991).

There were four categories of prostitutes at the time: "those who were kept in a house of prostitution under the supervision of an *ama* (mistress) or *amo* (master)"; "those who plied their trade by posting themselves in certain streets"; "those who went to the residence of their client"; and "those who serviced clients in their own homes" (Camagay, 1988, pp. 249-250). Prostitutes who were arrested were fined, imprisoned from a few days to a couple of months, subjected to lashing and other forms of corporal punishment, made to labour in public works projects, or were deported to the southern Philippines (Dery, 1991, p. 484). An offer of marriage could save a woman from deportation, "as marriage was also viewed as a means of reforming prostitutes" (Camagay, 1988, p. 247). The Spanish Governor of Jolo even requested the Governor-General to deport one hundred prostitutes to his island to become wives of soldiers there, on the grounds that "it would give the prostitutes the chance to start a new life and that in the long run, this would help create a new settlement which would be beneficial to the colonial government" (Dery, 1991, pp. 485-486).

After the revolution against Spain and the establishment of the first Philippine Republic, President Aguinaldo dealt with the problem of prostitution in 1898 by creating a Board of Health, which required all prostitutes to undergo a weekly medical examination. Those with venereal diseases were to be cared for, but the cost of taking care of them was to be borne by the brothel owners.

The American presence

The outbreak of the Philippine-American War in 1899 and subsequent American rule led to the further entrenchment and proliferation of prostitution, especially since the war worsened poverty, destroyed property and displaced many people. The presence of American soldiers (70,000 at its peak) provided a large market for women. The American officials saw prostitution principally as a health problem and regarded the measures to halt the alarming spread of venereal disease as a "military necessity" (Dery, 1991, p. 486).

The only time prostitution was expressly prohibited was in 1918, when the Commanding Officer of the United States Army in the Philippines disallowed all military and civilian personnel from "entering or residing in a house of ill fame". Such prohibitions were more honoured in the breach than in the observance, as some American and Filipino colonial officials were themselves brothel owners. The Japanese, who came to the Philippines to work in American construction projects, established a chain of brothels in a section of Manila. Bars, clubs and cabarets also became commonplace in Manila.

By far the most significant impact on prostitution in the Philippines was the establishment of United States military bases in the country. Two cities, Olongapo and Angeles, grew around the largest of these bases to cater to the "rest and recreation" (R&R) needs of the American soldiers. Olongapo, which used to be a small fishing village contiguous to Subic Bay, was converted into a naval base by the Americans and transformed into a city of hotels, saunas, massage parlours and prostitutes as a result of dramatic increases in demand brought about by the Korean and Viet Nam Wars. An idea of the magnitude of the demand can be gleaned from the fact that some 7,000 to 10,000 sailors would disembark from a single aircraft carrier and find their recreation mostly in the arms of Olongapo women. Angeles City used to be a "self-reliant town with a flourishing furniture manufacturing industry". It served as a landing base for the US Cavalry during the Philippine-American War, and evolved into the largest US airbase outside the United States (De Dios, 1988). Data collected in 1990 showed that in Olongapo, there were 615 registered R&R establishments employing 11,600 registered women entertainers and about twice as many unregistered workers. In Angeles City, there were about 1,567 registered R&R establishments with 5,642 registered women entertainers. The combined registered women entertainers therefore numbered more than 17,000 in these two cities (Manahan, 1991, p. 3).

With the historic decision of the Philippine Senate not to renew the bases agreement in September 1991, the bases were eventually closed. The last American soldiers left in 1992. The bases have since been converted into industrial and commercial estates, but prostitution still thrives because the women have not found alternative forms of employment. The local demand is still there. Even when military prostitution was at its height, certain bars in Olongapo and Angeles City were identified as for locals only.

Sex tourism and the export of women

Another trend in the sex industry which emerged in the 1970s was sex tourism. This was related to the overall orientation of the martial law regime instituted by President

Ferdinand Marcos in 1972; the outward-oriented strategy of development made tourism a top priority in the drive to earn foreign exchange. Government encouragement led to a sharp increase in the number of tour agents and tour guides. In the city of Manila, the number of cocktail lounges, bars and clubs also increased significantly. Prostitution houses catering to tourists sprouted in Manila and surrounding cities, each house having 200 to 300 women. In Manila alone between 1976 and 1986, the number of travel agencies and operators increased from 300 to 491, tour agents and guides from 1,550 to 8,120 and cocktail lounges, bars and clubs from 225 to 436. The number of "hospitality women" in Manila issued with health certificates jumped from about 1,700 in the early 1980s to more than 7,000 in 1986 (Manahan, 1991, p. 5).

With the number of visitors passing the one million mark for the first time and bringing in more than US$319.74 million in foreign exchange, 1980 was a peak year for Philippine tourism. Data from the Department of Tourism revealed that of the total number of tourist arrivals, more than two-thirds were males, but of these only about 12 per cent came for business purposes. Much of the tourism was sex-related, especially for the Japanese men, who arrived in groups. However, most of the money paid out by the tourists did not reach the women, but went instead to the Japanese tour agent, the local agent and the manager of the prostitution house. The women received only US$10 out of the US$60 normally paid by a Japanese tourist as "prostitution money" (Perpinan, 1981, p. 13). Sex tourism achieved such a high profile that it provoked a concerted protest from women's groups in the Philippines, Japan and other Southeast Asian countries. As a result, there was an appreciable decline in overtly organized sex tourism, which was replaced with semi-underground and more covert forms of sex tourism that have moved away from the capital city to smaller resort areas. The Philippine Plan for Gender-Responsive Development 1995-2025 notes that "the 'package deal' (for sex tourism) is very much alive, thanks to a conglomerate of interlocking air carriers, tour operators and hotel companies concentrating on the tourist trade" (National Commission on the Role of Filipino Women, 1995, p. 308).

The government of President Marcos also embarked on a vigorous programme of export of labour, again for the purpose of earning foreign exchange. By the mid-1980s, there was a marked trend towards the feminization of migration, and this trend is partly explained by the export of "entertainers", especially to Japan but also to Europe. Figures available for 1987 indicate that of the women registered with the Philippine Overseas Employment Administration, 17.5 per cent, or 31,579, were entertainers. Moreover, there tend to be more illegal than registered women going overseas. Many of these entertainers become prostitutes by force of circumstance (De Dios, 1990).

The interplay of economic, political and social factors

The historical perspective highlights not only the roots of prostitution in the Philippines but also the complex interplay of factors which led to its development and contributed to its entrenchment and proliferation. Many of the factors – economic, political and socio- cultural – were internally generated but tended to be exacerbated by external factors.

The economic motivation is obvious, not only for the sex workers but also for other actors in the sex sector. A number of studies on prostitution (for example, Moselina, 1981; Wihtol, 1982; Gabriela Commission on Violence against Women, 1987; Miralao et al., 1990; De Dios, 1991; Buklod Centre, 1992; Ofreneo and Ofreneo, 1993; National Commission on the Role of Filipino Women, 1995) highlight a pattern of poverty, unemployment, underemployment and inadequate incomes as "push factors" which drive women into the sector. These push factors interact with other facilitating factors, such as active recruitment by agents and sometimes deception, abduction or "conditioning rape" by agents serving the sex industry. There has also been significant migration from rural to urban areas or to foreign countries, as women search for better economic opportunities or are deceived or coerced into the sex sector. The series of natural calamities suffered by the Philippines in the early 1990s, resulting in a massive loss of land, property and jobs, also aggravated the economic problems. A growing sense of materialism, which has infected even rural villages, also cannot be discounted. Some Filipino families, dazzled by the appliances and electronic gadgets brought home by overseas workers, encourage their daughters to take their chances abroad, even if they have to risk selling their bodies.

Political factors have also played a role. Imperialism, militarism and racism provided the "geopolitical-economic" context of military prostitution and sex tourism (Perpinan, 1982). Colonial and racist attitudes continue to be cultivated on both the demand and supply sides of the prostitution relationship: many men from Western countries receive images, often pornographic, of the exotic, lusty but malleable women of the East, which often reduce the latter to "little, brown fucking machines" in their eyes, while many of the women who service them are taken in or sustained by the mystique of white men, their economic prowess, the prospect of "rescue" and a new and better life abroad, and the perceived higher status of those who attach themselves to Caucasian males and raise offspring with them. Internal political factors include militarization and the creation of new hamlets or villages to counter local insurgency, which led to the displacement of whole communities and the migration of women to prostitution centres. Government policies encouraging tourism and the export of labour have also been instrumental in facilitating the prostitution of women, leading some analysts to conclude that the state has effectively served as pimp (De Dios, 1991).

Socio-cultural factors are also important in explaining the development of prostitution. In Philippine society, most women are shaped by family, church and school to be dutiful daughters, virginal girlfriends, devoted wives and sacrificing mothers. Many prostitutes cite the need to repay their "debt of gratitude" to parents and support their natal and/or conjugal families as a major reason why they enter or stay in the sex sector. From the young women's viewpoint, *utang na loob* (debt of gratitude) requires taking on any type of work for the upkeep of the family, as they have an obligation to their parents who took care of them in the past. The premium placed on virginity, and the sense of unworthiness of those who have lost their virginity, have led many women to go into prostitution thinking that this is what they deserve (Calalang, 1985). *Hiya* (shame, disgrace) keeps women in prostitution despite the fact that they are exposed to abuses and brutalities; they feel that the situation they are in should be kept private to avoid embarrassment to themselves and their families. As a consequence, they avoid seeking help or trying to get out of prostitution, as they often feel that there is nothing more that can be done for their problem. However, the double standard of morality does not require men to be virgins before they get married. Many young men experience sexual initiation with prostitutes. When they get married, many do not feel morally compelled to be absolutely faithful to their wives. A lot of Filipino men tend to have two images of women: madonna and whore, virgin and vamp, "good girl" to marry and "bad girl" to bed. This helps to explain why there is such a strong local demand from men of all social classes for prostitutes.

The organizational structure and relations within the sex sector

The Project Group on Prostitution convened by the National Commission on the Role of Filipino Women (NCRFW) categorized three major visible actors in the sex sector: the "bought", the "buyer" and the "business".

The "bought" can be further categorized: by type of worker, by location of work, by nature and class of clientele, by level of visibility and/or formality and by extent of integration with the overall sex industry structure, which at its apex has been internationalized. Prostitutes may also be classified by sex and age. There are male prostitutes working mostly in gay bars and child prostitutes victimized mainly by foreign homosexuals and paedophiles.

Based on the degree of exploitation and independence, prostitutes can also be classified as follows: the self-employed, the employed, the enslaved and the exported.

At the top of the hierarchy are the self-employed prostitutes who operate independently or within a loose, pimp or patronage system, such as call-girls and prostitutes who cater to visiting foreign businessmen, local politicians and upper-class businessmen, or their clients. These women tend to be young and well dressed. Some operate "on call", servicing clients in hotels, motels or out-of-town resorts. They enjoy relative freedom compared to those working in clubs or brothels and may exercise some option of choice of clients and hours of work.

A sub-stratum, relative to apparent independence and individual choice, are the streetwalkers or freelancers (as they prefer to be called) who ply red-light district streets or selected public plazas and commercial areas. They may be jobless women, students or runaways who loiter in certain streets and third-class hotel lobbies. They accost men in the streets, approach them in sidewalk cafes and negotiate (with or without a pimp) with car-riding clients. These women, like the call-girls, are free of the restrictions of working inside an establishment. They do not have a direct employer-employee relationship, but they are more dependent on their relations with an intermediary for clientele, and have to share their profits with the pimps (who often pose as tricycle drivers and small shop or store owners).

The employed are the women working in bars, "a-go-go" joints, discos, night-clubs, cocktail lounges, restaurants, *karaokes*, saunas and massage parlours who are euphemistically termed "hospitality women" by the government. They have definite places of work or recruitment of business, definite managers/employers, definite work schedules, duties and responsibilities, and are subject to a definite set of house rules and regulations.

The lowest stratum, the enslaved, are the most exploited and tend to be those working in brothels or *casas*. Although these women tend to be registered as "food handlers" or "helpers" in the *casas*, they work as prostitutes and are guarded and virtually owned by their employers. Unlike the bar and club women, they have no regular working hours but are on call whenever there are customers. They cannot choose their customers, nor do they have any choice over the number they have to serve. They do not earn directly from customers but from whatever percentage of income the brothel owner decides to give them after deducting the cost of their lodging and maintenance (Miralao et al., 1990, p. 6). There are many known cases of illegal recruitment of young girls from the provinces, white slavery, imprisonment, rape and physical abuse, and abysmal living conditions. Sometimes the parents of the girls are the contractors.

A fourth category, the exported, has emerged in recent years with the trans-nationalization of the sex industry and the participation of international crime syndicates, such as the Japanese *yakuza* (mafia), in sex trafficking. Filipino women have been exported to Japan and other countries, mainly in Europe, as "entertainers", "mail order brides"[1] and "domestic helpers", but who actually end up engaged in prostitution in their places of destination (De Dios, 1991). A combination of push and pull factors explains the migration of Filipino women. The high unemployment and underemployment rates in the Philippines are important push factors. For instance, in 1991, in Metro Manila one out of every five able-bodied workers was unemployed, and over seven million workers were underemployed. The closure of the US bases in Angeles City and Subic Bay also threw thousands of women out of work without any livelihood alternatives. The major pull factor is, of course, the lure of much higher income potentials in other countries. Entertainers in Japan can earn US$1,500 to 2,000 a month, which is about 12 to 15 times the prevailing rate in the Philippines (De Dios, 1990, p. 36).

Of the above categories of prostitutes, only the second – hospitality women – is visible, officially recognized and accessible to research, advocacy, intervention and limited forms of social protection. Little is known about the self-employed or own-account workers or about those working in brothels (except in cases where they are "liberated" by police raids and the news is sensationalized in the press).

The "buyer" in the sexual transaction has been given less attention than the "bought". While the supply consists mostly of Filipino women, the demand comes from men of different nationalities, mainly Filipinos of all classes, who represent the clients or customers. Where there are military camps in a locality, prostitution tends to develop. Where there are industrial estates or tourist locations, there tend to be male executives, workers and visitors wanting to buy sexual services. Sexual transactions also occur at sea in anchored foreign or domestic ships and on shore with tourists or local fisherfolk. They take place in a string of bars lining red-light districts; in the pretentious "health clinics", such as saunas and massage parlours; in the "entertainment" establishments, such as discos, restaurants and *karaokes*; and even in dimly lit avenues and parks. The types of customers in the sex sector also vary according to the location of the sex establishments.[2]

Prostitution is also a "business", as there are those who derive financial gain from it. Apart from the women who earn a living, those who profit from the business include pimps, operators/maintainers of prostitution houses, tour operators (both local and foreign), recruiters and sometimes even corrupt police officers and politicians. Establishments known to be involved in the sex sector can be classified as follows:

(a) Establishments catering to tourists and upper- and middle-class locals:
- special tourist agencies;
- escort services;
- hotel room-service at high-class hotels;
- saunas and health clinics;
- casas (brothels);
- high-end (upmarket) bars, nightclubs and beer gardens.

(b) Establishments catering to middle- and lower-class Filipinos:
- hotel room-service in the lower-class hotels;
- saunas and health clinics;
- casas;
- bars, beer gardens and cocktail lounges;
- cabarets.

(c) Establishments catering to special types of customers (e.g. paedophiles, gays, women):
- special tourist agencies;
- escort services;
- casas;
- pick-ups, streetwalkers;
- special clubs (e.g. gay clubs).

An idea of the structures and relations within various parts of the sex sector can be gleaned from the brief descriptions below.

The bar economy in the Manila tourist belt

Today, the Manila tourist belt in Mabini, Ermita, is not the honky-tonk district that it once was, having been virtually closed down by the city government headed by

Mayor Alfredo Lim, an ex-army general. In the early 1990s, it was estimated that there were some 149,000 prostitutes in this area alone (Manahan, 1991, p. 9). An idea of how it was during its heyday is provided by one study:

The girls working in the bars can be described either as a-go-go dancers or as receptionists. Girlie bars are staffed mainly by receptionists, who sit or dance with customers and can leave the establishment with a customer once he has paid a fee – known as a bar fine – for the girl, as compensation to the management for the loss of the receptionist's service. A-go-go bars mainly employ dancers, whose work consists of dancing for short periods on the stage and sitting with customers. The dancers can also leave with a customer once the bar fine has been paid. The average bar in the Mabini district employs approximately 30 receptionists or dancers. In addition, the bars usually have several bartenders or waitresses, and one or several floor managers or *mamasans*, who act as intermediaries between customers and girls. In the tourist belt, there are approximately 140 a-go-go bars and girlie bars, employing an estimated 4,000-5,000 dancers and receptionists. ...

Going out with customers for the purpose of having sexual relations is an integral part of the girls' work, and there is a clear understanding on the matter between the girls and the management. The establishment receives the bar fine, which during the interview period ranged from P80-150 (US$3-5.80),[3] and the floor manager usually received a 5-10 per cent commission on the bar fine. Once the bar fine is paid, the girl is free to leave and negotiate a fee with the customer for her sexual services. In some establishments, the management will insist that the girl go out with any customer willing to pay the bar fine, but in most establishments the girl is allowed some discretion in going out with customers (Wihtol, 1982, pp.19, 32).

Another study on the bar economy in the adjoining Malate area, which also caters to tourists but mainly serves a domestic clientele, gives an idea of ownership patterns. Many of these bars were co-owned by foreigners married to Filipinos, who thereby complied with the legal nationality requirements for owning a business. Among these foreigners were Japanese, Chinese, Australians and Dutch (Stearn, 1987).

The combined efforts of the NGO STOP (Stop the Trafficking of Pilipinas), the Ermita Catholic Church and the Western Police District under General Lim led to police raids in the Ermita area of Manila in 1988. Efforts to close establishments directly or indirectly involved in the commercial sex industry intensified when Lim became Mayor of Manila in 1992. While these moves had an impact on the bar economy, they may also have pushed prostitution underground or into other areas rather than halting it.

The *karaoke* bars comprise the largest number of sex-related establishments and employ the most women. These bars are supposed to provide a training ground for Filipino women who wish to go to Japan as entertainers. In these bars, they learn the Japanese language, songs and customs: "The rules in the karaokes are very strict: they must kneel to pour the drinks, light cigarettes, and hand feed the customers (or be fined)" (Stearn, 1987).

Prostitution tourism not only flourishes in Metro Manila, but has also spread to other areas, such as Cebu Island, where there are direct flights to and from Japan. Undoubtedly, this has helped to make tourism one of the country's biggest foreign exchange earners.

Large numbers of Filipino women also go to Japan as "entertainers". Out of 125,400 foreign women entertainers in Japan in 1994, the majority were from the Philippines; and this number did not include the many more who entered Japan illegally. The trips of many of these women are arranged by crime syndicates. The lure, as mentioned above, is the possibility of earning much higher incomes in Japan.

The Olongapo "rest and recreation" structure

Another study (Moselina, 1981) gives an idea of ownership and control patterns in the sex industry in the mid 1970s. It shows the participation of foreigners and the extent to which the "rest and recreation" (R&R) business operators were integrated into local power circles:

Based on records of the Business Permit Section of the Mayor's Office, 75 per cent of the R&R establishments are Filipino-owned and/or operated (these are the smaller bars and beer houses); 19 per cent are Chinese-owned and/or operated; and 6 per cent are American-owned and/or operated. The accuracy of these figures, however, depends on whether or not the Business Permit Section has unwittingly allowed dummies to secure licenses for aliens.

In terms of the volume of capitalization, the Chinese control approximately 80 per cent of the city's R&R business. This means that they own the big clubs, hotels, sauna baths and massage clinics... As the local capitalist class, the R&R establishment owners and operators wield power, and influence much of the decision-making process in the city government. Many of the city ordinances enacted by the City Council are in the form of business regulations that work in their favour.[4]

The relations between the business operators and women employees reveal many violations of workers' rights, e.g. evasion of the minimum wage, no vacation leave, imposition of various regulatory fines (including fines for sneaking out or having steady boyfriends), non-remittance of social security contributions, no living allowances, no thirteenth month pay, no sick and maternity leave, shortchanging of commission slips, indiscriminate firing of employees and prohibition of self-organization (Moselina, 1981, pp. 26-27).

The working conditions remain the same in the 1990s. All sorts of regulatory fines are still being imposed by the management on the women. When they go out with their customers for "short-time entertainment" (for about three hours), the bar fine is P700 (US$27), of which only P300 (US$11.50) goes to them as commission. When they are absent or late, they have to pay fines or have their salaries deducted. When they have conflicts with customers or fellow workers, sanctions are again in the form of fines or deductions. When they have "steady boyfriends", these boyfriends have to pay "steady bar fines" of at least P3,000 (US$115) a month, of which only P1,200 (US$46) goes to them. When they transfer to another bar, they have to pay about P800 (US$31) for their "transfer papers" (Buklod Centre, 1992).

The sauna bath economy

Masseuses working in massage parlours and sauna bath establishments comprise a significant segment of the sex sector. Though, like hospitality women, masseuses regularly visit the government social hygiene clinics for health checks, there is relatively little documentation about them. They serve mainly middle- and upper-class Filipino customers, but the more prominent establishments attract rich Filipino-Chinese and foreigners like the Japanese and Taiwanese.

The massage parlour charges an entrance fee, some 10 per cent of which goes to the masseuse as commission. The fee varies from P100 to 300 (US$3.80 to 11.50), depending on the type of room. The more prominent establishments may charge as high as P1,500 (US$58). If the massage attendant in the average sauna bath depends solely on her commission, she would not have an adequate income. In order to earn good money, she has to provide sexual services which can fetch her anywhere from P50 to 200 (US$1.90 to 7.70) for a "hand job", P300 to 500 (US$11.50 to 19.00) for a "blow job" and P500 to 700 (US$19 to 27) for sexual intercourse. In a high-end establishment, she could charge as much as P1,000 (US$38.50).

Life in the cabaret

The structures and relations described above cater to the foreign and better-off local clients, but the ordinary, low-income Filipinos go to the cabarets. These are the humblest of the establishments, which employ "taxi dancers" who get paid per dance in the dimly lit halls and/or who agree to be "tabled" by their customers in completely dark cubicles where sex can take place. In the dance halls, there are also tables where the customers can take the women and pay a certain amount per hour for entertainment, which may include necking and petting, but at a rate lower than the cubicle rate. A survey of 281 women workers in 30 cabarets in Metro Manila was carried out by the Bureau of Women and Minors of the Department of Labour and Employment in mid-1976. Although the survey is old, it does provide an idea of the relations in such establishments:

Women workers are usually introduced to the operators of the dancing halls through a recruiter or *"nag-aalaga"* (caretaker). This *nag-aalaga* is responsible for the transaction of business with the operators regarding the conditions of work of these workers. The workers' wages are based on what they have earned for the night. The income is divided on a 50-50 basis between the operator and the worker. However, the worker is represented by the *nag-aalaga* who takes hold of the earnings in order to check off the debts of the girl under her custody. The remaining amount is given at the end of the month. With regard to the tips given by the customers, neither the management nor the recruiter gets a share (Bureau of Women and Minors, 1980).

Many of the taxi dancers do not have social security and health insurance. They are not given living or emergency allowances, overtime pay, holiday pay or maternity leave. They are subjected to disciplinary action for "tardiness, absence without permission, leaving the place of work without the employer's permission, insubordination, failure to have a smear test, and quarrelling with customers or co-workers" (Bureau of Women and Minors, 1980).

Rural prostitution

There are also reports of prostitution in rural areas. In areas such as Licab, Nueva and Ecija, for example, the women cite the saying *"Isang kaban, isang dagan"* (one *cavan*, which is an agricultural measure, one lay) to refer to the sexual trans-action during harvest time. The agricultural workers pay roving prostitutes with whom they have sex in the fields after work one *cavan*, i.e. one sack of rice, per transaction.

It is also likely that such prostitution is prevalent around mining sites, logging areas, military camps and tourist spots.

A survey of commercial sex workers

A survey of two major sub-sectors within the sex industry – the massage parlours and saunas and bars – was conducted for this study.[5] For the massage and sauna sub-sector, 50 attendants in Metro Manila were surveyed. The establishments in Metro Manila service mainly middle- and upper-class clients. Another 50 women working in beer gardens, cocktail lounges and bars of Laguna and Quezon provinces were also interviewed. These bars usually cater to all classes in these provinces, from slipper-clad customers to visitors driving fancy cars from Metro Manila. Both these sub-sectors cater mainly to local, rather than foreign, clients.

Demographic characteristics and background

The massage parlour and sauna attendants were all above 18 years of age, mainly between 18 to 30 years. Those working in the bars, however, were generally much younger; 16 per cent were under 18 and almost two-thirds were between 18 and 24 years. Some of those working in the bars appeared to be even younger than 15, their youth and good looks being the main reasons why the establishments hired them. Those working in saunas entered the job at a more mature age and tended to leave it at around 30. Over 60 per cent of the women from the total sample from both sub-sectors had completed secondary education. A few of the masseuses had even completed college. The main reasons for not completing their education were because they could not afford to do so or because they had to work to help support their families.

About 30 per cent of those working in the saunas were born in Metro Manila itself and another 18 per cent came from other urban areas. This is contrary to the finding of earlier studies, that most of the women engaged in the sex sector came from depressed rural areas. In the case of the bar workers, since the research areas – Laguna and Quezon – are still largely rural, it was not surprising that more than two-thirds of the women came from rural backgrounds, mainly from two of the most depressed regions of the country. These bar workers reported that the main reason for migrating from their depressed areas of origin to work in the sex sector was economic. They were recruited from their home towns for such work by employers or agents, were waiting for opportunities to work in Japan, or had to support children or other family members.

The low-income background and complicated family life of the women emerged vividly in the survey responses. In both sub-sectors, the fathers of the commercial sex workers were dead (more than 40 per cent) or were agricultural workers, traders or hawkers, factory workers or labourers, occupations that are generally low-paying in the Philippines. Their mothers were mainly housewives or engaged in low-paying occupations. Most women came from relatively large families, with between four to eight members. Most of them hid their occupation from their relatives or spouses. Some said their mothers knew about their job and had no choice but to accept it. However, only about 6 per cent of the women said their spouses or boyfriends were aware of their job.

About half of the masseuses interviewed were married with children, but most of them were separated from their spouses. The majority of bar women were also single parents, either married and then separated, or single with children. Most of the children stayed with the respondents or with the women's parents. Twenty-two out of the 100 women covered in the entire survey admitted having live-in partners for a number of reasons – monetary, protection, physical/sexual needs and so on.

Employment characteristics

Those working in saunas generally applied for the job on their own, with or without the assistance of friends or relatives involved in or familiar with the sub-sector. They were mainly walk-in applicants, since the saunas usually advertised in the media the need for female masseuses with or without experience. On the other hand, about 40 per cent of those working in bars got their jobs through the assistance of friends or relatives. Unlike in the sauna sub-sector, there was very little newspaper job advertising in the bar industry. The recruitment process relied heavily on word of mouth, by friends or relatives already working in the bars, or through active recruitment by owners, employers or agents.[6] Some 18 per cent of the bar workers were recruited by a recruitment agent or middleman contractor, and another 4 per cent were recruited directly by the employer.

Economic factors clearly represented the main motivation for entering the sex industry (see table 4.1). The pressure was especially pronounced in the case of those who had to support their parents, siblings or own children. The masseuses were much more likely to cite the well-paying nature of the job, whereas none of the bar workers gave this as a reason. Commercial sex work was the first job for slightly less than half those interviewed, with unemployment periods ranging from one to six months. Some of the bar girls could not be considered as unemployed before joining the sex sector, as they were below the legal age of employment (18 years) when they first entered. Those who were previously employed were most commonly factory workers, domestic helpers, sales girls or waitresses.

Most of the women reported that their first sexual experience was not related to the job and was usually with their husband or boyfriend. There were, however, women who were victims of incest or rape before they became commercial sex workers, with almost one-fifth of the women reporting that they lost their virginity by force. Other studies also reported a significant incidence of sexual abuse prior to entering prostitution.

Most of those interviewed had been working in the saunas for only between one and six months. Only one woman had been in the job for more than two years. The turnover of women in the sub-sector tended to be rapid, with women staying in the job for no more than two years. Some key informants mentioned that the women would work in the saunas for a few months, leave, then re-apply again and work for some more months. Other women moved from one sauna establishment to another. In contrast, most of the bar women had been in their jobs for more than six months. About 38 per cent had been working in bars for between one and two years, and

Table 4.1. Reasons for going into commercial sex work

Reasons	Sauna masseuses (%)	Bar workers (%)
Need to support poor parents	34	30
Need to support siblings	8	20
Need to support husband/boyfriend	28	0
Need to support own children	0	10
Need the income for own survival	0	28
The job is well paid	22	0
It is easy work	2	0
Like this kind of job	2	0
Do not have training or experience for other jobs	0	6
Bad sexual/emotional experience	0	2
No choice, forced into job	0	0
Other reasons	4	4
Total	100	100
Number	50	50

another 10 per cent for more than two years. The longer period of employment reported by the bar women was probably because they entered the sector at an earlier age than the masseuses.

The majority of women in both sub-sectors claimed they wanted to change their present jobs, saying they wished to get married, get another job, or save enough money to be able to avoid having to work or to return to their home towns. They did not indicate whether they thought they could earn as much in alternative occupations or how realistic their plans were.

Conditions of employment

The sauna establishments varied in the way they oriented their attendants on the nature of their job. In the smaller establishments, with 30 women or fewer, it was normally the owner or operator who explained the nature of the job. In the larger establishments, with from 60 to 500 women, the task normally fell on the staff, such as the floor manager. About 22 per cent of the sauna workers reported, however, that it was their co-workers who explained to them the terms of their employment. It was possible that the establishments did not explain clearly to the women some aspects of their job, which they presumed the women knew upon entry or would learn from their co-workers. For example, the new entrants were normally given a formal training or orientation in the art of giving a massage, and this training lasted from one day to one week, depending on the establishment. However, in the case of sexual transactions, some establishments were less open in their discussion of this aspect of the job. For example, more than a third of the sauna women said they were not told about the terms of payment for sexual transactions. Among the bar women, half learned about the conditions of their employment from the floor manager,[7] 20 per cent from the *mamasan,* 14 per cent from co-workers and 14 per cent from the employer.

Almost all the women (90 per cent of the masseuses and 86 per cent of the bar women interviewed) reported that there was no quota or target number of customers required by the establishment. The masseuses reported between two and four sexual transactions per week,[8] while for bar women, the frequency was between one and five, with the average about 2.3. In a focused group discussion among the masseuses, it was disclosed that the women usually had three to four customers in a day. They needed to have at least that number of sexual transactions per day, and not per week, because they received only about a 10 per cent share of the entrance fee paid by the customer. The entrance fee entitled the customer to the use of a room for one to one-and-a-half hours, or a cubicle and other facilities, such as a shower, bath tub jacuzzi or steam bath (depending upon the type of establishment), plus a massage by the attendant. Since the entrance fee ranged from P100 to 300 (US$3.80 to 11.50), the attendant's share would be only P10 to 30 (US$0.38 to$1.15) per customer. Even if she was able to massage four customers a day, she would receive only P120 (US$4.60) at most, which was still below the 1994 minimum daily wage of P130 (US$5). But if she engaged in sexual intercourse with one or two customers a day, she could earn an extra P300 to 500 (US$11.50 to 19.20), depending on the nature of the establishment (high-end or ordinary sauna), her "beauty" or attraction and the negotiation with the customers.

The massage parlours or saunas catered mainly to Filipino customers, the most frequent customers being Filipino-Chinese business executives, who were reported to visit some establishments two to three times a week. A number of Japanese, Taiwanese and other foreigners also frequented the more prominent establishments. The bar women also catered mainly to Filipino customers. Those interviewed claimed that they preferred Filipino customers, followed by Americans, Chinese and Japanese; the main reasons for their preferences were that such customers usually "were kind", "paid well" or "were clean". Their main complaints against other types of customers were that they "were dirty", "refused to use condoms", "gave small tips" or "forced them to engage in acts they did not like". Generally, the women did not care whether the customers were married or not, but more than a third considered it important that the man was rich.

The women in the massage parlours worked for at least 12 hours a day, although much of the time was actually spent waiting for customers. During these long waiting hours, they usually watched television in their waiting rooms, read comics, sewed garments or played games. Some of the masseuses worked for the entire week, while others worked only five days per week. Some of the massage parlours provided their employees with free uniforms (28 per cent), free lodgings (42 per cent), regular check-ups (40 per cent) and help in case of trouble with the law (78 per cent). Since the massage parlour attendants were supposed to be "self-employed", they were not provided with social security coverage or the other benefits guaranteed to formal sector wage employees under the Labour Code.

The massage parlours also enforced disciplinary rules, which usually included the following: no drinking in the establishment, no work under the influence of alcohol, no "under-time" (meaning that once they signed in for work, they could not leave till the sign-off time), full one-hour service for a customer, no rumour mongering, no quarrelling with each other, updated check-ups for venereal disease (two to four times a month) and maintaining silence at work.

Those working in bars had shorter hours of work, between six and eight-and-a-half hours per day. Almost three-quarters of those interviewed reported working the entire week without a day off. As part of their work benefits, they received lodging (60 per cent of those interviewed), food (40 per cent), free medical treatment (24 per cent), regular medical check-ups (42 per cent) and help in case they were arrested (62 per cent).

Incomes and expenditures

The women working in the massage parlours received about 10 per cent of the entrance fee paid by a customer. Some establishments, especially the larger ones, issued the corresponding stubs of customers' receipts to the women for accounting purposes. Generally, the women were really expected to earn their incomes from the provision of sexual services to customers. The income from the so-called "extras" in the massage business ranged from P50 (less than US$2) for a "sensation" or masturbation job to P700 (almost US$27) for intercourse. Hence, for servicing one to three customers a day, a woman could earn both commissions and extra compensations from a low of between P60 and P180 (US$2.30 to 6.90) to a high of above P2,100 (US$81) per day. The attendants in VIP rooms in the high-income range establishments could reportedly earn as much as P4,000 (US$154) a day, which was more than a sales clerk would earn in a whole month.

More than half the masseuses earned above P3,000 (US$115) a month. In light of the earlier observation that the women were too shy or reluctant to acknowledge the actual number of sexual transactions they had, these figures were likely to be very conservative. A minimum monthly income of P5,000 (US$192) and an average monthly income of P7,500 (US$288) was estimated to be the more likely figure. Strikingly, 15 out of the 50 masseuses interviewed claimed that they could not calculate the amounts they earned.

The women working in bars earned their income from commissions on women's drinks (roughly 20 per cent per drink), tips from customers, payment from the establishment if they danced as naked models (although in some establishments, this was considered part of their regular duties) and payment for sexual services. The bar women were not salaried workers. Forty-six per cent said they earned as much as P2,000 to 4,000 (US$77 to 154) per month based on commissions alone. Another 26 per cent reported earning only between P500 and 1,000 (US$19 and 38). In terms of monthly income from sexual transactions, 18 per cent earned between P1,000 and 2,000 (US$38 and 77); 36 per cent earned between P2,000 and 4,000 (US$77 and 154); and another 18 per cent earned above P4,000 (US$154).

The women reported that they themselves determined their expenditure patterns. The main item of expenditure for the masseuses appeared to be food, followed by lodging, clothes, transportation, cosmetics, leisure activities, cigarettes and alcohol. They also normally remitted between P1,000 and 2,000 (US$38 and 77) per month to their families. Their total expenditures tended to be around P5,000 to 6,000 (US$192 to 230) per month, which explained why many of the women reported that they had no savings. Those who did have some savings at the end of each month had less than P1,000 (US$38). More than two-thirds said they had borrowed money and 42 per cent said they still had debts to repay.

The bar women also had roughly the same expenditure pattern. About a quarter of them spent 50 per cent of their earnings and another quarter spent more than 75 per cent of their earnings on themselves. The remainder went to their families and to pimps. About 44 per cent of the bar women claimed they had no savings at all. Sixty per cent said they had borrowed money and 40 per cent still had outstanding debts. Those who did have some savings kept them in the form of jewellery or cash.

Health and medical attention

Almost all the masseuses and bar women interviewed said they had received information on the possible health dangers related to their work. The main sources of such information were health workers, the media and co-workers. Very few of the massage parlours or bars provided detailed health information to their workers. There was a generally high degree of awareness of STDs. Eighty per cent of the masseuses and 70 per cent of the bar women interviewed knew about AIDS. However, 60 per cent of the bar women claimed that they had yet to receive full information about various health issues related to the nature of the jobs.

The masseuses reported that they were required to go twice a month to the government health clinics (social hygiene clinics), where they were given a coloured card certifying that they were safe for their customers. However, only 28 per cent went to the government clinics; the others went to private hospitals or clinics. Some sauna establishments arranged for regular doctors' visits and also checked weekly to ensure that the women did not have any venereal diseases. The masseuses had to pay for their own medical expenses. If they were sick, they were asked by the establishment temporarily not to report for work. Among the bar women interviewed, more than half reported that they underwent weekly check-ups, which were usually arranged by their employers or managers. Thirty-six per cent said they went to private clinics or hospitals, and 56 per cent went to government clinics. Some floor managers paid for the check-ups for the women. Cases of abortion were not uncommon in the industry. Eighteen per cent of all the women interviewed in both sub-sectors reported having had an abortion, and some more than one.

Those women who reported knowing about AIDS also said that they knew that condoms should be used as a preventive measure. Yet 82 per cent of the masseuses admitted that during the last five times they had had sex, a condom had not been used. Of these, 30 per cent said that their customers did not want to use condoms.

Among the bar women too, only 52 per cent reported that they insisted on the use of condoms. Again, customer refusal was the main reason for the non-use of condoms.

Sexuality

The survey also asked questions about the attitudes of the women towards and experience of sex with the customers. More than half the masseuses indicated that they did so "with a heavy heart" or felt forced, about a third said they did not feel anything, and another 20 per cent said they were conscience-stricken because they still considered sex with customers a sin. Fifty-four per cent of the bar women said they did not feel anything when they had sex with their customers; the remainder said they had sexual transactions with a heavy heart.

In terms of their normal experiences with customers, the bar women were more likely than the masseuses to describe the sexual transaction as fast and bereft of any preparations. On the other hand, 46 per cent of the masseuses (as compared to 32 per cent of the bar women) claimed that the customers displayed concern or affection. Thirty-eight per cent of the bar women and 18 per cent of the masseuses also said that some customers forced them to engage in acts against their will. About half the bar women and over a third of the masseuses reported that they had been subject to violence or harassment, most commonly from the police but also from city officials and gangsters. The violence was normally in the form of degrading treatment, including being physically battered, and verbal abuse. Six per cent of the masseuses and 8 per cent of the bar women also claimed to have been raped.

The scope and significance of the sex sector in the national economy

It is extremely difficult to get reliable data on the scope and significance of the sex sector in the national economy, for a number of reasons. Since prostitution is illegal, there are no official statistics on it, except those from police arrests, and such figures are extremely limited. Research on prostitution is far from comprehensive and is usually confined to certain sub-sectors, geographical areas or particular aspects of the problem. Furthermore, there are risks involved in investigating underground structures and networks where criminal syndicates abound (Calalang, 1985, pp. 14-15).

The available estimates tend to be partial and inconclusive. One way of trying to arrive at an estimate is to look at occupational classifications, but this approach is frustrating and inaccurate. For example, in the Philippine Standard Occupational Classification, hospitality women and related workers are lumped together with guides, undertakers and embalmers, medical helpers and ushers under "service workers not elsewhere classified". Such service workers numbered some 168,000 in 1989, but since they represent just one group in this broad sub-classification of service workers, hospitality women and related workers would account for a smaller number. It is not possible to estimate how much smaller the figure is; and it also cannot be said that all hospitality women engage in sexual transactions.

Another possible approach is to look at the statistics from police stations and social hygiene clinics where the women are supposed to have their regular medical check-ups. Yet many of the prostitutes do not go to the social hygiene clinics, preferring instead to go to private clinics whose records are not available. The available data from the social hygiene clinics do, however, indicate some striking features. For example, the number of visits by men to the Venereal Disease Control Section of the Manila Health Department was only 2,997, as compared to 42,412 by women for the year 1992 (comprising visits by 550 housewives, 30,293 hospitality women and 11,569 masseuses).

The sex sector is part of both the formal and informal segments of the economy. Therefore, only the hospitality women and masseuses of the bigger establishments are likely to be registered with the social hygiene clinics. Streetwalkers, taxi dancers of the cabarets and women working in clubs in small towns, honky-tonk bars and brothels are not registered at all. There is also the growing phenomenon of *akyat barko* (climbing ship), a form of prostitution where the women actually go aboard commercial vessels to serve the seamen in the major ports.

The available literature yields a low estimate of 100,000 and a high estimate of 600,000 prostitutes in the country (Tan, 1990). The research team for this study put the figure at somewhere between 400,000 and half a million commercial sex workers. This is based on a crude and simple assumption that 1 per cent of the urban population and 0.5 per cent of the rural population are engaged in some form of prostitution.[9] The basis for arriving at the 1 per cent formula was as follows. In Quezon City, which is not exactly a tourist destination area, the Office of the Vice-Mayor estimated that there are more than 5,000 masseuses in the sauna industry and at least twice this number in the bar industry, which comprises hundreds of beer gardens, disco pubs, music bars and cocktail lounges that cater to all types of customers. If the number of streetwalkers, taxi dancers and seasonal prostitutes is estimated to be the same as the number of masseuses, then there would already be around 20,000 women involved in prostitution in Quezon City, which had a population of 1.67 million in 1990. However, there are areas with higher concentrations of prostitutes, such as the former US military bases and the tourist destination spots. Even small rural towns in the provinces around Metro Manila have a fair share of sex-related establishments. In the countryside, places with higher concentrations include mining sites and logging areas. Of course, there is no way of determining whether the actual figure is nearer 400,000 or 500,000 or even higher or lower. A recent report to the United Nations Children's Fund estimated that there are 300,000 women in prostitution (Cueto, 1997). Another study reported that male prostitutes have been growing in numbers, but gave no estimate of the total number of male prostitutes (Ahlburg et al., 1997).

Whatever the estimates are, prostitution in the Philippines can be considered a full-fledged industry, directly employing hundreds of thousands of hospitality women. Factoring in the services of male and child prostitutes – as well as "entertainers" who work both in the country and abroad – further increases the numbers. Assuming that there is an equivalent number of pimps, waiters, cashiers, security personnel and other workers engaged in activities related to the industry, the number of persons dependent on the sex sector is clearly significant.

Legislation covering the sex sector

In practice, ever since colonial times, the State has always adopted an ambivalent attitude towards the sex sector. On the one hand, it outlaws prostitution in its legal statutes. The act of prostitution is illegal under the Penal Code. On the other hand, it allows and even licenses, through local city and municipal ordinances, the operations of beer joints, massage parlours and other establishments known to be fronts for prostitution, giving the impression that the State promotes, legitimizes and regulates prostitution. The State also requires sex workers, again through local ordinances, to submit themselves regularly to medical examinations for the detection of STDs, in exchange for which they get coloured cards guaranteeing that they are safe for their customers. In the case of women wishing to work as "entertainers" abroad, the government even provides a screening mechanism for accrediting them.

It is in the shadow of such ambivalence that corruption tends to thrive. Harsh and intermittent measures, such as bar closures after highly publicized raids, which punish the women prostitutes but allow the male operators and customers to go free, reinforce the government's ambivalent posture. Worse still, these measures make the prostitutes vulnerable to stigmatization through media sensationalism and to harassment by policemen while they are in detention. The uncertain status of the sex establishments is one reason why a large part of the sector is underground and difficult to monitor. The laws related to prostitution lend themselves to ambiguities with regard to their interpretation and enforcement. They also tend to be patently discriminatory and unevenly implemented.

Prostitution and the Penal Code

In the Philippines, the 1965 Revised Penal Code (article 202, section 5) states that "for the purpose of this article, women who, for money or profit, habitually indulge in sexual intercourse or lascivious conduct are deemed to be prostitutes". In the words of the Philippine Development Plan for Women 1989-1992, "such a definition is not only discriminatory towards women, it also subjects the law to arbitrary interpretations and implementation. And since parameters are absent in determining what 'profit' and 'lascivious conduct' mean, the criminalization of prostitutes is largely dependent on who judges the case." The more recent Philippine Plan for Gender-Responsive Development 1995-2025 also makes the point that "by this definition, prostitution applies only to women. The provision is silent with regard to the pimps, bar operators, clients and others who are involved."

Article 202 refers not only to prostitutes but also to vagrants.[10] Available records show that charges of vagrancy are much more common[11] because they are easier to prove than prostitution. The penalty for vagrancy is the same as that for prostitution: for a minor offence, a fine not exceeding P200 (US$7.70); and for a repeated or major offence, a minimum period of imprisonment or a fine ranging from P200 to 2,000 (US$7.70 to 77.00), or both, based on the discretion of the court.

There are two other articles in the Revised Penal Code of the Philippines which relate to prostitution:

Article 340: Corruption of Minors: Any person who shall habitually work with abuse of authority or confidence, promote or facilitate the prostitution or corruption of persons under age to satisfy the lust of another shall be punished by correctional imprisonment in its minimum and medium period, and if the culprit be a public officer, he shall also suffer the penalty of temporary absolute disqualification.

Article 341: White Slave Trade: The penalty of correctional imprisonment in its medium and maximum periods shall be imposed upon any person who, in any manner, or under any pretext, shall engage in the business or shall enlist the services of women for the purpose of prostitution.

Article 340 is important because many prostitutes are actually less than 18 years of age. Article 341, on the other hand, is consistent with the United Nations Convention on the Suppression of the Traffic in Persons and Exploitation of the Prostitution of Others. The Philippines is the only one among the four Southeast Asian countries studied which has ratified (in 1952) this Convention, that seeks to punish any person who "(a) procures, entices or leads away, for purposes of prostitution, another person, even with the consent of that person; or (b) exploits the prostitution of another person, even with the consent of that person". The parties to the Convention also agree to punish any person who "(a) keeps or manages, or knowingly finances, or takes part in the financing of a brothel; or (b) knowingly lets or rents a building or other place or any part thereof for the purpose of the prostitution of others".

Implementation and enforcement of the above-mentioned laws, however, tend to result in a double standard. Women are often the ones punished, while the male operators in the sex industry (e.g. the club operators and pimps) remain free. The most that happens is that the establishments are closed after a raid, but these can easily reopen in another area under another name.

Labour law and prostitutes

Under article 138 of the 1974 Labour Code, "any woman who is permitted or suffered to work with or without compensation, in any nightclub, cocktail lounge, massage clinic, bar or similar establishment, under the effective control or supervision of the employer for a substantial period of time as determined by the Secretary of Labour, shall be considered as an employee of such establishments for purposes of labour and social legislation". This means that hospitality women (a category which includes women who are employed as hostesses, masseuses, attendants, waitresses or dancers in any nightclub, bar, cocktail lounge, cabaret or similar establishment) are covered by all provisions affecting labour (Calalang, 1985, p. 7).

As succinctly put by the Philippine Development Plan for Women, "such legislation is, however, of no help at all to most of these women who enjoy none of the benefits accorded to legislated workers" (p. 138). In Olongapo City, for example, a detailed sociological study clearly showed that the women workers did not enjoy minimum wages, living allowance, thirteenth month pay, vacation, sick leave or maternity leave. They could not have access to social security because contributions were not remitted by their employers. They could not organize themselves since this was prohibited (Moselina, 1981). A 1991 survey of Olongapo and Angeles City, conducted by the Bureau of Working Conditions of the Department of Labour and Employment under Operation LEAP (Labour Enforcement and Productivity), found a large number of violations of minimum wage and other regulations.

There is ambiguity too in the designation of agencies charged with protecting the rights and welfare of hospitality workers. The Bureau of Women and Minors of the Department of Labour and Employment was originally designated as the agency responsible for implementing the Labour Code provision described above. It used to run briefing seminars for women workers in the hospitality industry. The briefing had strong spiritual overtones, and during the course, religious medals were given to the women. There were also efforts to give the women and girls a sense of belonging, to train them in such skills as typing and hairdressing so that they could find alternative employment, and to organize them into a service association and credit unions. This programme, however, was temporarily suspended for evaluation in December 1982, resumed in a different form soon after President Aquino took office in 1986 and eventually cut due to lack of resources and a change of priorities of the Department of Labour and Employment.

The Labour Code and the agency responsible for its implementation operate on the assumption that hospitality workers are legitimate workers only in so far as they do not engage in prostitution, which is illegal under the law. Those who are reimbursed for sex are no longer workers with the accompanying rights, but criminals who must suffer the consequences of their criminal act. The term "sex worker" becomes a contradiction, because once a worker admits to engaging in sexual transactions, her (his) rights as a worker can no longer be pursued.

Officials of the Department of Labour and Employment argue that it is another government agency, the Department of Social Welfare and Development, which is mandated to take charge of prostitutes. The Department of Social Welfare and Development is supposed to take care of all disadvantaged women (estimated to number over 4.3 million), of whom "victims of involuntary prostitution" are just one category out of many. The Department's focus so far has been only on the rehabilitation of those women who have been rescued from prostitution dens.

Behind the raids in Manila and Quezon City

A discussion of legislation and its implications in the Philippines would be incomplete without an assessment of the raids in Manila and Quezon City in pursuance of both old and new ordinances.

Police raids in the Ermita area of Manila began in 1988. When the head of the Western Police District became mayor four years later, the drive to clean up Ermita intensified and resulted in the closure of most of the night spots in the area, the displacement of some 5,000 hospitality women and other staff, and the dislocation of some 35,000 others who were directly or indirectly employed in the area. The *coup de grâce* came in February 1993, complete with placard-bearing demonstrators. Previously, the bars had been able to reopen after the raids, by obtaining court injunctions; this time Mayor Lim refused to re-issue operating licences from January 1993 (MacBeth, 1993).

The City Council of Manila approved two additional ordinances giving legal sanction to the actions taken by Mayor Lim. Ordinance No. 7783, dated 9 March 1993, prohibits the establishment or operation of businesses providing certain forms of amusement, entertainment, services and facilities in the Ermita-Malate area. The prohibited businesses are those "where women are used as tools in entertainment and which tend to disturb the community, annoy the inhabitants, and adversely affect the social and moral welfare of the community, such as but not limited to sauna parlours, massage and *karaoke*, beerhouses, night clubs, day clubs, supper clubs, discos, cabarets, dance halls, motels and inns". Owners of such businesses in the area were given three months to "convert into curio and antique shops, souvenir, handicraft, art galleries, record and music shops, restaurants, coffee shops, flower shops, music lounges and sing-along restaurants, and theatres". The penalty for violation could be imprisonment for one year, a fine of P5,000 (US$192) or both. Subsequent violation and conviction would result in the closure of the business premises.

The second ordinance, No. 7791, dated 11 June 1993, prohibits "sexual relations with, and solicitation or procurement of prostitutes and other related acts". Section 2 of the ordinance states that "it shall be unlawful for any person: (a) to have sexual relations with a prostitute for some consideration including payment but not limited to sums of money; (b) to solicit, procure, pimp or pander; and (c) to act as a middle person or go-between for a third person and a prostitute in any place in the City of Manila for purposes of prostitution". The penalty for violation is a fine of P5,000 (US$192), imprisonment for one year, or both.

This ordinance was seen as a response by the city government to the criticism that the crackdown on prostitution had resulted mainly in punishing the women while leaving their clients, procurers and pimps free. Public criticism was, however, not limited to this point. The title of a contemporary newspaper article, "Beyond Lim's reach, flesh trade thrives",[12] was very revealing. The closures only drove the industry underground (some bars which offer prostitutes still operate clandestinely in the tourist area) or to other areas (to localities just outside Manila, Cebu City and Puerto Galera in central Philippines, or as far away as Hong Kong). Instead of bar prostitution, there is more ship prostitution (where the prostitutes actually board commercial ships anchored in Manila Bay), street prostitution and park prostitution (notably in the skating rink in Luneta Park).[13]

In Quezon City, there was a furore when the biggest sauna parlour, which was employing some 500 massage attendants and other employees, was ordered to close, first in May and then again in August 1993. This was mainly at the initiative of the Vice-Mayor who, during the period when he was the Acting Mayor, decided to implement the Quezon City Ordinances No. 9303, dated 22 August 1972, and No. 9837, dated 24 April 1973, to regulate the establishment and operation of sauna parlours. These ordinances state that entrances to the compartments within establishments should have curtains rather than doors, and that partitions between compartments or cubicles should be made of light wooden materials with one foot of clearance from the floors and at least six feet of clearance from the ceiling. Various local NGOs supported the efforts of the Vice-Mayor. The case went to the Court of Appeal, and the massage parlour and the Quezon City government attempted to work out a compromise agreement. Under this, the former would remove all doors and locks in its massage compartments, do away with the "aquarium" or showroom for clients to choose the women, open its doors to female clientele and employ men and handicapped attendants. They would also provide the massage attendants with employment contracts with at least monthly wages, commensurate and proportionate with the income of the establishment (which was reported to be P100,000 or US$3,846 a day, of which only 8-10 per cent went to the attendants), and provide supplementary income benefits by creating or encouraging a workers' cooperative.

Legalization and regulation attempts

Because of the dissonance between the prohibitionist law on the one hand, and the ambiguity and abuse inherent in its implementation on the other, there have been some attempts at legal reform. In the early 1980s, there was a move to legalize prostitution, but this did not go far because of vigorous Church opposition. More recently, the regulation of prostitution in connection with AIDS control became the subject of public discussion. A bill was filed in the Philippine Congress in 1992 seeking to set up red-light districts where prostitutes would have to undergo compulsory registration and medical check-ups. Brothels would also be licensed and subject to inspection by the Department of Health.

In a policy workshop jointly organized by the Task Force on Prostitution and the Government Organizations–Non-Government Organizations Network on Violence against Women and Prostitution, in February 1993, the proposed bill was discussed and rejected on four grounds. First, compulsory registration and health checks or segregation in specially designated red-light districts discriminates against and stigmatizes the commercial sex workers. Most prostitutes do not want their families or friends to be aware of the nature of their work. They are also concerned that registration records could be used against them even when they have left the sector. To avoid having their names and faces recorded in official registers, the prostitutes may be driven underground, thus exacerbating the very problems that legalization is intended to solve. Secondly, registration or regulation may not bring everyone in the sex sector under the purview of the law. If all workers are not registered, the aim of legalization in order to prevent the spread of diseases would be defeated, since there would be no effective way to regulate health measures or protect such workers. The ones most likely to be exploited, the unregistered workers, would also fear seeking protection. It is also a fallacy to believe that compulsory health checks for prostitutes will control the spread of AIDS. Many others are vulnerable to the disease. Thirdly, objections were raised by women's NGOs and human rights groups that legalization violates the human rights of prostitutes by giving official sanction to the commoditization of women's bodies and sexuality for sale and profit by the sex industry. They also argued that regulation usurps the dignity of the prostitute by expropriating her sexuality and assigning control over it to the State. Finally, legalization may, in fact, lead to an increase in both the supply and demand sides of the commercial sex sector, from those who previously refrained because of the illegality of the activity (Ofreneo and Ofreneo, 1994, p. 25).

The proposed bill for the legalization of prostitution was withdrawn in March 1993. In its stead, concerned groups in the Philippines have called for the decriminalization of the prostituted, for an end to police harassment, and for prostitutes to be entitled to the working conditions and welfare benefits provided for in the country's labour code and industrial relations system. This is also the recommendation of the Philippine Plan for Gender-Responsive Development 1995-2025: "decriminalization means the abolition of sexist discrimination in general and removing the culpability and criminality which the law places specifically on women prostitutes. It will entail repealing all articles in the Revised Penal Code and the Child and Youth Welfare Code that refer to prostitutes as criminal offenders. Local ordinances should also not further victimize prostitutes." (National Commission on the Role of Filipino Women, 1995, p. 312.) The Plan calls specifically for the repeal of Article 202 on vagrants and prostitutes. It also calls for the strengthening of Article 341 of the Revised Penal Code against "white slavery" (which it recommends calling something else to remove the racist connotation), in line with the view that prostituted persons are victims, and those who victimize them should be penalized. The Plan stresses that "decriminalization of the prostituted should go hand in hand with the apprehension and prosecution of agents, recruiters, traffickers, pimps, procurers, establishment owners, customers and others who derive sexual gratification, financial gain and advancement, or any other benefit from the prostitution of others" (p. 312). It notes that once prostitutes are no longer treated as criminals, there should be no impediment to the recognition, protection and assertion of the rights of workers in the "hospitality industry", and to the effective implementation of Article 138 of the Labour Code. To date, however, Article 202 has not been repealed, there has not been any change in Article 341 of the Revised Penal Code, and Article 138 of the Labour Code is still poorly enforced.

Social programmes affecting the sex sector

Most of the programmes directed at the sex sector have been in the areas of health, "rehabilitation" or renewal, and education and advocacy efforts. Government agencies and NGOs dealing with such programmes differ in their approach, coverage and effectiveness. Some offer an integrated and comprehensive package of services, while others choose to focus on particular areas, depending on their expertise, experience and available resources.

Health programmes

In the Philippines, the health programmes relating to government regulation of the sex sector have traditionally aimed at making the prostitutes "safe" for their male clients. The procedures are meant to monitor the incidence of STDs, to identify those who are infected, and to issue or regularly update the coloured health cards that the hospitality girls and masseuses are required to carry when they work. The procedures are generally paid for by the workers themselves, although some establishments do cover the costs. The Philippine Plan for Gender-Responsive Development 1995-2025 describes the present system of mandatory medical check-ups imposed by local ordinances as "discriminatory and oppressive to prostituted women because it is not meant to protect their health but that of their customers. The underlying assumption is that it is alright for them to get infected by customers who do not have to prove they are 'clean', provided the infection is detected immediately and is not transferred to subsequent customers." (National Commission on the Role of Filipino Women, 1995, p. 310.)

The government social hygiene clinics operate in only a few urban areas and tend to be understaffed; they are not able to service large segments of the commercial sex sector. Also, since the social hygiene clinics offer "judgemental" health care (in the sense of being limited to STD testing and treatment), and since women attending the clinics are liable to be stigmatized because they are clearly identified as working in the sex sector, they may be reluctant to go to these clinics. Many of the prostitutes rely on private clinics, which are often of questionable quality and have been described as "hole-in-the-wall operations that prey on prostitutes, charging exorbitant fees for ineffective or excessive treatment" (Tan, 1987).

The Department of Health has initiated a National AIDS Control Programme, but owing to the constraints imposed by Catholic values, the programme has been limited to relatively low-profile public information, counselling and voluntary anonymous testing. The Department attempted to popularize condom use, but met formal opposition on moral grounds from the Church. Ironically, the controversy generated by the issue resulted in greater media attention, thereby indirectly aiding the awareness-raising campaign. The programme has also been hampered by the lack of coordination with and cooperation from local government and other public agencies. For example, when the United States military bases closed, there was no monitoring of the whereabouts of the HIV carriers among the bar women who were dispersed. The same problem emerged after the "clean-up" campaigns of the sex establishments by the mayor of Manila.

NGOs in the Philippines have been complementing government efforts in the fight against AIDS, including conducting outreach work in bars and among the high-risk groups. For example, Kabalikat has a centre in the bar area of Ermita-Malate where prostitutes can drop in for information, counselling and advice. It also does outreach work in bars and clubs, providing information on AIDS and STDs, counselling and referrals for medical care, livelihood and vocational or non-formal education. Talikala, an NGO based in Davao City, focuses on a health programme, including an AIDS drama shown in bars and clubs. Because its focus is on health, the management of the bars and clubs do not feel threatened. Members of the NGO also help out in the government-run social hygiene clinics.

"Rehabilitation" and renewal programmes

The Department of Social Welfare and Development (DSWD) runs rehabilitation centres "for women rescued from prostitution dens". These women are housed in centres located in different cities under the Substitute Home Care Programme for Women in Especially Difficult Circumstances. The women enter the programme in three ways: by walking in, through referral from government organizations and NGOs, or through outreach or actual rescue operations. The prostitutes stay in the centres together with victims of domestic violence, rape, incest and illegal recruitment. The length of stay varies from a week to two years; but on average, the women stay from three to six months. For some women, the centres provide temporary residential care or shelter, which enables them to immediately leave violent or hazardous situations and to have a place to stay while they work out their problems.

Upon entering the centres, the women are given medical and physical examinations for contagious diseases, STDs, drug abuse or other impairments. They also undergo psychological evaluations. While in the centres, the women undergo skills training and do subcontracting jobs if they wish to earn an income. They also attend group and individual sessions on self-enhancement, stress reduction and spiritual formation. Counselling services are also provided. Those suffering from drug addiction and STDs are referred to government hospitals. Other types of referral services, provided by other government agencies, such as legal aid, are also available. Those who have court cases (they often act as witnesses against bar owners) are provided with free legal services and transport to and from the court hearings. After leaving the centres, the women are returned to their families and assisted with reintegrating into society. Community-based services, such as self-employment assistance, community participation skills development, counselling and referral services, are available to assist the women to reintegrate. Social workers in the communities monitor their progress and provide reports to the DSWD.

Although the range of rehabilitation and resocialization facilities appears large, the number of prostitutes covered by the DSWD programme represents a mere drop in the ocean: 198 in 1991, 257 in 1992 and 69 for the first half of 1993. Clearly, the resources and the territorial spread of the DSWD programme, which is not even exclusively for prostitutes, are woefully inadequate compared to the magnitude of the problem. The stress of the Department is on "rehabilitation", although some attention is also given to the preventive aspect through the DSWD's community-based approach, which includes information dissemination, skills and productivity enhancement, and capability building for "disadvantaged women".

Filipino NGOs are also active in rehabilitation and resocialization programmes. The Third World Movement against the Exploitation of Women (TW-MAE-W) runs three drop-in centres for women in distressed situations. Those who wish to leave the hospitality/sex industry are brought to a halfway house, the Nazareth Growth Home, in Quezon City, where they undergo skills training and value formation sessions. Graduates of these sessions then go on to the Bethany Home, which provides housing and aftercare, especially for those suffering from HIV/AIDS. The NGO Gabriela has networked with other NGOs to establish drop-in centres for the prostitutes. The NGOs include Buklod in Olongapo City, Talikala in Davao and Dayang in Quezon City. These centres are, however, basically to provide the prostitutes with places for discussion, counselling and relaxation. For example, before the Mount Pinatubo eruption in 1991, the Buklod drop-in centre provided health courses, consciousness-raising and skills training for women, as well as night care for children. After the eruption and the economic dislocation following the closure of the US military bases, Buklod concentrated more on socio-economic programmes, such as training in sewing and subcontracting jobs to provide alternative employment to women in need. Buklod still conducts consciousness-raising workshops for women, provides counselling services and monitors educational support for vulnerable children, mostly Amerasians.

Education, awareness-raising and advocacy programmes

The approach and efficacy of programmes designed to educate and advocate on behalf of prostitutes depend on the orientation of the government, religious, civic or cause-oriented organizations which run them.

In the 1970s and early 1980s, the Bureau of Women and Minors of the Department of Labour and Employment ran a briefing seminar for hospitality women "to impart information on social labour legislation, strengthen the moral fibre of the girls in this 'dangerous' occupation, awaken their awareness as self-respecting citizens, contribute to the socio-economic development of their families and the country as a whole, and to impart tips on how to entertain and serve well without prostituting themselves" (Calalang, 1985, p. 27). The programme was, however, allocated very limited resources and was discontinued in 1982. In the mid-1970s, the Department of Labour and Employment also helped to educate and organize hospitality workers in Olongapo into cooperatives and credit unions. These efforts were, however, strongly opposed by operators of the hospitality establishments, who "resented the idea of their workers organizing themselves. Workers identified with the cooperatives were either dismissed or suspended and became victims of intimidation and harassment" (Calalang, 1985, p. 2). After resuming briefly in 1986, the programmes were discontinued due to resource constraints and a shift in the Department's priorities.

The DSWD has made efforts to prevent the sexual exploitation of migrant women through networking activities with NGOs, and through deploying social workers at the international airport to monitor minors travelling abroad. It also helps to train law enforcement officers, beginning with women in the police force, to ensure better handling of the victims of prostitution.

A number of Filipino NGOs are also very active in advocacy and awareness-raising work. The pioneer in feminist advocacy was the TW-MAE-W, which was founded on Human Rights Day, 10 December 1980. Soon after, in January 1981, it initiated synchronized demonstrations in the ASEAN capitals against the "sex-ploitation" of women, principally by Japanese male tourists. In February of the same year, TW-MAE-W was also the first to draw worldwide attention to military prosti-tution, against which it launched a campaign (termed CAMP International) in Nairobi at the NGO Forum in 1985. The TW-MAE-W also conducted compre-hensive research on the problem of prostitution. Through its efforts, "women's groups in industrialized countries joined hands with Third World women to confront issues regarding marriage bureaus, migrant workers, international beauty contests, child prostitution, women workers, Islamic suppression of women, whoredom created by the US bases, nudist resorts, the importation of Third World entertainers" (Calalang, 1985, p. 18). In recognition of its role, the TW-MAE-W was granted consultative status in the United Nations Economic and Social Council in 1985. Now it not only engages in campaigns against prostitution and AIDS but also in direct services for "distressed women".

STOP was founded by socio-civic and religious groups in 1983. Its campaign is "directed primarily against the pimps, protectors, agents, recruiters, managers and brothel owners from all sectors behind the trafficking/exploitation of women and children" (Calalang, 1985, p. 15). It has been concentrating on a programme called "stopping at the source" by sending social or religious workers to the provinces or to piers, meeting inter-island vessels to try to dissuade women and girls from migrating to Manila or other urban centres, warning them of the dangers of city life (Gabriela Commission on Violence against Women, 1987). STOP also lobbies for legal reform and for the formulation of laws, rules and regulations, and ordinances which are protective of and beneficial to women and children. It has also lobbied for the wider application of Manila Ordinance No. 7791 (against clients and procurers of prostitutes) by writing to women councillors of other city and municipal governments.

Gabriela aims "not to persuade or remove girls from prostitution" but, rather, it "endeavours to educate and organize prostitutes towards empowerment where they are, until such changes in the political, social and cultural structures are effected that will eliminate the reasons for prostitution". This is based on its fundamental belief that women go into prostitution not by choice but because of poverty, and that only decent employment with decent pay can stem the tide of prostituted women.[14]

Other Filipino feminist groups involved in research, education and advocacy work on prostitution within an empowerment perspective are Kalayaan, WEDPRO and the Women's Resource and Research Centre (WRRC). Kalayaan and WEDPRO, for example, have conducted feasibility studies and designed transition programmes to create employment options for prostituted women, principally in the previous US military base areas of Angeles and Olongapo (see Miralao et al., 1990). WEDPRO also launched a signature campaign addressed to the members of Congress, for the decriminalization of prostitution. A joint GO–NGO Network on Violence against Women and Prostitution has also been established, which holds monthly meetings and workshops, mainly on policy issues.

Notes

[1] At least several hundred "mail order brides", whose marriages are arranged for material gain, leave the Philippines each year. For the period 15-31 August 1989 alone, there were 389 would-be brides of Japanese men interviewed by the Commission on Filipinos Overseas (De Dios, 1990).

[2] For example, in the Manila area, Quiapo caters to Chinese, low-income Filipinos and taxi drivers; Binondo to Chinese businessmen; Makati to Filipino businessmen, Arabs, Europeans and Japanese; Divisoria to drivers and stevedores; Ermita and Malate to Germans, Australians, Dutch, Arabs and Japanese (Manahan, 1991, p. 12).

[3] The rate of exchange is taken at 26 pesos to US$1, but there have been fluctuations over time. During the 1980s, for example, the rate of exchange was sometimes over 30 pesos to US$1.

[4] For example, ordinances that prohibited soliciting on the streets were "intended to make sure that solicitation of customers takes place only inside the clubs, so that by means of drinks and fines, club owners and operators are assured of income" (Moselina, 1981, p. 25).

[5] The interviewers were asked to limit to a maximum of five the number of respondents per establishment. They were also encouraged to seek creative ways of establishing contacts within the establishments, e.g. by befriending the security guards, cashiers and bar managers; getting the permission of owners; drinking with the women in the bars, etc. These tasks turned out to be difficult, as many of the establishments and the women themselves were wary of such surveys, mindful as they were of various raids by police officers and the sensationalized media stories. The surveys were reinforced by unstructured interviews with key informants, such as the managers, who shed light on the nature of operations of the establishments. Focused group discussions involving some respondents from both groups were also conducted to clarify information, especially about the nature and frequency of sexual transactions, and to elicit comments on a draft bill on the regulation of prostitution.

[6] A bar owner told the research team that he had an effective way to recruit new women. He asked those already working in his bar to recruit new workers when they were taking vacations in their home towns and offered them rewards in terms of reimbursing the transport costs of both the recruiters and new recruits, plus P100 (US$3.80) commission for every new recruit. Under this system, most of the recruits turned out to be relatives or friends of the bar women.

[7] The floor managers in the bars play a special role, in that a growing practice is for the owner/operators to exercise minimal supervision over the women and to concentrate on managing the business aspects. The responsibility for supervising the women is given to a manager or a group of floor managers.

[8] These figures were low, and were probably due to the reluctance of the respondents to admit a greater number of sexual transactions, as indicated by the fact that 60 per cent of them did not answer the question on the number of sexual transactions.

[9] In 1990, the urban population was estimated to be 26,245,568 and the rural population 35,234,612. Based on the above assumption, the number of prostitutes in urban areas in 1990 would have been about 263,000 and in rural areas about 176,000, giving a total of about 439,000.

[10] Vagrants are described in the following way: (i) any person having no apparent means of subsistence, who has the physical ability to work and who neglects to apply himself or herself to some lawful calling; (ii) any person found loitering about public or semi-public buildings or places or tramping or wandering about the country or the streets without visible means of support; (iii) any idle or dissolute person who lodges in houses of ill fame; ruffians or pimps and those who habitually associate with prostitutes; and (iv) any person who, not being included in the provisions of other articles of this code, shall be found loitering in any inhabited place belonging to another without any lawful or justifiable purpose.

[11] For example, during the period 1972-75, the annual number of vagrancy cases in Metro Manila ranged from 3,950 to 4,492, as compared to between six and 26 cases of prostitution for the same period.

[12] Philippine News and Features, *Philippine Daily Inquirer*, August 1, 1993.

[13] There were also uglier accusations. An article in the *Far Eastern Economic Review* reported that there were people saying that the intention of the mayor was "to open up choice del Pilar real estate for overseas Chinese investment" because if the issue was a moral one, "then why hasn't he shut down the clubs and the whorehouses in Chinatown?" (MacBeth, 1993).

[14] Information provided by an official of Gabriela in an interview for this study.

PROSTITUTION IN THAILAND

5

Wathinee Boonchalaksi and Philip Guest

Historical and social factors behind the development of the sex sector

There is no clear evidence as to when prostitution in Thailand became widespread. During the Ayuddhya period (1350-1767), prostitution was legal and taxed by the government (Mettarikanond, 1983). Prostitute houses were situated in the area occupied by the Chinese community in the ancient capital of Ayuddhya. The prostitutes served both local and foreign customers. There has been a close association between prostitution, migrant communities and economic development throughout Thai history.

In the reign of King Rama I (1782-1809), the Chinese community again figured prominently in the recorded history of prostitution in Thailand. As male-dominated Chinese migration into Thailand increased (Skinner, 1957), prostitution flourished, and was geographically concentrated in Sampeng, a Chinese locality of Bangkok. Sampeng remained the most well-known place for prostitution in Thailand up to the reign of King Rama IV (1852-1868). Most of the prostitutes were Chinese, and the Thai prostitutes working in the area would adopt Chinese names (IPSR, 1991). As the Thai economy developed and new communities of foreigners were established, prostitution also expanded, with the prostitutes adapting to the characteristics of their new customers. For example, as a community of Europeans grew in the Bang-rak area, it attracted prostitutes who often adopted foreign names in order to identify with their clients. Prostitution was not, however, confined to serving the foreign communities. In addition to prostitution in the capital city of Bangkok, there was a well-documented sex industry operating in regional centres. For example, during the reign of King Rama V (1868-1910), prostitution was an activity that was taxed in a number of provinces. The tax was euphemistically termed a "road tax" (Mettarikanond, 1983).

The most common form of prostitution during the reigns of King Rama IV and V involved "stationed women". These women were essentially slaves, who could be sold by their owners. Women were commonly purchased to serve in "houses of prostitution" – the forerunner of the Thai brothel today. In these houses, a manager supervised the female slaves, ensuring that they observed proper manners in serving their clients.

Reports indicate that the houses were very well managed; stealing was forbidden and clients who might forget their belongings had them returned. These houses also served a variety of other functions, such as gambling (Mettarikanond, 1983).

After King Rama V abolished slavery in 1905, some slaves voluntarily became prostitutes, and there was an increase in the numbers of prostitute houses in many parts of the country. In 1908, the Contagious Disease Prevention Act was passed to register prostitute houses and to maintain order in them. According to this Act, every house operating as a brothel had to hang a lantern at the front door. Although there was no stipulation under the Act as to the lantern's colour, the example used in the announcement of the Act was green, and this colour was adopted. Hence brothels became known as green-lantern houses, and prostitutes were called green-lantern women. Houses with green lanterns had to pay tax and therefore had legal status (Mettarikanond, 1983). There were also "illegal" prostitutes who did not stay at a registered house but who, instead, solicited clients at gambling centres, lottery centres or theatres.

In brief, the development of prostitution during the nineteenth and early twentieth centuries in Thailand was linked to the large-scale immigration of Chinese workers and to the institution of slavery. On the one hand, the men in the growing migrant communities were ready to purchase sexual services; on the other hand, the bonded status of many women meant that there was a supply of prostitutes. Prostitution was profitable, legal and, to some extent, acceptable in Thai society.

The recent development of prostitution

Currently, the sex industry in Thailand is highly visible, economically successful, internally differentiated and illegal. Ironically, since the 1960s the main policy issue has been how to legally reduce the size of the industry while, in fact, this period has seen the fastest growth of the industry, often under the indirect patronage of the government. The pattern of economic development (including the expansion of the tourist industry) and gender relations in Thai society have interacted to create the conditions for a flourishing sex industry. A complex set of interrelated changes associated with economic development and gender roles has operated to provide an increasing supply of women for the sex sector. For example, Blanc-Szanton (1990) argues that the combined effects of agricultural transformation, changes in inheritance rules (so that property must now be equally divided among sons and daughters rather than going primarily to daughters) and the proletarianization of the labour force have adversely affected the position of women in society. Women are forced to migrate and enter urban employment, in which they are easily vulnerable to exploitation and in which remuneration rates are low. They are still expected to continue to support their parents, siblings and even their children.

The poor income-earning opportunities for women with low levels of education, the desire to provide substantial support for their families and a relatively tolerant attitude towards prostitution in some segments of Thai society help to ensure that some of this labour supply will be directed towards the sex industry. A demand exists in the sex industry because of the social acceptance of men buying sexual services, the increased disposable income of a large and growing segment of the Thai population, and the development of tourism, which tends to promote the sex industry.

A sex industry has developed because of the large amounts of money that can be made. Still, there has been a lack of research on the economic interests behind the development of the sex industry in Thailand. Information on the involvement of the police or "influential people" in the sex trade comes mainly from press reports, which frequently suggest that even if the authorities do not actually own the establishments, they provide both protection to the industry and, in many cases, moral support.[1]

Three major factors can be linked to the growth of the sex industry in Thailand: gender roles, economic development and tourism.

Gender roles and prostitution

The position of women in Thai society has been the subject of much debate (Keyes, 1984; Hongladarom and Guyot, 1983; Yoddumnern-Attig et al., 1992), partly because of the complexity of defining women's status. A common assessment, based on socio-economic indicators such as education and labour force participation, is that Thai women enjoy relative equality with men (Limanonda, 1992). Economic development has enhanced women's economic roles and reinforced their autonomy (Soonthorndhada, 1992). However, there are a number of factors which run counter to these trends and which have created an ideology in which a woman's beauty (and body) is considered her major asset.

Chief among these factors has been the expansion of upper-class values associated with the roles of women. Thai women from lower socio-economic classes, especially those in rural areas, have always had major economic roles and a high degree of autonomy. Much of Thai society, especially in the north, is matrilineal, with the youngest daughter expected to inherit the family's agricultural holdings (Potter, 1977). In upper-class Thai society, women were totally separated from economic activities and were expected to pursue "feminine" interests (Santasombat, 1992). Many of these interests were focused on pleasing their husbands. Furthermore, polygamy was widely practised by upper-class Thai men and was viewed as a prerogative of position and economic success. Men expected to be served by women (Santasombat, 1992).

The stress placed on feminine values found in the upper class has spread throughout Thai society, even though there have been concurrent improvements in female education and access to modern sector occupations. The stress placed on beauty and service to men was reinforced by the mass media. Since the time of King Rama V, the cinema and newspapers and, more recently, television have highlighted the physical aspects of Thai women. This was indirectly supported by the government. For example, one objective of the first Miss Thailand Beauty Contest held in 1934, was to promote cooperation with the new government (Kobkitsuksakul, 1988). The contest was seen as a tool to encourage women's participation in national development, but used beauty as the measure of women's success. The Miss Thailand contest has since become very big business, with beauty schools established to turn out beauty queens.

Other factors associated with women's roles in Thai society also help to explain the supply of women available to work in the sex industry. A number of researchers have drawn attention to the deeply-rooted cultural expectation that Thai daughters contribute in any way they can to the support of their parents (Podhisita, 1985; Yoddumnern, 1985; Pramualratana, 1990; Yoddumnern-Attig et al., 1992). This expectation, when it occurs in conjunction with an economic structure which provides relatively high rewards for work in the sex industry, can represent a strong motivation for young women to enter prostitution. The link between support for parents and prostitution in Thailand has been emphasized by a number of researchers (Phongpaichit, 1982; Malikaman et al., 1983; Wongchai et al., 1988). The obligation felt by daughters towards their parents tends to be strongest in the northern region of Thailand and results from an interplay of local customs and matrilineal practices.

The link between prostitution and obligations as a daughter is only one aspect of the value placed on the sexuality of Thai women. Another relatively common finding is that many Thai women enter prostitution because they lost their virginity before marriage (Skrobanek, 1986) or separated from their spouses (Thaipakdhi, 1973; Wongchai et al., 1988). In both instances, their sexuality lost the value that is associated with socially accepted roles (as bride and wife), but retains an economic value which can be accessed through working as a prostitute.

The view that men are sexual predators, and that their sexual appetites must be satisfied if the virtue of "good" women is to be protected, is also common in Thai society. This is reflected in comments made by male respondents in a study on rural Thailand (Havanon et al., 1992) and also in statements made by officials.[2]

Patterns of economic growth and the sex sector

Role expectations and other social and cultural factors related to prostitution operate within an economic structure that influences the supply of women willing to work in the sex industry, and also affects the demand for commercial sexual services. The patterns of economic development in Thailand over the last 30 years have contributed to the growth of the sex industry and the types of services available.

Economic development in Thailand has had a strong international orientation. In the 1950s and 1960s, this was closely related to investments made in Thailand by the United States. These investments were mainly undertaken for strategic reasons, but the result was large transfers of money and men into the country. Most of these men were military personnel who came to Thailand for short periods of time, either to serve at US military bases established in Thailand or on rest and recreation (R&R) leave from the Viet Nam War (Santasombat, 1992).

During the Viet Nam War period, Pattaya, one of the centres most famous for prostitution in Thailand, first developed a visible sex industry. Pattaya was selected as an R&R centre for American soldiers. Restaurants, shops, hotels, bars and nightclubs expanded rapidly from North to South Pattaya. After the American withdrawal from

The sex sector

Viet Nam, Pattaya survived and expanded on the basis of tourists, although a naval presence can still be seen when American warships dock for crew shore leave.

However, a more important influence has been the domestic economic policies that have attempted to transform Thailand's agricultural economy into an economy with a high proportion of its national product derived from the export of industrial goods and the provision of services (Santasombat, 1992). Thailand's economic reform programme has been lauded as a great success (Sahasakul, 1992). The Thai economy expanded at one of the fastest sustained rates in the world over the decade from 1985 to 1995, the incidence of poverty decreased, and there has been significant human resource development. However, the shift in emphasis from agricultural to industrial exports, and from import-substitution to export-led growth, resulted in a shift in the spatial concentration of development efforts and in the demand for labour. The strategy of economic restructuring was pursued in conjunction with extracting surplus from the agricultural sector for industrial investment, subsidizing urban dwellers in order to keep urban wages low, encouraging foreign investment and promoting tourism.

Some negative outcomes of this development strategy have been increasing inequality among regions and social groups in the country, marginalization from economic development of some groups, and the increased commercialization and enhanced materialism of Thai society. These processes are apparent, for example, in the contrasting patterns of urban and rural development. Poverty in Thailand is overwhelmingly rural-based, and the differences between urban and rural levels appear to have increased. The incidence of rural poverty was at least five times higher than that of urban poverty in the 1980s, compared to a ratio of about three for the mid-1970s (Hutaserani, 1990). Regional inequalities in income also widened over the decade of the 1980s. The northeast and the north, the two poorest regions in the country, became poorer in relative terms, mainly because the policies of export-led industrial growth concentrated industries in Bangkok and the central regions. Sussangkarn et al. (1988) argue that increases in rural incomes in the 1980s resulted mainly from a movement out of agriculture. Much of this movement was geographical as well as occupational, with migrants flocking to Bangkok and contributing to rural households through remittances.

Thailand's process of economic development has resulted in the inevitable commercialization of the rural economy. Nearly all villages are now electrified and exposed to television, and transportation links have made movement between areas easy and cheap. The rural population has become increasingly integrated into the urban economic and media markets. However, there has not been a concurrent expansion of rural employment opportunities, especially since the mechanization of agriculture has reduced the need for labour inputs. The economic effects of these changes can be seen in both increased levels of tenancy in the Central region due to indebtedness, and higher aspirations for consumer goods. These changes have affected females in the rural labour force more than males. As in many other countries, increasing productivity in agriculture in Thailand has been associated with decreasing opportunities for agricultural wage employment for women and increasing opportunities for men (Thitsa, 1980).

On the other hand, the structural adjustment policies pursued by the Thai government have expanded urban employment opportunities for women, especially in the export-oriented industries. The growth of urban economic opportunities has led to increased levels of female migration. Migration to urban centres in Thailand is dominated by women, and this domination has increased over time (Phongpaichit, 1993; Guest, 1992). Unfortunately, female rural-urban migrants are confronted with low-paid urban jobs, which, while adequate to meet the costs of urban living, provide them with little additional money to remit to their families. In urban areas, female migrants are also away from the strict social control of parents and community members. The desire to earn more money and a loosening of social control may influence young women to enter prostitution (Sattaporn, 1975; Malikaman et al. 1983).

Most of the research on prostitution in Thailand has concentrated on the economic reasons why Thai women become prostitutes. There has been hardly any research on the effects of economic development on the male demand for the services of prostitutes. The literature which traces the expansion of the Thai sex industry to the involvement of foreign men, either as military personnel on R&R or as tourists, views the economic power of these men as an important causal factor (Phurisinsith, 1976; Godley, 1991). However, similar attention has not been given to increases in the disposable income of Thai men. As noted earlier, wealth in Thailand has traditionally been associated with increased sexual access to women, usually in the form of taking "minor wives". Economic growth in Thailand over the last three decades has considerably expanded the size of the Thai middle class, especially in urban areas. While the practice of taking a minor wife (*mia noi*) continues for some men, the increased spending power of males often seems to be used now to obtain sexual services on a temporary basis under enjoyable, and in many cases luxurious, circumstances. This trend has been associated with the establishment of new sectors of the sex industry, such as member clubs. Economic development has not only increased the size of the sex sector, but has also resulted in an increased diversity in the settings where sexual services are offered.

One of the main developments of the sex industry in Thailand over the last decade has been an apparent increase in both the number of prostitutes being recruited from neighbouring countries to work in Thailand and the number of Thai women working as prostitutes in other countries in East Asia and Europe. Japan has been a major destination for Thai prostitutes. The government allocated over 5 million Baht (US$200,000) to programmes to discourage women from going to Japan for prostitution.[3] Several thousand Thai prostitutes are also believed to be working in Europe, particularly in Germany (Skrobanek, 1986). Many of these women are recruited from the sex industry in Thailand by German men, while others are forced into prostitution because of failed or sham marriages with Germans.

It has been estimated that there are more than 200,000 Thai prostitutes working outside Thailand (IPSR, 1991), a number which, if accurate, would exceed the number of Thai women working in the sex industry in Thailand. This estimate, however, appears to be based more on supposition than on fact, and a number less than 100,000 would appear to be more plausible. It is true that more and more Thai prostitutes are seeking opportunities outside the country. In part, this must be viewed as a consequence of the internationalization of the Thai economy.

For several decades Thailand has promoted international tourism, with Thai sex workers being a major attraction for some tourists. The contacts made between the tourists and sex workers in Thailand has inevitably established a counterflow of women to the countries of origin of the tourists. It is not a coincidence that the two countries most renowned for having sex tour packages to Thailand – Japan and Germany – are major destinations for Thai prostitutes. Skrobanek (1986) notes that Thai prostitutes are highly valued in Europe because they are willing to work for lower fees and because they are less emancipated (i.e. more submissive) than women of other nationalities.

There has also been an increase in the number of foreign prostitutes working in Thailand. Considerable publicity has been given to the large numbers of women from Myanmar and southern China working in brothels in Thailand.[4] Local officials in Chiang Mai estimate that between 25 and 35 per cent of those entering the sex sector in northern Thailand are migrants from northern Myanmar, and that some 40 to 60 per cent of them are already HIV-positive. Women returning from the Thai sex industry with HIV have also been found in the Chinese province of Yunnan, in Shan State and in central Myanmar (Lintner and Lintner, 1996).

Tourism and prostitution

There have been consistent annual increases in the number of international tourist arrivals over the last three decades.[5] The income obtained from tourism comprised almost 5 per cent of GDP in 1991 (TDRI, 1992). The development of the tourist industry has also expanded employment in the service sector. In Thailand, tourism is a major earner of foreign exchange, providing a large number of jobs in the hotel and restaurant sector, in commercial enterprises, as well as in the commercial sex sector.

There has been much publicity given to the sex tours arranged for foreign tourists. Although organized sex tours appear outwardly to have declined in recent years, mainly because of public pressure from international women's groups, they still occur. For example, some massage parlours in Bangkok offer special rates to tour groups from Asian countries. The role of foreign tourists in patronizing prostitutes is highly visible, because of the concentration of the activities of commercial sex workers catering to foreign tourists in a few areas. In Bangkok, there are Patpong and several areas in the Sukhumvit area (e.g. Soi Cowboy and Nana Entertainment Plaza). Outside Bangkok, there are Pattaya and sections of the resort island of Phuket, as well as Hat Yai in the south, which caters mainly to Malaysian tourists. This visibility has led several researchers to link the existence of the sex industry to foreign tourists (Truong, 1983; Sereewat-Srisang, 1987).

Numerically, however, foreigners are probably only a small proportion of the customers of the commercial sex market.[6] They do dominate as customers for certain sectors of the industry, most notably the beer bar and "a-go-go" sectors, but, as will be noted later, these are relatively small sectors. Most clients of prostitutes in

Thailand are Thai men. The influence of foreign tourists on the sex industry does not stem from the numbers who frequent prostitutes. Instead, the influence derives from the perception of policy makers and politicians that commercial sex is a major factor in bringing tourists to Thailand and that, therefore, the sex industry should be, at a minimum, ignored and, in some cases supported, but not banned.

Every government in recent times has espoused policies of support for tourism. The implications and strength of such support were most clearly seen in the attempts by the government to publicly minimize the threat of AIDS in order not to deter tourists from visiting the country (Cohen, 1988). There were a number of statements by Ministers requesting that stories about AIDS be toned down in order not to scare tourists away.

Government support for tourism has been more direct in some instances. In 1980, a Deputy Prime Minister made a speech at a conference of provincial governors in Thailand, in which he said that in order to increase tourism the governors should promote sex-oriented entertainment in their provinces.[7] Such attitudes still tend to prevail. For example, in March 1993, the Governor of Songkhla, a southern province, was reported as supporting the idea of prostitutes being prevented from returning home during the Thai New Year period (Songkran), and instead being made to participate in the annual Songkran parade because "their participation would make the procession more colourful, particularly when they are in Hawaiian dress or scantily clad ... I think they will attract foreign tourists".[8] This desire to see the sex industry flourish in order to encourage the inflows of foreign exchange helps to explain the government's supportive attitude towards the entire sex industry, not just that segment frequented by foreign tourists. Another form of government support for the sex industry is financial, although indirect. For example, a significant component of the sex industry is associated with hotels, restaurants and tour companies. These are the same establishments as those supported by tourism promotion campaigns paid for by the government.

On the other hand, the government has reacted very vigorously against international reports which suggest that Thailand has a prostitution "problem". For example, in 1993, there were three instances in which international attention was focused on Thailand's sex industry. On all three occasions the government made official protests. The first occasion was a *Time* magazine article on prostitution which included a picture of a Thai bar girl on the front cover, and which stated that there were two million prostitutes working in Thailand. Soon after the *Time* article appeared, the *New Longman Dictionary of English Language and Culture* was published, which described Bangkok as a city "often mentioned as a place where there are a lot of prostitutes". Thai authorities were successful in persuading the publisher to withdraw the dictionary and amend the entry for Bangkok. The third incident was a programme on BBC television that identified Thailand as one of the most dangerous tourist destinations. The danger referred to both physical violence and the possibility of contracting AIDS.

The protests by the Thai government must be viewed partly in terms of attempts to protect national honour, but there was also obvious concern that the stories would affect tourism and foreign investment. Some government officials did admit that in many respects the stories, although exaggerated, identified a problem that needed to be addressed through policy actions. But the more common reaction was denial of anything unique about the Thai situation. Thai politicians and businessmen face a dilemma. While they are aware that the sex industry is an important tourist attraction for some individuals, they also perceive that too much focus on prostitution could depress other segments of the tourist market. Consequently, indirect promotion of the sex industry, coupled with public denial of the size of the industry, have gone hand in hand. The government has, however, shown increasing commitment to eliminating child prostitution, including dealing harshly with foreign paedophiles (as discussed in Chapter 6).

The organizational structure of the sex sector

Sexual services in Thailand can be purchased through a number of institutional arrangements. The diversity of such arrangements seems to have increased over time, especially to serve specific market niches. Some of these niches are based on socio-economic status, some on nationality, while others rely on perceived lower health risks in order to attract clients.

The increasing internal complexity of the commercial sex sector in Thailand is a relatively recent development. In some cases it is easy to trace the ancestry. Prostitute houses have become what are known as brothels. The opium houses became traditional tea rooms, which more recently have turned to providing sexual services in addition to tea. In many other cases, the new ways of packaging commercial sex were imported from overseas, although often in an adapted form. Massage parlours and nightclubs became popular venues for obtaining sexual services or contacting prostitutes during the 1960s. Beer bars and dance clubs also appeared at this time. During the period of the Viet Nam War, being a *mia chaw* (rented wife) to American soldiers was popular in those provinces where US air bases were situated. This form of prostitution expanded to include tourists spending at least several weeks in Thailand. There are certain hotels in Bangkok where women can be picked up for this purpose (Phongpaichit, 1982).

More recently, there has been an expansion of "indirect" prostitution. Prostitutes now work as waitresses, as salesgirls in department stores, as golf caddies and in a variety of other sectors where they can meet potential customers. Those operating in restaurants are, more often than not, working with the full knowledge of their employer, who, in many cases, is paid directly by the customers for the sexual services of their employees.

The following partial list of places where prostitution is currently practised in Thailand provides some idea of the variety of locales:

- traditional brothels;
- hotels and motels;
- tea houses;
- massage parlours;

Table 5.1 Number of commercial sex workers by sector of employment, Thailand, 1979-1996

Year	Brothels	Hotels	Bars and nightclubs	Massage parlours	Teahouses	Others	Total
1979	13 456	4 962	6 775	10 140	128	6 061	41 522
1980	16 798	4 516	5 792	6 272	144	8 058	41 580
1981	14 729	6 608	6 198	12 308	2 336	9 177	51 356
1982	10 138	3 218	6 107	16 034	2 452	8 681	46 630
1983	11 716	6 244	5 997	12 764	2 915	7 948	47 584
1984	19 911	6 420	7 638	15 775	1 488	13 610	65 839
1985	23 550	7 388	6 905	15 758	2 854	14 992	71 447
1986	26 681	9 140	5 828	16 466	2 619	19 952	77 677
1987	27 680	8 596	5 843	11 385	2 252	21 254	77 010
1988	28 047	7 639	5 656	14 148	2 267	25 214	82 971
1989	27 842	6 967	6 330	14 044	2 219	27 724	85 126
1990	29 148	7 034	5 848	13 627	2 244	27 177	85 078
1991	21 712	3 845	6 020	12 317	1 510	29 004	74 048
1992	20 786	4 370	6 536	10 431	1 658	31 595	75 376

Source: Ministry of Public Health

- call-girl and escort-girl services;
- bars, nightclubs, "a-go-go" bars, cocktail lounges;
- restaurants;
- public places (streetwalkers); and
- other places (e.g. golf clubs, discos, pubs and members' clubs).

Data from the Ministry of Public Health provide an indication of the size of different sectors of the sex industry (see table 5.1). Several significant changes in the relative shares of the different sectors can be observed. The sector which is largely patronized by foreign tourists – the bars and nightclubs – appears to have experienced an increase in numbers. Brothels, the other sector in which there is some foreign custom, although largely confined to areas bordering Malaysia, grew considerably over the decade of the 1980s and then declined very substantially through the 1990s. Similar declines can be observed for the hotel sector. The brothels and cheap hotels cater mainly to low-income Thai men. The decline might be due to fears concerning AIDS and to police crackdowns. In many cases, the reduction of brothel prostitution involved a shifting or redefinition of the sector; for example, from a brothel to a "restaurant" or discotheque, although business continues as usual.[9] In one location, the shift was explained as a means by which the sex establishment owner could employ the younger girls that customers desired, while at the same time allaying the customers' fears about AIDS. Because of media campaigns, there has been a strong tendency in the minds of customers to link AIDS with brothel and hotel prostitutes. There has also been a shift from other sectors, although these shifts are not as large as those noted for the brothels. For instance, the number of sex workers in massage parlours reached a peak of 16,000 in 1986, but dropped to around 10,500 in 1992 and has since picked up again. Tea houses, a relatively small segment of the market, were most popular during the middle of the 1980s.

Two-star hotels which supply prostitutes are located primarily in Bangkok and in the larger provincial cities. The prostitutes are usually freelance and are not harassed by the management of the hotels since they bring in customers. These women wait in places such as the hotel coffee-house. In some up-market hotels, including some of the five-star hotels in Bangkok, hotel staff such as doormen and bell-boys solicit customers. If the hotel guests are interested, the sex worker will come to their room.

In low-income-range hotels, many of which are distinguished by a prominently displayed number rather than a name, prostitutes are directly employed. These hotels also rent out rooms on a short-term basis to commercial sex workers, who pick up their clients in other locations, such as bars. In most hotels the short-time rental is for two to three hours. These types of hotel are common both in Bangkok and in the provinces. A variant on of these hotels, which is similar to Western-style motels, is also available. They can usually be identified by having curtains pulled over the client's car, that can be driven right to the door of the room, which the person subsequently rents. Such arrangements, which may be used for both commercial and non-commercial sexual liaisons, protect the customers' anonymity.

Brothels are found in Bangkok but are more common in the provinces. They are a traditional rural venue for sexual services. Prostitutes in brothels work for the owner, and usually receive a fixed percentage of the fee paid by the customer. Brothels vary widely in the working conditions and the freedom provided to the workers. There have been many stories in the press about young girls imprisoned in brothels and forced to work against their will. This is particularly true in many of the border provinces. Women confined in this manner are often illegal immigrants from southern China and Myanmar, and hence are not likely to try to escape. On several occasions in 1993, police raids on brothels in provinces, such as Ranong in the south, reported rescuing large numbers of prostitutes from neighbouring Myanmar. In another case in Tak, a province bordering Cambodia, of the 69 women released from a brothel, 29 were Cambodian nationals and one was Vietnamese.[10] While raids on brothels receive a large amount of publicity, in most brothels workers are free to come and go as they please.

More than two decades ago tea rooms mainly served tea. Now they are more likely to offer sexual services. Most tea rooms are in the Yowarat area of Bangkok. Clients are mainly Sino-Thais. The establishments have acquired a reputation of employing very young women, and they are infamous for being able to provide virgins at very high prices. They mainly operate in a similar fashion to brothels.

Massage parlours for sex services first appeared in Thailand in the 1960s, rapidly becoming popular and increasing in number. They are mainly frequented by middle-income Thai men, although there are several in which foreigners account for a large share of the clients. Sexual services are available in several ways: orgasm by massage; "body massage" (the women use their nude bodies to massage the customer); and sexual and oral intercourse. A complete service usually includes body massage and intercourse. Sexual activities normally take place within the establishment. The women sit behind a glass partition where they can be viewed by the customers. The customer selects the woman he wants, often with the help of staff members who highlight the special ability of each of the workers, and she is summoned to accompany the customer to a room. Women are hired by the hour or for a fixed period (from 90 minutes to two hours). The women working in the establishments are often subject to strict rules and can be fined for infractions. They are commonly recruited to work in the parlours by agents, with whom they share their earnings. These agents often work as *cheer kheek*, i.e. workers employed by the parlour to provide customers with information to help them in their selection of a woman.

There is a popular story of how call-girls originated in Thailand. When Field Marshal Sarit Thanarat was Prime Minister, from the late 1950s to the early 1960s, he was well-known for his relationships with film stars and models. It is said that in order to protect their reputation he used the telephone to arrange meetings for sex. After his death, these arrangements were revealed and the telephone became a fashionable means of contacting prostitutes, a trend that was perhaps aided by the increasing availability of telephone services. The telephone numbers of call-girls are usually restricted to small groups of customers, although there are also publications supplying the numbers. These publications include "girlie" magazines sold at news-stands. Tourist magazines in English, available free at the airport and in hotels, also include telephone numbers of escort agencies. In some cases, the call-girls can be contacted through telephone paging services.

There is a wide variety of bars, cocktail lounges and nightclubs where it is possible to obtain the services of a prostitute. Apart from individual bars and clubs, there are areas which cater to particular groups. For example, in Bangkok, foreign tourists go mainly to bars in the Patpong area or on Sukhumvit Road. Within these two areas, there is further differentiation according to nationality. Japanese tourists are more likely to go to Thaniya Plaza, while Western tourists go to Patpong, Nana Entertainment Plaza and Soi Cowboy. There are also bars on Soi Nana which cater mainly to Arab customers. Scattered throughout Bangkok are bars, nightclubs and cocktail lounges which cater to Thai customers. There are also areas with a concentration of bars mainly for Thais, for example, on Sutisarn Road. Bars of all varieties are also found in the major tourist resorts of Pattaya and Phuket.

When bars first developed as places for meeting women, the hostesses often only chatted with customers. In the Thai language they were called "partners" or "hour-sitting hostesses". Their duties more overtly included offering sexual services during the Viet Nam War. Other types of entertainment, for example, erotic dancing and sex shows, were also introduced around this period. "A-go-go" bars were reported to have first made their appearance in Bangkok around 1967, and were established in Patpong in 1969.

It is possible to get sexual services, particularly oral sex, within the premises of some bars. However, sexual services are normally arranged by paying the establishment a fee to take the worker out of the bar to a hotel, and then negotiating payment for sexual services with the woman herself. In other bars, total payment for sexual services is paid at the bar, and the bar manager pays the prostitute an agreed percentage. Bar hostesses can also make money by getting customers to buy them drinks, for which they receive a commission (around 20 baht or US$0.75 cents per drink). In nightclubs in which sexual services can be arranged, the singers are also often prostitutes. Arrangements can vary from women working on their own, to situations where the nightclub management is involved in managing the services of the women employees.

The sector which has gained in terms of the numbers of workers is the "other" category. From around 15 per cent of sex workers in 1979, it comprised almost 40 per cent in 1992 and about 47 per cent in 1996. This sector covers what is often referred to as "indirect" prostitution, operating under the guise of some other activity. However, in most cases, knowledge of their real activities is no secret. The "other" category contains a wide variety of venues for commercial sex. By far the largest component involves women working out of restaurants. More detailed 1996 data made available by the Ministry of Public Health indicate that 13,732 commercial sex workers operated from restaurants, 171 from hairdressing or beauty salons, 7,336 from cafes and coffee shops, 322 were call-girls and 8,778 operated from discos, pubs, *karaoke* bars and cocktail lounges. The move from direct to indirect prostitution is a trend which is probably an outcome of official pressure and of customer demand. One consequence of the trend is that it is now more difficult for concerned groups such as health officials to gain access to the sex workers. They first have to identify the women involved and then in many cases have to approach the workers individually, rather than going through the owner or manager of the establishment, since the latter can disclaim any responsibility for the sexual activities of employees.

Karaoke bars, in which visitors can sing along to music videos, are a relatively recent development. Many of these bars provide hostesses, and private rooms can be hired. Not all *karaoke* bars or all hostesses are involved in the sex industry, but in many bars it is possible to arrange to pay for sex with a hostess, although this is typically a privately negotiated arrangement between the customer and the woman.

It is also possible to pick up prostitutes in some public places. In Bangkok, there are several areas which are well known, or were previously well known, such as the foot of Memorial Bridge, Pramane Ground, Hua Lampong railway station and Wong Wian Yiisipsong Karakada. Normally, sex takes place at nearby hotels. Prostitutes working from public places are usually streetwalkers who cannot easily get employment in establishments, for example because they are too young or too old, or have a noticeable addiction to drugs.

Restaurants, especially garden restaurants (with tables set in open grounds), are also important places of assignation. Generally, the owner employs waitresses who also operate as prostitutes. In some places, rooms are available at the back of the restaurant for sexual activities. In other cases, the customer has to take the woman to other locations. It is not difficult to identify such restaurants: many have more waitresses than they have tables. This form of prostitution is growing rapidly, especially in the provinces.

Other places of assignation include hairdressing salons, golf clubs (in Thailand, golf caddies are usually women) and discotheques. Escort agencies also advertise their services in both English and Thai newspapers. A more up-market venue is what is known as a "member club", although it is rare for these clubs actually to restrict their visitors to members. They are located in hotels and along some of the larger streets in the inner city of Bangkok. They usually have dining services, live bands and attractive, well-educated hostesses. Some only cater for one nationality, for example, there are numerous Japanese-only member clubs.

A survey of commercial sex workers

The segmentation of the commercial sex industry in Thailand clearly makes it difficult to generalize about prostitution in Thailand. It is necessary to examine different sectors in some depth. In this chapter, two sub-sectors – rural brothels and Bangkok massage parlours – were chosen for in-depth analysis. A structured questionnaire was administered by the researchers, assisted by university students, to purposively selected samples of female sex workers in each sub-sector. In both sub-sectors, several establishments were visited and in each of these establishments unstructured interviews were also conducted with the owners or managers. Interviews were also held with government officials whose responsibilities brought them into contact with the sex industry.

The rural brothel sample

The area selected for the study of rural brothels was in a province approximately four hours' drive north of Bangkok. Major roads to the northeast and north run through this central region province. According to the 1991 Department of Health Statistics on sex establishments, there were 52 prostitutes working in six brothels in the town. All six brothels were operating during the time the survey was conducted (five days in December 1992). All 48 women working in the six establishments during this five-day period were interviewed. Another four women working in a brothel in a nearby town were also interviewed, giving a total of 52 rural brothel workers from seven establishments in the sample.

The town in which the brothels were located is small, with a population below 10,000. Unlike the other main centre for brothels in the province, brothels in this town did not depend on long-distance truck drivers and people from other provinces for their main custom. Most of the clients were local, coming from the town itself and neighbouring areas. Nearby, there were several very large factories producing cement or involved in extractive industries. A number of large factories were also being built. These industries provided one source of customers. The town is also a famous religious site, particularly revered by Sino-Thais. The visitors to the temple, especially during festival time, provided a valued seasonal source of clients. For regular customers, however, the brothels relied on locals.

The brothels were grouped around a road intersection, not far from the temple and commercial area of the town. It was not difficult, when driving through the area at night or in the afternoon, to recognize the function of the buildings in which the brothels were located. In the early evening, many of the young women sat out in front of the establishments. Later in the evening, the places were brightly lit. They closed around three in the morning. The brothels were not segregated from the rest of the community. There were shops and houses next to some of the establishments. Children played on the street and people went about their normal activities in the area of the brothels.

The brothels were run down in appearance, although similar to other buildings in the area. Inside they were unattractive and relatively dirty places. They all basically had the same layout. In the front was an area where the customers could view the women, who were partitioned off by an open metal grate. The women sat behind this grate engaged in their own activities – putting on make-up, chatting, sewing and so on. The women had numbers affixed to their clothes. Clients indicated their selection by the number of the woman. After making a choice, the client and the chosen woman went to rooms in the back of the establishment. The rooms in which the women received clients were also the rooms in which they lived. Each woman decorated her own room, normally with a bed, a fan, a bedside table, a wardrobe and posters of semi-naked women and, sometimes, posters of male pop stars.

The first brothel in the town was established about 30 years ago. This establishment, with the original owner, was still operating and – in terms of the number of customers – appeared to be the most popular. According to the owner, before the brothel was established there were prostitutes working out of rented rooms, but they had to deal with the authorities on their own, and hence most were happy to join the brothel when it started. Soon after the first brothel commenced operation, other brothels opened. While some establishments opened and then subsequently closed, there had always been at least six establishments operating. A few years ago there were about 10 brothels in the town. The cost for sexual services was 30 baht (US$1.25) when the first brothel opened.

A family network linked three of the six establishments. One establishment, which had been operating for about 25 years, was run by a woman in her sixties. One of her daughters owned another establishment, while her 22-year-old grandson owned another, which he inherited from his mother. These family linkages undoubtedly contributed to the cooperation that existed among all the establishments. The owners met regularly to decide on common policies, such as prices and how to deal with customers who refused to use condoms. It was decided that no establishment would accept a customer who refused to use one, and it did seem that this united front had been successful in enforcing what appeared to be almost universal use.

There was pessimism shown by all brothel owners regarding the current level of business. They did not link this to pressure from police for them to close down, but rather saw it as related to the fear of AIDS and an economic downturn. All said that they did their best business about five years prior to the survey, when there was an economic boom and when AIDS was not yet a concern. Several of the owners claimed that the effective ban on hiring women under the age of 18 was also hurting business, because most of the customers wanted to have sex with younger women. It is important to note that while there had been a drop in customers, the owners said that there was no difficulty in obtaining women to work in the brothels. The problem was seen as one of a lack of demand rather than of supply. Several of the younger owners expressed a desire to get out of the business but said that they had no other skills.

Bangkok massage parlours

Bangkok has a wide variety of massage parlours. The main distinction is between those establishments which offer traditional massage and those offering other forms of massage. In many traditional massage establishments sexual services are not available. According to Department of Health statistics, Bangkok accounts for around 60 per cent of the commercial sex workers employed in non-traditional massage parlours in Thailand. However, only 22 per cent of the sex workers in establishments which were classified as offering traditional massage worked in Bangkok. The massage parlours which functioned to provide a setting for commercial sex varied in size from very large buildings with hundreds of rooms, also offering dining and nightclub-type entertainment facilities, to small establishments in nondescript buildings. Massage parlours also tended to be spatially concentrated. For example, in Bangkok, over half of the establishments were located in the Ratchadamri area. The average number of sex workers in a Bangkok massage parlour was just under 100, although several had over 250 employees each.

Four establishments were chosen for the survey. In order to get a range of establishments which were in rough proportion to the price distribution outlined in the Department of Health's listing of commercial sex establishments, two massage parlours from the middle-price category, one high-price establishment and one low-price massage parlour were selected. All establishments were located in the Ratchadamri area. A total of 36 interviews were completed in the medium-price massage parlours, ten in the low-price parlour and eight in the high-price establishment.

While the cost and services available varied from one massage parlour to another, the method of operation was basically the same (Sureeman, 1988). The women sit behind a glass partition, while on the other side of the partition customers stand, or in some places sit drinking and eating, until they make their selection. Each woman has a number, and it is this number that the customer uses to inform the staff which woman he wants. The woman is then called out and, after the customer pays the fee to the massage parlour, they go to a room in the building. The room contains a bed and a large bathing area, normally with mirrors on the walls and ceiling. Food and beverage service is available in the rooms. The women normally do not live in these rooms.

The two middle-price massage parlours had about 100 to 120 women providing sexual services, although only 70 to 80 would turn up on any one night. The high-price establishment had 200 to 300 women workers, although only 100 or so were regular workers. The low-price massage parlour had about 40 rooms in regular use. The four establishments all had restaurants with live entertainment. Aside from the sex workers there were many employees, including men who helped customers to make a decision about which women to choose, cleaners, waitresses (for the restaurant and for room service), cashiers, parking valets and security guards. The number of support staff exceeded the number of women employed to provide sexual services.

All four establishments surveyed had been operating for over ten years with one, the high-price massage parlour, in operation for 20 years. The massage parlours occupied prime real estate, probably some of the most expensive land in Bangkok. Apart from the value of the land, there was also substantial investment in buildings and furnishings. While all four managers complained that business had fallen from the peaks experienced several years ago, a fall they attributed to a combination of economic downturn and fear of AIDS, there had been no trimming of staff and there were no plans to close. While statistics indicated a reduction in the number of commercial sex workers employed in massage parlours, discussions with managers suggested that the decline was concentrated at the low-price end of the market and that at the high-price end there might even have been an expansion.

Demographic characteristics

Because of the nature of the work, women in the sex industry are generally young. The mean age of the 106 women interviewed was 23.1 years, with those working in brothels on average almost two years older than those working in the massage parlours (24 as compared to 22.2 years). In both sectors, several women aged over 30 were interviewed. These women generally entered the profession late in life, usually as a result of marriage problems.

One surprising aspect of the age distribution was that three workers were under the age of 18. The police, especially in the rural area surveyed, were very strict on checking ages and had sent some young girls home not long before the survey. However, it was not unusual for the workers to obtain identity cards on which their ages are misstated. The brothel owners often highlighted the preference that customers have for very young women. Because of the recent crackdown on under-age prostitutes, owners were quite wary of employing anyone who could not produce evidence of being over 18 years or who did not look to be over 18. In the massage parlours, however, the managers did not express any strong customer preference for very young women.

The levels of education of the sex workers were similar to those of other rural women but were much lower than those of rural-urban migrants in general (see table 5.2). While 15 per cent of the brothel workers and 17 per cent of the massage parlour workers had completed some secondary education, the corresponding national figure for rural women aged from 20 to 24 years was 15 per cent, while for rural-urban migrants aged from 20 to 24 years it was 24 per cent.

A striking finding was that 79 per cent of respondents in the brothel sub-sector and 48 per cent in the massage parlours had been married before, or were currently married. These findings contradict the popular perception that the sex industry is composed of young single women who are lured into prostitution. In fact, many

Table 5.2. Percentage distribution of educational attainment

Educational attainment	Sex workers		Rural population	
	Brothels	Massage parlours	All rural (age 20-24)	Rural-urban migrants (age 20-24)
No education	13.5	1.9	3.7	1.3
Primary	71.2	79.6	75.6	55.0
Secondary	15.4	16.7	15.2	24.4
Tertiary	0.0	1.9	5.5	19.2
Number	52	54	2 127 800	111 800

Source: Interview data and Ministry of Education.

women entered the sex industry after the failure of their marriage. Table 5.3 shows the present living arrangements and fertility of the "ever-married" respondents. More than half the respondents in the rural brothels had children, but only six out of the 54 women interviewed in Bangkok massage parlours were mothers. Most of the children did not live with the mother, being mainly looked after by the respondents' mothers. However, several women working in the brothels looked after their own children. The attitudes of the owners towards children living with their mothers on the premises varied considerably among establishments. Some owners said they would not accept any worker who had a child with her, while others had no objection. Women who were looking after their own children were doing so because they had no other child care options.

Almost all respondents were recent migrants, and they came mainly from agricultural backgrounds. There was a high degree of geographical concentration of origin of the women interviewed. Almost 60 per cent were born in the northern region, and another 20 per cent came from the northeast. The rest were from Bangkok or the central or southern regions. Most of the variation in origin was among, rather than within, establishments. For example, two of the seven brothels specialized in hiring women from the north, while several others preferred to hire women from the northeast and central regions. Of the four massage parlours covered in the survey, one had no women from the north, while the other three had more than 75 per cent from the north. There were a number of explanations for these patterns. Social networks were the main mechanism through which the women were recruited. Once a link with an area was established, it served to channel women, including sisters, to particular establishments. There was also a demand factor. An often-expressed belief in Thai society is that northern women are the most beautiful, partly because of their fairer complexions. This view was expressed by the managers of the establishments. However, three brothel owners indicated that they did not like hiring women from the north because they would usually demand money in advance of employment (up to 20,000 baht or US$800) and then would sometimes not stay long.

While none of the brothel owners claimed to be directly involved in recruiting from the north, a local official suggested that active recruitment did occur. The massage parlours did not normally engage in direct recruiting, although private

Table 5.3. Current marital status, fertility and child-care arrangements of "ever-married" women

Characteristics	Sub-sector (percentage distribution)	
	Brothels	Massage parlours
Marital status		
Living with spouse	3.8	13.0
Separated	63.5	11.1
Divorced	1.9	24.1
Widowed	9.6	0.0
Single	22.2	51.8
Number	52	54
Have children	53.8	11.1
Living arrangements of children		
With respondent	17.9	0.0
With partner/ex-partner	3.6	16.7
With respondent's parents	46.4	66.7
With partner's/ex-partner's parents	10.7	16.7
Other arrangements	21.5	0.0
Number	28	6
Responsibility for care of child if living with respondent		
Respondent herself	40.0	0.0
Partner/ex-partner	0.0	0.0
Respondent's parents	20.0	0.0
Hired help	40.0	0.0
Number	5	0

Note: Total may not equal 100 due to rounding.

agents were active in supplying workers to massage parlours and then taking a cut of their earnings (often against an advance paid to the parents of the women).

The sex workers came not only from particular regions but also particular provinces within these regions. Approximately 35 per cent of all sex workers sampled were from two northern provinces, Chiang Rai and Phayao. Furthermore, most workers originated from particular districts within these two provinces. These patterns might be expected to result from the purposive sampling design where, because of the existence of strong social networks and recruiting patterns, different establishments would end up with large proportions of their employees originating from the same area. However, it is likely that the patterns also reflect an industry-wide reality. For example, eight of the 54 respondents working in the massage parlours came from Dok Kham Tai district in Phayao. This district is famous in Thailand for the numbers of sex workers it exports, and there is even a popular song entitled *"plaeng saaw dok kham tai"* (song of the

Table 5.4. Characteristics of sex workers by region of birth

Characteristics	Region (percentage distribution)		
	Northeast	Central/south	North
Current mean age	24.8	24.1	22.1
Mean years of education	5.9	5.7	5.5
Percentage ever married	95.0	83.0	45.0
Percentage with children	75.0	21.0	22.0
Percentage ever married and living with husband	10.0	15.0	14.0
Number	20	24	62

young women from Dok Kham Tai) about girls from this district coming to Bangkok. This district was also given special attention as a source area of massage parlour workers in Phongpaichit's (1982) classic study of massage parlour workers.

None of the respondents interviewed were from other countries, although there has been a great deal of recent concern that sex workers from neighbouring countries, especially from Myanmar and China, were being brought into the country. These women were often very vulnerable because of language difficulties and because it was difficult for health workers and other government workers to communicate with them. They were more likely to be found in the brothel sector than in massage parlours, since communication with customers is more important in the latter sector. All the brothel owners interviewed stated that they had never had workers from other countries, although they did know of such workers in brothels in other areas of the province. Several did mention, however, that they had employed hill-tribe women. There was a local community of several thousand Hmong, from which some young women had previously come to work in the brothels. Because of crackdowns on child prostitution, and since only a small percentage of the Hmong had identity cards to establish their age, they had all been sent home.

The survey revealed substantial differences in the characteristics of the prostitutes from different regions, especially between those from the north and those from the northeast. Women from the north tended to be younger, less educated, more likely to have never been married and less likely to have children (see table 5.4). These findings coincided with the statements of brothel owners who claimed that women from the northeast largely entered the occupation because of a failed marriage and a consequent need to support their children, while women from the north were more likely to be supporting their parents. Women from the central/southern regions formed an intermediate category, with over 80 per cent ever-married, but only 21 per cent having children. Much of the available literature, which has concentrated on sex workers from the northern provinces, has emphasized the importance of obligations to parents, and the need to meet these obligations through remitting money. It has been noted that this is a strong motivating factor for young northern women to enter the sex industry (Muecke, 1989).

For northeastern women, however, entry into the sex sector appears to be related more to a need to provide for their children. Phongpaichit (1982) notes that the attitude of northeastern villagers and parents towards women who had gone to work as sex workers was much more intolerant than that of northern villagers. This attitude extended to potential husbands of women who worked as sex workers. A woman from the northeast who enters the sex industry is reducing her chances of marriage in a society in which marriage and children are still considered very important.

The survey results indicated that sex workers in both sub-sectors came from impoverished family backgrounds, especially in the northern region. Many had already married and borne children themselves, although few of the marriages remained intact. The women were generally young and had a limited education. Important differences in the characteristics of women could be observed by sector of employment and by region of origin. These differences suggested that certain factors operated to attract women into the sex industry, and channelled these women into different sectors of the industry.

Work experience, entry into the sex industry and job mobility

Half of the respondents in the massage parlours and 29 per cent of the respondents in the brothels stated that a job in the sex industry was the first employment that they had ever had. These percentages were overstated, however, as many of the respondents did not consider work on the family farm or in home industries as employment. Almost half of the brothel workers and 22 per cent of the massage parlour workers had previously worked in agriculture. A further 17 per cent of the massage parlour respondents worked in home or cottage industries and 11 per cent as domestic maids.

Unemployment did not seem to be a factor prompting women to work in the sex industry. Only 12 per cent of brothel workers and 22 per cent of massage parlour respondents reported a period of actively looking for work before entering the industry. The period of unemployment was usually less than one month.

About a third of the women first became commercial sex workers before they reached the legal age of 18. Nearly one-fifth of the women currently working in brothels commenced working between the ages of 13 and 15. This did not mean, however, that they worked continuously after first entering the industry. Several of the women received a large amount of money by having sex for the first time when they were very young. This was normally arranged through an agent and occurred in a hotel; the girl returned home afterwards and did not enter the industry for another few years. The money was usually paid to the parents or other family members. Many more of the massage parlour workers lost their virginity through commercial sex than was the case with the brothel workers; their first sexual encounter often occurred in a massage parlour, and they continued work afterwards. Women from the north entered the industry at a younger age than women from the other regions.

Most of the massage parlour workers who entered the sex industry in their late twenties or early thirties were employed in the low-price establishment where both sexual services and regular massages were provided. Although all the respondents

Table 5.5. Method of entry into the sex industry

Method of entry	Sub-sector (percentage distribution)	
	Brothels	Massage parlours
Introduction by friends	53.8	63.0
Self-arranged	17.3	24.1
Arranged by owner of establishment	1.9	1.9
Agent or middleman	13.5	7.4
Forced	13.5	0.0
Responded to advertisement	0.0	3.7
Number	52	54

Note: Total may not equal 100 due to rounding.

from the low-price massage parlour offered sexual services, many did not begin to do so until after having been employed for a considerable time providing regular massages. Many of the older workers did not offer sexual services, while others did so on an irregular basis.

The main reason for becoming prostitutes was economic, although the types of economic factors varied. Brothel workers were more likely to say that they became prostitutes to earn money to raise their children, while massage parlour workers were often motivated by the opportunity to earn a high income. These differences were related to the regional origins of the workers. Women from the northeast were much more likely to say that they needed to raise a child, while women from the north were more likely to state that their parents were poor.

The majority of respondents voluntarily became prostitutes (see table 5.5), mainly to support family members. Only seven women working in brothels claimed to have been forced into commercial sex activities. Almost 60 per cent were introduced by a friend, while another 20 per cent learnt about the availability of work through an acquaintance returning to their home village and then made their own arrangements to enter the establishment. Others were recruited by agents or establishment owners, or responded to advertisements. The majority of workers in brothels reported that while their families knew of the nature of their work, they did not approve. Those working in massage parlours were less likely to face family disapproval.

In summary, women working in brothels or massage parlours generally entered the sex industry at a young age. Most obtained their knowledge about the industry and an introduction to employers through friends who were already in the same occupation. Once in a particular sector of the industry, they were likely to stay in that sector and, especially in the case of massage parlour workers, stayed for a relatively long time in the same job. Brothel workers, however, shifted jobs quite regularly, although most moved between jobs that were at the lower-income end of the sex industry. The limited amount of inter-sectoral mobility appeared to be related to the operation of social networks that restricted flows of information about opportunities in other sub-sectors.

Working conditions

Almost all of the brothel workers and 82 per cent of the massage parlour workers stated that they knew the type of work they would be undertaking before taking up their current job. In many cases, the knowledge was based on past experience in the sector. In addition, friends who had worked in the establishment, or other women currently working there, explained the activities to them before they took up the job. The survey results highlighted the importance of social networks in providing information about working conditions. Once the women arrived in the establishment, they were generally given information about the types of duties they were expected to perform and the conditions of employment. In three of the four massage parlours surveyed, new workers were provided with training in basic massage techniques and in providing services to customers, before they commenced work.

All the brothel workers interviewed claimed that they had complete freedom to select their own customers. In-depth discussions with establishment owners and the workers themselves revealed that they rarely exercised this right. The reasons for rejecting customers were usually because they were drunk or old. It did appear that the workers would be supported by the management in situations where they did not want to go with a client. For nearly all brothel workers, however, there were strong economic incentives not to reject clients, since they were paid according to the number of customers they serviced. In the massage parlours, where there was greater emphasis on customer satisfaction, it was much harder to define freedom of choice to select customers. The only "acceptable" or "good" reason for rejecting a client was when the worker was acquainted with the client outside her work role, such as if the prospective customer lived in the same apartment block or was from the same home village.

Due to the greater amount of time spent with customers, massage parlour workers had, on average, only about half the number of customers of the brothel workers. The number of customers in a normal week was significantly higher than in the week prior to the survey (see table 5.6), the main reason being that some women were menstruating. This partly explains the large range in the number of customers reported for the week prior to the survey; for the brothel workers it was from 0 to 60 customers, while for massage parlour workers it was from 0 to 28.

Table 5.6 indicates that the amount of time the women actually spent with customers was small in relation to the total working day. The hours during which brothel workers generally received customers were from about 7 or 8 p.m. to 2 or 3 a.m. Massage parlour workers started earlier, about 5 or 6 p.m., and worked until about midnight. Weekend hours were longer, and workers were normally required to work at the weekend, when there tended to be more customers. Brothel workers expected to spend about 20 minutes with each customer, while massage parlour workers spent from around 90 minutes to two hours. In both sub-sectors, most of the time at work was spent waiting for customers.

In a normal week, the women worked every day. At no establishment surveyed were paid holidays given. The brothel workers were free to work as many or as few days as they wanted, while the massage parlour workers were provided with

Table 5.6. Mean and median number of customers

Reference period	Sub-sector			
	Brothels		Massage parlours	
	Mean	Median	Mean	Median
Last week	22.8	20	12.8	13
Average day	4.2	4	2.4	2
Average week	26.0	25	16.0	16
Number	52		54	

incentives to work 20 or more days a month. The women took from three to five days off each month during their menstruation. Many also took long breaks to return home, or simply because they did not want to work. Another reason for taking time off work was illness, although women were not paid if they were sick, even if the sickness was an outcome of their work.

Incomes and expenditures

Most of the women entered the sex industry for economic reasons. In exchange for working in an occupation which is disapproved of by most of society, and which can have severe and well-recognized health risks, the workers expected to obtain an income greater than they could earn in other occupations for which they would be qualified. Other studies have also documented the high incomes that could be earned by the prostitutes (Phongpaichit, 1982; IPS, 1993). The mean income of all the women surveyed was about 20,000 baht (US$800) per month, with a mean of 35,000 baht (US$1,400) for women working in massage parlours and of 6,000 baht (US$240) for brothel workers. Median incomes were somewhat lower, reflecting the influence of the high earnings of several workers in each sub-sector. The highest monthly income for a woman in the brothel sub-sector was 15,000 baht (US$600), which, disregarding a relatively small contribution of tips, corresponded to 300 customers per month. The highest monthly income in the massage parlour sub-sector was 91,500 baht (US$3,660), obtained by an employee of the high-price establishment and based on receiving approximately 70 customers over the previous month. Very few workers had other sources of income.

Table 5.7 shows gross earnings. Net earnings (after deductions by employers, agents or officials) was roughly the same as gross earnings for brothel workers. There was a substantial difference of about 2,300 baht (US$92) between average gross and net earnings of massage parlour workers. The deductions in the massage parlours were in the form of fines for coming to work late or for not working on a weekend. Some of the women also made substantial payments to their agents, typically about half of their earnings. In some cases, the agents worked in the establishment as *cheer kheek* (those helping customers to choose the women).

Table 5.7. Percentage distribution of gross income in the month prior to the survey

Income (baht per month)	Sub-sector	
	Brothels	Massage parlours
Below 3 000	15.4	0
3 000-4 999	26.4	0
5 000-6 999	25.0	5.6
7 000-9 999	21.2	1.9
10 000-14 999	9.6	16.7
15 000-19 999	1.9	13.0
20 000-24 999	0	5.6
25 000-29 999	0	3.7
30 000-34 999	0	7.4
35 000-39 999	0	7.4
40 000-44 999	0	1.9
45 000-49 999	0	3.7
50 000-54 999	0	9.3
55 000-59 999	0	7.4
60 000-64 999	0	7.4
65 000 and above	0	9.3
Mean (baht)	5 959	35 526
Standard deviation (baht)	3 223	21 651
Median (baht)	5 000	26 500
Number	52	54

Note: The rate of exchange at the time of the survey was approximately 25.3 baht per US$.

The variation in earnings was greater in the massage parlour sub-sector than among brothels. The relative lack of differentials in earnings among the brothels might help to explain the lack of mobility among different establishments in the rural area studied. In Bangkok, however, workers moved between different massage parlours. The massage parlour owners claimed that price differentials were not due to the perceived quality of the workers, but were instead related to the luxuriousness and physical amenities of each establishment. However, within each massage parlour, there was a clear ranking system of workers. Both middle-price parlours in the sample had two classes of workers: the normal and the *dara* ("stars"). The *dara* were considerably more expensive and were selected on the basis of a combination of physical appearance and personality characteristics (such as having a light complexion, being over 165 centimetres tall and having good manners). The term "star" was also used in the rural brothels and referred to those women who received the most customers.

The method of receiving income varied between the sub-sectors. In the rural brothels, payment was based on the number of clients the prostitute entertained. Each client paid the establishment 100 baht (US$4), for which they expected to spend about 20 minutes with the brothel worker. This time period was normative, rather than fixed by regulation. The number of clients was entered into a book, and the women were paid at the end of the night, based on how many clients they had. They received 50 baht (US$2) per client. Several women also accepted clients on a nightly basis (receiving from 200 to 300 baht or US$8 to 12). They also made some money on drinks commissions and on tips, but these were irregular and not large. In the massage parlours, payment methods were intended to encourage the women to work on a regular basis. For example, in the two middle-price massage parlours, there were four components of payment. The first component was paid at the end of the working night, and was a portion of the fee paid by the client to the establishment. The second was in the form of coupons redeemable at the end of the month for each client. The third was extra incentive payments given after a woman had received more than 41 customers during the month; the amount of the incentive increased for every ten extra customers. Fourth, commissions on drinks and food were also given, although they tended to be very small. Overall, it was possible for a prostitute to receive between 50 and 60 per cent of the money paid by a client, but to do so, she had to work regularly.

At the end of each night at the high-price massage parlour surveyed, the workers received 1,000 baht (US$40) from the 1,600 baht (US$64) paid by a customer for two hours of service. There was also an incentive payment based on the number of hours worked (40 baht or US$1.60 per hour) and an additional 800 baht (US$32) if a woman worked more than 160 hours during the previous month. There were no food or drink commissions.

At the low-price massage parlour, the system of payment resembled that which, according to informants, was previously the industry standard. Customers paid for a massage by the hour (90 baht or US$3.60 an hour), with a usual period of two hours. The masseuses received 20 baht (US$0.80) an hour from this. An extra fee for sexual services was subject to negotiations between the woman and her client. Commissions were available on food and drinks, but these were rarely worth more than 50 baht a day. There were also monthly incentive payments based on hours worked, with a minimum payment of 800 baht (US$32) for working 124 hours, and a maximum of 3,000 baht (US$120) for over 221 hours in the month.

Most massage parlour employers retained part of the women's earnings until the end of the month as a means of disciplining or controlling the workers. Several workers reported being fined for coming to work late. The main reason given by the management for retaining some of the earnings was that the women would otherwise spend it all in one night by going to the disco or giving money to their boyfriends, and then having nothing left to pay the rent or to send home at the end of the month. This paternalistic attitude was also reflected in comments by one manager who claimed that he had to be like a father to the women, giving them advice, loans and so on.

Earnings in both sub-sectors far exceeded any income that might be earned in other occupations by the women, who commonly had only a primary level of education. The majority of women at equivalent levels of education were engaged in the agricultural sector or were self-employed in the service sector (NSO, 1988).

Most of the women were conscious of the income loss they would face if they moved to another occupation. Only 6 per cent of the women thought that they might be able to obtain equivalent earnings in an alternative occupation. When asked about the types of occupations they would consider as alternatives, the brothel workers were most likely to mention agriculture, factory employment and sales (mostly as vendors). In contrast, no respondent from a massage parlour considered working in a factory, although almost 20 per cent said that they wanted to work in a beauty shop or as hairdressers. A small number in both sub-sectors had not thought about entering other occupations, either because they were happy in their work or because they had no wish to do anything else.

In terms of benefits, brothel workers were provided with accommodation, food, legal help and loans from the owners. Massage parlour workers received less in terms of benefits, although they had much higher incomes than the brothel workers. Most massage parlour workers were provided with uniforms and medical treatment, although the costs were often deducted from their incomes. Most workers thought that they could obtain loans from their employers and would be given legal help if they encountered a problem linked to their work.

The types of benefits available clearly had an influence on the expenditure of workers. The expenses listed in table 5.8 refer to a normal month over the previous year. The mean total monthly expenses were 4,717 baht (US$189) for the brothel workers and 28,300 baht (US$1,132) for the massage parlour workers. These amounts were roughly 15 per cent lower than the mean take-home pay for the previous month. Some of the differences in expenditure patterns were directly related to the living arrangements of the workers. Nearly all the brothel workers lived on the premises and, apart from paying a utilities charge in several of the establishments, had no accommodation expenses. Massage parlour workers, however, allocated on average about 10 per cent of their expenditure to accommodation. Both groups spent a considerable amount on food. Although the brothels provided their workers with meals, these were very basic and the workers reported often going out for snacks. Those in massage parlours had large expenditures on cosmetics and transport (because it was more convenient, or even necessary, for the women to use taxis to go home when the massage parlours closed after midnight).

Since their expenditures were less than their incomes, 70 per cent of brothel workers and 90 per cent of massage parlour workers reported having some form of savings. The most common kind of savings was cash, with mean cash savings of brothel workers at 3,468 baht (US$139) and of massage parlour workers at 46,800 baht (US$1,872). The next most popular form of savings was the purchase or the building of a house. About a quarter of the brothel workers and half of the massage parlour workers owned houses, typically back in their home villages. In several cases, they owned more than one house. Some workers also had land and farm animals.

Remittances and the purchase of houses, land and other property by the sex workers both helped their families and insured their own futures by providing resources to their families. The women commonly specified the use to be made of the money they sent home or that they brought with them on their frequent return

Table 5.8. Mean monthly expenditure and percentage distribution by category of expenditure

Expenditure items	Sector			
	Brothels		Massage parlours	
	Baht	%	Baht	%
Clothes	671	14	2 256	8
Food	775	15	3 525	12
Cigarettes	195	4	201	1
Alcohol	56	1	246	1
Accommodation	203	4	2 863	10
Transport	109	2	1 839	7
Cosmetics	232	5	2 244	8
Leisure	45	1	499	2
Remittances	1 841	39	6 151	22
Savings	541	11	8 074	29
Other	158	3	380	1
Total	4 714	100	28 279	100
Number	52	52	54	54

Note: Totals may not equal 100 due to rounding.

trips. Especially for the brothel workers, the money was mainly for raising their children. The amount of the remittances was large relative to total expenditures and in absolute terms. On average, brothel workers remitted 1,841 baht (US$74), while massage parlour workers remitted 6,151 baht (US$246) per month. Another survey of sex workers in a variety of sub-sectors and geographical areas recorded monthly remittances of between 2,000 and 4,000 baht, or US$80-160 (IPS, 1993). In comparison, the legal minimum wage for workers in areas outside Bangkok was less than 100 baht (US$4) per day. Remittances from the women working in the sex industry therefore provided families with a relatively high standard of living. Phongpaichit (1982) described how the earnings of daughters in the sex industry provided families in the north and northeast with the chance of being upwardly mobile. No other industry would provide the opportunity for young uneducated women to send regularly these large amounts of money to their rural families.

The role of industry gatekeepers

Since prostitutes are engaged in activities regarded as illegal, they are prone to exploitation and harassment from numerous sources. Perhaps because of this potential for harassment, women are willing to join the sex industry establishments rather than operate on their own, even though this means receiving only a portion of the money that customers pay for their services.

Workers in both sub-sectors surveyed were well protected from outside harassment. Because there were more layers of protection, women working in the massage parlours were less likely than those working in the brothels to experience some form of trouble in their work. Workers in the massage parlours did not live there, and had their customers screened by the *cheer kheek*. All massage parlours had security personnel and a variety of other staff who acted as buffers against any trouble. The management could also screen out customers they thought would upset the workers.[11] Another possible reason for the greater security of the masseuses was that the massage parlours were often frequented by influential customers. The owner of the high-price establishment commented, "I don't have any trouble (with police and officials), many are customers". Since the brothel workers lived where they worked, the community could identify them as prostitutes, and they had only the owner standing between them and harassment. Even so, only 11 out of the 52 brothel workers surveyed reported having experienced any problems, and these were mainly from the police, or from customers who wanted them to perform acts they objected to. The majority of incidents was solved through the intervention of the owner.

It was the owners/managers who dealt with outsiders, these normally being officials who had some role to play in regulating the activities of the sex industry. For example, health officials appeared to have very good relations with the owners/managers, and regularly organized meetings to provide health-related information to the workers. With the police, however, there was a potential for conflict. When asked, none of the managers of the massage parlours said that they had any arrangements with the police to ensure that their businesses operated smoothly. All reported that the police regularly visited the establishments to check that the workers were above the legal age of 18. All brothel owners, however, admitted making payments to the local police.

Health and medical attention

Two-thirds of the respondents reported having experienced some form of health problem related to their work. Brothel workers, who normally serviced more clients, were more likely to have experienced health problems than massage parlour workers. Sixty per cent of the brothel workers reported having had gonorrhoea, 10 per cent had contracted syphilis and 60 per cent had experienced an infected or abraded vagina. The women working in brothels relied on government services for information about health issues and treatment for health problems. In nearly all cases, brothel workers who had a health problem obtained free treatment from the Health Department. The massage parlour workers, however, paid for their own treatment from private doctors.

Almost all of the respondents from both sub-sectors reported having received health information related to their work. Three-quarters of the brothel workers had received information from a government health official; others from friends or customers. In contrast, the massage parlour workers relied less on government health officials. Instead, they obtained information from the owner/manager of the establishment they worked in, from the media or from friends. For brothel workers, the health information they received was normally about how to protect themselves against diseases, including AIDS. Massage parlour workers were more likely than brothel workers to have also received information on family planning and abortion. This may help to explain why the incidence of abortions was higher among the brothel workers than the massage parlour workers. One quarter of the respondents from the brothels reported having undergone an abortion, compared to 11 per cent of those from the massage parlours. Only five out of the total of 19 women from the whole sample who had undergone abortions had had more than one abortion.

Health checks are one way to reassure clients that the prostitutes are safe, and careful monitoring of their health also ensures that they are available for work. In both sub-sectors surveyed, health checks were mandatory and were arranged on a regular basis. In the brothels, the checks were conducted on a weekly basis by the Health Department. The workers from each brothel went for their checks on a designated day of the week, and if they did not keep their appointments, the health officials sent someone to find out why they were absent. In the other sub-sector, one of the massage parlours operated its own clinic, another arranged for a doctor to come to the establishment, and the other two establishments arranged for their workers to be checked at nearby private clinics. The health checks were compulsory for the massage parlour workers, who were also required to pay for the checks. The frequency of the health checks varied. In two of the establishments it was three times a week, in another twice a week and in the fourth it was once a week. Blood tests for AIDS were done every three months in both sub-sectors.

The concern about HIV/AIDS was universal, shared by the owners/managers, the workers themselves and, according to the workers, the customers. All of the 106 respondents in the survey had heard about AIDS and were aware of the precautions they could take to minimize the risks of infection. Eighty-seven percent of the massage parlour workers, and all except three of the brothel workers, said they used condoms all the time as a precaution. Other precautions that were reported included refusing to engage in oral sex (brothel workers only) and careful washing after sex. Those who reported that condoms were not used in the last five times they had had sex claimed that it was because their customers refused to use them. In the brothels, the concern about the workers contracting AIDS was very strong, and the owners had taken a united stand against customers who refused to use condoms. In the massage parlours, although condom use was supposed to be compulsory, one manager said that it was up to the workers, since he did not know or want to know about what went on in the rooms; and one *cheer kheek* indicated that if a customer was a regular, and was considered respectable, it was not necessary for him to use a condom.

The scope and significance of the sex sector in the national economy

One of the problems encountered in efforts to formulate policies related to the sex industry is that there is no clear idea of the number of persons involved. For example, the kinds of labour market policies required will vary substantially depending on whether there are 65,000 or 2.8 million prostitutes (the approximate low- and high-range estimates available from the literature). The links between prostitution and the economy also require some estimate of the number of ancillary workers employed in the industry, while the potential health impact of activities associated with the sex industry has to be based on an estimate of the number of customers of sex workers.

One basis for estimating the numbers involved would be the population most likely to be employed as prostitutes. According to the 1990 census, there were 8.3 million women in Thailand aged between 15 and 29 years. While there are male prostitutes, these make up a relatively small proportion of the total number of prostitutes (Muecke, 1990; and Brinkmann, 1991). While there are undoubtedly both younger and older female prostitutes, the age range from 15 to 29 years captures the group for which prostitution is most likely (for example, Sittirai and Brown, 1991, claim that most female prostitutes are aged from 15 to 24). Approximately one-third of these 8.3 million persons, or somewhat less than 2.8 million, live in municipal areas or large districts which are considered to have some urban characteristics. As it is generally agreed that the majority of prostitutes in Thailand operate from urban areas, the validity of some of the available estimates could be called into question. For example, the figure of 2.8 million urban females aged 15 to 29 is approximately the same as the highest estimate of prostitutes in the country (cited by an NGO, the Coalition against Trafficking in Women) but this would mean that all women between 15 and 29 living in urban areas would be prostitutes.

Based on interviews and other sources, Godley (1991) provides estimates of the number of prostitutes. She indicates that the most commonly cited figure is around 700,000 women. This is in the range of 500,000 to 1 million that Muecke (1990) cites from other sources. This number of 700,000 constitutes around 8.5 percent of all women aged from 15 to 29 and about 25 per cent of urban women in that age group. One of the few studies which attempted to rigorously estimate the number of prostitutes, based mainly on ethnographic methods, produced an estimate of between 150,000 and 200,000 prostitutes (Sittitrai and Brown, 1991). If 175,000 was taken as the estimate, this would constitute 2.1 per cent of all women aged from 15 to 29 and around 7.3 per cent of urban women in this age range. These percentages, especially the latter, are plausible. The police department estimate is also in the range of 150,000 to 200,000.[12]

The estimate which is the lowest, but also the most systematically derived, was obtained from the Venereal Disease Section of the Ministry of Public Health. The Ministry regularly undertakes surveys of sex establishments in order to determine the number of women working in such establishments. Interviews conducted with health officials in a provincial area suggest that considerable care goes into these surveys.[13] The sex establishments are identified through women and/or men coming in for venereal disease checks. If the person is tested positive, and contracted the disease through a commercial sexual encounter, the health officials contact the establishment (or the prostitute if she operates on her own) to obtain information on the number of workers, prices charged, and so on. The health officials also arrange for the workers to have free health checks. The statistics are collated and sent to Bangkok twice a year.

Table 5.9. Number of sex establishments, workers and sex workers, January 1997

Region	Number of sex establishments	Number of workers	Number of sex workers
Bangkok	1 421	36 473	26 361
North	1 112	9 054	4 664
Northeast	1 192	11 355	5 060
Central	2 199	29 844	17 760
South	1 835	17 536	11 041
Total	7 759	104 262	64 886

Source: Bhatiasevi, 1997.

The figures provided by the Ministry of Public Health which were reproduced in table 5.1 provide a valuable indication of changes over time and among sectors in the number of commercial sex workers, even though they are underestimates (Havanon et al., 1992). The pattern during the 1980s was one of a general increase in the total number of commercial sex workers, with stagnation between 1982 and 1984, which coincided with a period of slow economic growth, and a decline after 1990. The peak, of some 85,000 workers, was reached in 1989 and 1990. Economic recession cannot account for the declines after 1990, and alternative explanations, such as the fear of AIDS and shifts from direct to indirect and less easily detected prostitution, are the most likely explanations. However, even with the declines experienced since 1990, current numbers of prostitutes are much higher in both absolute and proportional terms than they were a decade earlier. Data from the national survey conducted by the Ministry of Public Health in January 1997 indicated that there were 64,886 commercial sex workers in some 7,759 establishments (see table 5.9).

The largest concentration of prostitutes was in the Bangkok and central regions. Table 5.9 also shows that prostitutes accounted for about 60 per cent of total workers in the establishments where sexual services could be obtained; other workers were support staff. A report on the 1997 survey (Bhatiasevi, 1997) indicated that out of the total of 64,886 commercial sex workers, 2,237 were male and 12,607, or about 16 per cent, were non-Thai, mainly from Myanmar. The survey did not, however, take into account the age of the sex workers. An official of the Communicable Diseases Control Department of the Ministry of Public Health clarified that questions related to age and nationality were sensitive, so that data on these aspects tend to be less reliable. He also explained that due to the difficulties and problems of data collection, there could be a margin of error of about 20 per cent, which could bring the total number of sex workers to some 74,000.

The actual number of sex workers is difficult, if not impossible, to estimate, especially because of the rapid turnover of workers in the sex industry. An estimate of the number working as prostitutes at a particular time will be much lower than an estimate based on an interval, for example, one year. As suggested above, a plausible range of the number involved in prostitution at a point in time is 150,000 to 200,000. Results from small-scale surveys of sex workers in Thailand suggest that the median length of employment as a sex worker is between 18 months and two years (Guest, 1993). Hence, in any one-year period it could be expected that between 200,000 and 300,000 women work in the sex industry.

It is even more difficult to estimate the total numbers involved in the sex sector. In Thailand, the people likely to benefit economically from the activities of the sector, apart from the sex workers themselves, are: (a) parents of sex workers (through remittances); (b) owners, managers and other employees of sex industry establishments; (c) those working in tourism-related industries; and (d) public officials who receive payments from the sector.

If we assume a ratio of at least two workers in the sex industry to every commercial sex worker (this ratio is probably higher in some sectors of the industry, such as massage parlours and member clubs where there are many support staff, and lower in other sectors), and at least four family members of each commercial sex worker directly benefiting through remittances, the numbers of people with financial connections already exceeds 1.2 million (assuming a total of 200,000 commercial sex workers). These numbers, conservative as they are, indicate the potential economic dependency of a large part of Thai society on the sex industry. Employment is also generated in the hotel and restaurant industries by the activities of the sex sector. This indirect effect on employment is likely to be higher than the direct effects.

As most of the sex industry is located in urban areas, while most sex workers are from rural areas, the industry provides a major source of income for many rural households through remittances. A recent survey found that the average remittance from a commercial sex worker was 3,000 baht (US$150) per month. This is almost three times the average monthly wage available in agriculture in 1991 (TDRI, 1993). Assuming the total number of commercial sex workers to be 200,000, this implies an annual transfer from urban to rural areas of 7.2 billion baht (US$288 million) – an amount that dwarfs the budgets of many development programmes funded by the government. For example, it is eight times the amount earmarked for rural job-creation schemes designed to stop migration to Bangkok.

The number of customers of the sex workers is also difficult to establish, although there have been efforts to do so. Brinkmann (1991) reports on other studies which estimate that 4.6 million Thai men regularly frequent prostitutes. He makes his own estimate of 500,000 foreign tourists annually visiting prostitutes. Survey-based results from a variety of studies (see review in Weniger et al., 1991) also suggest very high levels of contact with prostitutes. The results include estimates that more than 75 per cent of a sample of young Bangkok men and almost one-quarter of men in stable relationships had visited prostitutes during the previous 12 months. Therefore, the numbers suggested by Brinkmann (1991) appear feasible. The Deputy Director-General of the Communicable Disease Control Department reported that more than 30 million condoms are now being used annually in Thailand, compared with only about 4 million some 10 years ago.

In summary, much of the Thai population is directly touched by prostitution, either through working as prostitutes, financially benefiting from prostitution or paying for the services of prostitutes. These groups vary in size, with the sex workers comprising the smallest group and the customers of sex workers the largest group.

Legislation covering the sex sector

Thailand has had three main legal statutes directly related to prostitution: the Contagious Diseases Prevention Act of 1908, the Prostitution Suppression Act of 1960, and the Entertainment Places Act of 1966. Besides these three Acts, the Penal Code of 1956 (sections 282-286) provides that those who are convicted of procuring persons for prostitution or profiteering from prostitution can be jailed and fined (for a discussion of the legal status of prostitution in Thailand, see also Malikaman et al., 1983; Jamnarnwej, 1984; Saisawat, 1986; Working Group on Public Welfare, 1989; Prukpongsawalee, 1991). The Prostitution Suppression Act of 1960 was replaced by the Prostitution Prevention and Suppression Act of 1996.

The Contagious Diseases Prevention Act was enacted during the reign of King Rama V as a result of the perceived increase in the number of prostitutes. The Act was intended to control places of prostitution because of the frequent occurrence of fights and brawls at brothels. Also, as the title of the Act suggests, there was concern with sexually transmitted diseases. The Act did not make prostitution illegal and was only intended to control the public order and health effects of prostitution. Brothels and prostitutes were subject to registration and were required to pay certain fees to the State.

The Act was abolished in 1960, when the Prostitution Suppression Act came into effect. The Prostitution Suppression Act was enacted in part because of pressure from the United Nations, which was campaigning internationally for the abolition of prostitution, especially in conjunction with the Convention on the Suppression of the Traffic in Persons and the Exploitation of the Prostitution of Others. To date, however, Thailand has not ratified this international convention. Under the Prostitution Suppression Act, prostitution was defined as the act of promiscuously rending sexual services for remuneration; and prostitutes, as well as all who were involved in arranging or profiting from the act (including owners, managers or keepers of entertainment parlours who allow their premises to be used for prostitution), were liable for punishment. Although the law was intended to suppress prostitution through making it an illegal activity, the thrust of the majority of provisions was the reform of prostitutes. Sections 11 to 16 of the Act provided, for example, that convicted prostitutes "should be given medical treatment, vocational training or both", "be committed to an assistance centre [for a period] not exceeding one year from the day the person has satisfied the sentence of the court", "be penalized if they seek to flee the centre", and so on.

The Entertainment Places Act of 1966 is designed to control the operation of establishments which endanger the morals of the community, through empowering the police to close a place in which commercial sex is offered. The Act regulates nightclubs, dance halls, bars and places for "baths, massage or steam baths which have women to attend male customers" by requiring them to obtain operating licences from local police, and expressly prohibiting them from using the premises for prostitution.

It also provides for the Social Welfare Department to send prostitutes to rehabilitation centres where they are to receive occupational training. However, the Act has been rarely used, with the exception of the provision for "rehabilitation" for prostitutes after completion of punishment. Instead, the Prostitution Suppression Act of 1960, which had lighter penalties, was employed in the limited number of cases where offenders were actually prosecuted (National Commission on Women's Affairs, 1985). The Entertainment Places Act has also been used selectively. It has been rare for the owners of the sex establishments or other persons in the industry, apart from the prostitutes, to be prosecuted.

The Entertainment Places Act is still in force today, but the Prostitution Suppression Act has been replaced by the Prostitution Prevention and Suppression Act, which was adopted in October 1996 and came into force in December 1996. The new Act is the result of growing awareness of the weaknesses of past legislation[14] and the concern for more effective measures to eradicate child prostitution. It became a reality largely as a result of the work of the National Committee for the Eradication of Commercial Sex, set up under the National Commission on Women's Affairs in the Prime Minister's Office. The Act went through several revisions, with initial drafts including provisions for registration and the carrying of health cards by prostitutes.

Under the Prostitution Prevention and Suppression Act as adopted (for details of the Act, see National Committee for the Eradication of Commercial Sex, 1996), prostitution is still illegal. Prostitutes are, however, subject only to a small fine. Section 6 provides that "whoever approaches, solicits, introduces, follows or importunes another person on a street, a public place or any other place, for the purpose of prostitution and if such act is overtly or shamelessly committed, or causes nuisance to the public, shall be punished with a fine not exceeding 1,000 baht (US$40)". The list of places that can be inspected has been extended (compared to the previous Act) to include airports, dockyards, railway stations, bus terminals, service premises, factories and other public places.

The new Act focuses punishment on those responsible for drawing women and children into prostitution rather than on the prostitutes themselves. While the prostitutes are liable only to fines, those found guilty of procurement, trafficking, pimping, advertising or soliciting, including through the media, are punishable by a prison term and heavier fines. More severe penalties are imposed where physical force or any form of threat is used to detain, confine or force a person to perform the prostitution activity. Where such offences are committed by an administrative official, police official, government official or someone working in the rehabilitation services, the Act has a special provision for imposing a heavy prison term (from 15 to 20 years) and a fine (300,000 to 400,000 baht, or US$12,000 to 16,000). The Act also has various provisions for the rehabilitation of prostitutes (which are described in the following section). The main concern of the Act, however, is eradication of prostitution through coercion and child prostitution (of both boys and girls below 18 years of age). The provisions for dealing with child prostitution are described in Chapter 6.

A number of additional amendments have also been proposed to strengthen the legal instruments against trafficking of women and children for the purpose of commercial sexual exploitation. For example, the proposals include revision of the Penal Code (the Extraterritorial Jurisdiction and Trafficking Amendment) to allow Thailand to "prosecute every offender who procures, deceives or traffics an adult or child of either sex for an indecent sexual act for the purpose of sexual gratification of another person, no matter where the offence is committed, and what nationality the offender is. The proposed amendment shows the policy and perception of Thailand that the said offences are universal and very serious crimes" (National Committee for the Eradication of Commercial Sex, 1996, p. 26). As of July 1997, the Extraterritorial Jurisdiction and Trafficking Amendment was before Parliament.

Social programmes affecting the sex sector

Since prostitution has received a great deal of political and media attention in Thailand, a wide range of "solutions" have been proposed for dealing with the "prostitution problem" (see, for example, Malikaman et al., 1983; Hantrakul, 1985; Skrobanek, 1986; Working Group on Public Welfare, 1989; IPSR, 1991; Ungphakorn, 1990; Muntarbhorn, 1992). The proposed "solutions" are mainly directed towards women as prostitutes, and disregard men. Those that focus on men typically stress the short-term strategy of invoking legal penalties or the long-term social strategy of changing men's attitudes towards women, although how this is to be done is not made at all clear. Economic pricing policies, such as increasing the price of sexual services, are rarely encountered. Most programmes are based on the assumption that women enter the sex industry out of poverty, lack of occupational skills or because they are tricked into entering. Hence the solutions are formal education (to improve their labour market chances), vocational training, income support and informal education so that they are less likely to be tricked. Other motivating factors, such as high income differentials between sex work and alternative occupations, are rarely discussed in a policy context. Finally, there is very little attention given to alternative institutional arrangements for the sex industry. For example, private ownership is assumed to be the rule; arrangements that have been tried in other countries, such as state control, workers' cooperatives and community control, have not been considered. Thailand does, however, have a closely regulated system for controlling health conditions within the sex sector.

Health programmes

The Ministry of Public Health has implemented both information campaigns for the commercial sex workers and a system of registering commercial sex establishments in order to provide their workers with health services. Health checks are carried out widely and frequently in the organized sex sector, especially when compared with the situation in the other Southeast Asian countries. In Bangkok, for instance, municipal regulations require the sex establishments to ensure that their workers undergo weekly checks for STDs as well as blood tests every three months for HIV, and implementation and enforcement of these regulations is relatively strict. The survey for this study found that, even in rural areas, the Health Department conducts weekly health checks of the brothel workers. The workers from each brothel go for their checks on a designated day of the week and if they do not turn up as scheduled, health officials are sent to find out why they did not appear. While the Health Department provides free services, some sex establishments arrange for their workers to be checked by private practitioners, and in other cases the prostitutes pay for their own medical checkups. The Venereal Diseases Section of the Ministry of Public Health undertakes a twice-yearly survey of sex establishments in order to determine the number of workers who should receive health coverage.

In addition, Thai NGOs have been playing a very active role in awareness raising and in distributing large numbers of free condoms in bars and nightclubs. They have also developed wallet-sized cards for sex workers to give clients, to convince them to use condoms. The messages on these cards are translated into a number of languages to make them useful with foreign tourists.

"Rehabilitation" and "protection and vocational development" programmes

Under the provisions of the Prostitution Suppression Act of 1960, the Department of Public Welfare was empowered to provide institutionalized care of persons referred to under the Act as "socially handicapped women". Women who were sent to the rehabilitation institutions included prostitutes convicted under the Act, those rescued from forced prostitution and women who voluntarily sought assistance. The aim of such care was stated to be: controlling the spread of venereal diseases, suppressing prostitution and providing vocational training, adult education, counselling and follow-up services, in order that such women could earn a living in an alternative occupation after leaving the rehabilitation institution. Under normal conditions, the women were not kept in the institution for more than one year. Two public institutions were mainly responsible for providing such rehabilitation: the Kredtra Karn home in Nontaburi province and the smaller Narisawad home in Nakhon Ratchasima. In both centres, women were provided with adult education at the first and second level (equivalent to obtaining a grade 4 primary school education) and vocational training, mostly involving the production of handicrafts. Vocational courses were either of six- or nine-month duration. In the first year after their release from the institution, the women were contacted by officials of the Department of Public Welfare at three-monthly intervals to assess their living conditions and to determine whether they required further assistance.

Compared with the estimated number of Thai women working as prostitutes, the number of women passing through the two homes was very small. In the 1992 budget year, the two rehabilitation homes provided shelter for a total of 591 women and 26 dependent children. During the first three years of the 1990s, a total of 1,164 women stayed at the two homes. Even when the most conservative estimate of female prostitutes is adopted, this would constitute less than 1 per cent of the women working in the sex industry during the period. Nonetheless, the Department of Public Welfare claimed a high degree of success in being able to rehabilitate commercial sex workers. For the period 1990/92, the Department released the results from a survey of the women to indicate that 80 per cent had not returned to prostitution within one year of being released. The validity of these results is, however, very questionable, as the survey was based on self-reports of those women who could be traced, or, where the women could not be directly located, based on reports of others who claimed to know the situation. Also, the results referred to the period within a year of release, but did not provide any indication of the long-term success of the programme. Press reports and conversations with the commercial sex workers suggest that the rehabilitation programmes are viewed with some fear, and are considered to be of little practical value. The fear is based on being institutionalized for a period of up to one year and the stigma attached to being institutionalized. The educational and vocational training programmes are seen as providing limited opportunities for obtaining well-paid alternative employment.

The rehabilitation institutes that were established under the Prostitution Suppression Act, 1960, have now been converted to "protection and vocational development places" under the new Prostitution Prevention and Suppression Act. The new Act provides that prostitutes picked up by the police and who are below 18 years of age should first be sent temporarily to a primary shelter. The primary shelter will consider factors including the personality, educational background, reason for entering prostitution and performance in an aptitude test, to determine whether the individuals should be sent to a suitable protection and vocational development institute, or be released. Those placed under the protection and vocational development programme should stay for a period not exceeding two years. If a girl escapes from the primary shelter or from the protection and vocational development institute during this period, the responsible officials have the authority and duty to pursue the girl, if necessary with the assistance of the police, so as to bring her back to the shelter or institute. Prostitutes over the age of 18 years cannot be forced, but can, if they so wish and if it is considered appropriate in the opinion of the court, be sent to a protection and vocational development place.

Under the new Act, the "protection and vocational development place" can be not only a rehabilitation home run by the government but also a place established by other foundations, associations or institutes for welfare protection and vocational development of vulnerable women and girls. "Protection and vocational development" is defined as covering "mental rehabilitation, medical treatment, vocational skills training and development and other development for improvement of the quality of life".

The Prostitution Prevention and Suppression Act, 1996, also has specific provisions for the establishment of a Committee for Protection and Vocational Development (CPV), comprising the Director-General of the Public Welfare Department as the chairperson, representatives of a large range of government departments (Employment, Local Administration, Community Development, Non-Formal Education, Royal Thai Police, Skills Development, General Education and Vocational Education), the Central Juvenile and Family Court, the Office of the National Primary Education Commission, the National Youth Bureau, the National Commission on Women's Affairs, and other experts, including some from NGOs with expertise and experience in dealing with the problems of prostitution. The extensive composition of the CPV reflects the current Thai approach, which regards prostitution as a problem concerning a wide range of government departments and requiring effective cooperation between the public and private sectors. The CPV is given the authority to coordinate plans, projects, systems and practices between government and private agencies involved in the prevention and suppression of prostitution, as well as to develop policies and programmes for the protection and vocational development of former prostitutes.

Education, awareness-raising and advocacy programmes

The Office of the National Commission on Women's Affairs, with support from the Danish government, has initiated two innovative programmes as part of preventive and development efforts aimed at reducing the number of women and children at risk of being drawn into the sex sector (National Commission on Women's Affairs, 1995, p. 8). The Education and Training Programme for Teachers, Parents and Young Girls at Risk has multifaceted components for: (a) scholarships which are offered to young girls from northern Thailand (a major source area for prostitution because of severe poverty and social attitudes) to ensure that they remain in the educational system until age 18, completing either secondary school or vocational training; (b) directing the girls away from traditional areas such as hairdressing or dressmaking to occupations with better opportunities; (c) sex education; (d) improvement of self-esteem, so that the girls will be able to resist pressure to enter the sex sector; (e) changing the attitudes of family members, many of whom currently push their daughters to enter the sex sector; (f) training and credit, to enhance income-earning abilities, since financial need is a driving force behind such attitudes of families; and (g) involvement of teachers and monks as community leaders, in helping to restore traditional values and respect for the rights of women and girls.

The second programme is the Use of Mass Media to Eradicate Child Prostitution. Since changing the public's attitudes is seen as one of the key factors in preventing child prostitution, the programme consists of: (a) the production of short films shown at prime time on three of Thailand's most popular television stations; (b) radio broadcasts and the distribution of posters and pamphlets; and (c) panel discussions involving prominent persons in the regions in which child prostitution is known to be a problem.

Several universities in Thailand have developed projects to work with prostitutes and groups at risk. One of the universities in Thailand, Chiang Mai University (which is located in the north), has implemented a programme involving: (a) an intensive education, counselling and publicity campaign to disseminate information about prostitution and AIDS; (b) trained counsellors in schools who target girls at risk, reinforce the prostitution and AIDS-awareness campaign and advise the girls' families; and (c) modest scholarships for vulnerable girls from poor families, and assistance with skills training and job opportunities so that those at risk are aware of alternatives to working in the sex sector.

NGOs in Thailand have also targeted their awareness-raising and advocacy programmes at groups of women considered to be at risk. For instance, the Foundation for Women provides information and counselling for women seeking work in foreign countries and/or intending to marry foreigners; it also coordinates with international organizations to provide assistance to Thai migrant women with problems in foreign countries. The Club for Northern People assists in preventing the sale and trafficking of women, mainly through awareness raising, informal education, vocational training to enhance employment opportunities and income support.

Notes

[1] A sample of reports from the English-language press regarding the involvement of government officials in the sex industry suggests the involvement of Members of Parliament in providing Thai women to the Japanese sex industry (*Bangkok Post*, 19 March 1993), and the involvement of police and government officials in the murder of a prostitute in Songkhla (*Bangkok Post*, 11 November 1992).

[2] For example, a senior police official recently argued that sex crimes would increase if brothels were banned. He was quoted as saying "the rate of rapes and other sex-related crimes might sky-rocket if these men find no place to satisfy their sexual desires" (*Bangkok Post,* 11 November 1992).

[3] *Bangkok Post*, 22 December 1993. Although estimates of the numbers of Thai women working as prostitutes in Japan have been as high as 70,000 (*Bangkok Post*, 19 March 1993), this would appear to be an overestimate. The Japanese government estimated that there were around 100,000 illegal immigrants in Japan around 1991 and, based on detention of illegal immigrants, Thailand contributed only about 10 per cent of all illegal immigrants and around 25 per cent of female illegal immigrants (Nagayama, 1992).

[4] *Bangkok Post*, 6 August 1992.

[5] Since 1960, when there were 81,000 visitors, the number of tourist arrivals has increased more than 50 times; in 1970 there were 628,000 international tourists, in 1980 the number had reached 1.8 million and in 1990, 5.3 million arrived. Figures for 1991 indicated a slight downturn to 5.1 million, of whom 65 per cent were male (*Bangkok Post*, 21 February 1993).

[6] In 1991 the average stay of an international tourist was seven days. Of the 5.1 million tourists, approximately 3.3 million were male. Even if the unrealistic assumption that each international male tourist visited a female prostitute each day they were in Thailand was adopted, in conjunction with a conservative estimate of the number of commercial sex workers, it can be seen that international tourists are not the major contributors to the total number of clients in the sex industry.

[7] *Matichon*, 18 October 1980.

[8] *The Nation*, 18 March 1993.

[9] Referring to the brothel sector in the southern province of Ranong, Sombat Raksakul, a columnist for the *Bangkok Post*, writes: "When the pressure is on from higher up to get rid of a sleazy old brothel in Ranong, the owner picks up the phone and calls a decorator. Before long, he or she is the proud proprietor of a 'restaurant', a 'cocktail lounge' or a 'discotheque'. But for customers, it's business as usual" (*Bangkok Post*, 13 September 1992).

[10] *Bangkok Post*, 20 January 1993.

[11] For example, at one parlour it was stated that Westerners were not admitted. Any Westerner who wanted to enter was told that it was a member's club and only members were admitted. Japanese and other Asian customers were admitted. Another possible reason for the ban was to deflect the workers' concern about AIDS. In the training provided for workers in that particular establishment, they were told that there was a high level of AIDS among Western tourists.

[12] Several estimates are available from the police department. The highest estimate of 500,000 is based on the number of registered entertainment establishments and is likely to be too high, as some establishments hold more than one licence. If they are closed down by the police they can reopen with another licence. Also, the list is cumulative: establishments get added to the list but are not taken off when they close down. The estimate of 150,000 to 200,000 was based on a survey of establishments.

[13] The estimate of sex establishments and workers provided for the survey area covered in this study coincided with the study team's own assessment and those of other people interviewed in the area. The number reported by health officials for the massage parlours surveyed in Bangkok was in rough agreement with the number reported to the study team by the management of the massage parlours. Where understatement of the number of prostitutes does occur, it is most likely to happen in those places where the prostitution is "indirect", i.e. where the main function of the establishment is something other than commercial sex. This could happen in the case of restaurants, discos, etc.

[14] For instance, enforcement of the Prostitution Suppression Act was difficult because the definition of "place of prostitution" was vague. Also, the Act did not explicitly exempt from punishment persons who had been forced into prostitution; customers were not liable to punishment. Penalties provided for under the Act were light, especially when compared to those under the Penal Code.

CHILD PROSTITUTION 6

Lin Lean Lim

While in the case of adults it may be possible to make the distinction between voluntary and enforced prostitution, child prostitution "constitutes a form of coercion and violence against children, and amounts to forced labour and a contemporary form of slavery" (World Congress against the Commercial Sexual Exploitation of Children, 1996). In the words of Vitit Muntarbhorn, the former United Nations Special Rapporteur to the Commission on Human Rights, on the Sale of Children, Child Prostitution and Child Pornography, "I do not pass judgement on the pros and cons of adult prostitution. However, child prostitution is inadmissible – it is tantamount to exploitation and victimization of the child because it undermines the child's development. It is detrimental to the child both physically and emotionally, and is in breach of the child's rights" (Muntarbhorn, 1996a, p. 10). This chapter explains why child prostitution differs from – and should be considered a much more serious problem than – adult prostitution. It also describes child prostitution as part of the overall commercial sex sector. It is important to draw attention to how child prostitution is linked to the mainstream sex industry because, as with adult prostitution, there are strong economic and social bases as well as vested interests involved: "there is someone, some system behind the trade, which is benefiting from this" (Otaganonta, 1990). Children are clearly more helpless against these established structures and vested interests than adults, and therefore more vulnerable to serious sexual and economic exploitation and inhuman treatment.

The definition and magnitude of child prostitution

Child prostitution is defined by the current United Nations Special Rapporteur on the Sale of Children, Child Prostitution and Child Pornography as "the act of engaging or offering the services of a child to perform sexual acts for money or other consideration with that person or any other person". The stress of this definition is that child prostitution is not "committed" by the child but by the person "engaging or offering the services of a child" (United Nations, 1995, pp. 5-6). This definition has been refined in the recent discussions of the Working Group on a Draft Optional

Protocol to the Convention on the Rights of the Child, on the Sale of Children, Child Prostitution and Child Pornography as "the act of obtaining, procuring or offering the services of a child or inducing a child to perform sexual acts for any form of compensation or reward (or any acts that are linked to that offence) (even with the consent of the child)" (United Nations Economic and Social Council, 1996, p. 27).

Child prostitution is one of the two main aspects of the sexual exploitation of children, the other being child pornography. The sexual exploitation of children has been defined as the use of children for the sexual satisfaction of adults. "The basis of the exploitation is the unequal power and economic relationships between the child and the adult. The child is exploited for his/her youth and sexuality. Frequently, though not always, this exploitation is organized by a third party for profit" (Muntarbhorn, 1996b, p. 1). Child prostitution tends to be closely linked to child pornography, which refers to the visual, written or audio depiction of a child for the sexual gratification of the user, involving the production, distribution and/or use of such material, as well as pornographic performances using children. Young girls are not the only victims of commercial sexual exploitation; there has been a notable increase in the number of young boy victims, especially in sex tourism.

The international definition of a child is that given in Article 1 of the United Nations Convention on the Rights of the Child: "every human being below the age of 18 years unless under the law applicable to the child, majority is attained earlier". There are various complications when applying this age criterion at national and local levels. For instance, since marriage confers the age of majority on an individual, the Convention is no longer applicable to such an individual. In Indonesia, an under-age person is commonly defined as someone without a *Kartu Tanda Penduduk* (Residential Registration Identification Card) because the card is usually given to someone who has already reached 17 years of age, but married girls under 17 can legally obtain the card, leading to some confusion among brothel owners and government officials over what exactly constitutes the minimum age of a prostitute. Many countries have also set the legal age of consent for sexual intercourse at an age below 18, which would mean that the customer is exempt from criminal responsibility if the child victim consents, even if she or he is under 18. In Malaysia, the Women and Girls Protection Act, 1973 makes it a criminal offence to have sexual relations with a female below the age of 16 years, with or without her consent, but child prostitutes are those under 21.

As with adult prostitution, it is not possible to have precise figures on the extent of child prostitution. The 1996 report of the United Nations Special Rapporteur on the Sale of Children, Child Prostitution and Child Pornography estimates that about one million children in Asia are victims of the sex trade (United Nations Commission on Human Rights, 1996, p. 7). Globally, child prostitution is estimated to net US$5 billion annually (United Nations, 1995, p. 13). Although it is a global phenomenon, child prostitution is reported to be most serious in Asia and Central and South America, while increases have been noted in most other parts of the world.

A 1992 field survey of a major brothel complex in Indonesia found that about one-tenth of the workers were below 17 years of age. Of those aged 17 years or above, almost one-fifth became prostitutes when they were under age 17 (see Chapter 2).

A 1994/95 survey of Indonesia's registered prostitutes found that 60 per cent were aged between 15 and 20 years (ECPAT, 1995). The 1995 ECPAT report also notes that recent developments in Indonesia include street children selling sex for survival, and boys selling sex in the tourist resorts.

No comprehensive estimates are available for child prostitution in Malaysia, partly because of the underground nature of the sex sector and strict law enforcement. One study found, however, that during the period 1986-90, of the 2,626 women and girls rescued by the Malaysian police from brothels, bars, massage parlours and houses of prostitution, 50 per cent were under 18 years, and the rest between 18 and 21 years (Bruce, 1996, p. 31). There have also been several media reports of sex rings recruiting teenage schoolgirls to persuade their classmates to enter the profession.

The most frequently cited figures for child prostitution in the Philippines are between 30,000 and 60,000.[1] However, a recent report submitted to the United Nations Children's Fund puts the number of child victims of prostitution at 75,000 (Cueto, 1997). Several studies have focused on Filipino street children who sell sexual services. In addition to prostitution among street children, three other types of child prostitution have been identified: prostitution with the use of pimps, brothel prostitution and prostitution with parents as contractors (Srisang, 1990, p. 56). ECPAT (1995) cites the case of a town in the Philippines which became so well known in the late 1970s and early 1980s for its paedophile visitors that it attracted boys from poverty-stricken neighbouring areas in search of employment. Documented cases of child prostitution in various cities in the Philippines confirm a "clear and definite relationship between the inflow of tourists and the sexual exploitation of Filipino children" (UNICEF, 1995, p. 64).

Child prostitution actually has a long history in Thailand (Rutnin, 1992), although public concern over the problem only escalated after the government of Prime Minister Chuan Leekpai, who had long been an advocate of efforts to improve the education and health of children, took office in September 1992. Estimates of child prostitution vary so greatly that the Task Force to End Child Sexploitation in Thailand[2], in collaboration with Chulalongkorn University, held a seminar with academics and social workers in 1992, in an attempt to arrive at a consensus on the magnitude (Panyacheewin, 1992). ECPAT (1993,1995) uses estimates ranging from 200,000 to 800,000. However, if there were 800,000 child prostitutes and 3.07 million persons in Thailand aged between 15 and 19 years of age around 1990, this would have meant that one in every four teenagers was in the sex trade, a highly unlikely situation (Panyacheewin, 1992). The Ministry of Public Health provides a much lower estimate of about 13,000, based on surveys of commercial sex establishments and workers. Guest (1993) estimates that there are approximately 30,000 to 35,000 child prostitutes in Thailand – an estimate that roughly coincides with the official figures provided by the National Commission on Women's Affairs.[3] It has also been estimated that of the child prostitutes, some 10 per cent are boys (Otaganonta, 1992). A survey of prostitutes in brothels found that nearly one-fifth had started work between the ages of 13 and 15 (see Chapter 5). There has also been an increasing incidence of trafficking in under-age girls from ethnic minorities and from neighbouring countries, such as Myanmar, China, the Lao People's Democratic Republic and Cambodia (ECPAT, 1995; Asia Watch and the Women's Rights Project, 1993). More than half of the girls rescued in police raids of brothels in recent years were from Myanmar or China.

Child prostitution is reported to be on the increase in many other parts of Asia, such as China, Viet Nam, the Lao People's Democratic Republic and Myanmar. Child prostitution has also been prevalent for a long time in South Asia. In Cambodia, a major study conducted in Phnom Penh and 11 provinces in 1995 estimated that at least one-third of the commercial sex workers were between 12 and 17 years of age. Researchers familiar with the situation in Cambodia considered this a low estimate because of the difficulties of gaining access to the very youngest girls in brothels (Gray et al., 1996, p. 6). In Sri Lanka, child prostitutes are estimated to be 30,000 in number and are expected to increase to 44,000 by the year 2000 (UNICEF, 1995, p. 75). Sri Lanka has been advertised as a centre for male child prostitution in American and European magazines (Goonesekere, 1993, p. 15). The male child prostitutes are found especially in the coastal resort areas of Sri Lanka. In India, studies indicate that the proportion of children among prostitutes has increased, so that in 1995 it was about 25 to 30 per cent. Many of these children became victims of prostitution before the age of 15, and most are from the scheduled castes and tribes or from neighbouring Nepal and Bangladesh (Sinha, 1996, p. 6). Human rights activists estimate that between 200 and 400 young women and children are being smuggled every month from Bangladesh and Pakistan; their numbers have been on the increase since the mid-1980s (Shamin,1997).

How child prostitution differs from adult prostitution

The subject of prostitution elicits a wide range of responses. While opinions vary sharply regarding adult prostitution, it must be recognized that there are crucial differences between adult and child involvement in the sex sector.

One view is that all prostitution, whether of adults or children, is enforced or involuntary and coercive. Some human rights advocates argue, for example, that it does not matter whether prostitutes are 18 years and above, because all prostitution involves coercion of one kind or another; therefore it should be regarded as a violation of human rights and as one of the most alienating forms of labour. Many prostitutes actually entered the trade when they were under age and remained trapped into adulthood. Their entry into the sex sector as children, and their continued involvement in commercial sex, may compound the trauma and problems they encountered as children. The United Nations Convention for the Suppression of the Traffic in Persons and of the Exploitation of the Prostitution of Others, 1949, declares that prostitution and the traffic in persons "are incompatible with the dignity and worth of the human person and endanger the welfare of the individual, the family and the community". In this view, both adult and child prostitutes are victims of human rights abuses, and should accordingly be protected from such abuses and exploitation. Even then, the degree of victimization would be greater, the younger the prostitute was. Accordingly, child prostitutes need extra protection and special treatment.

Another view, however, is that adults can voluntarily go into prostitution as the occupation of their choice. As discussed in greater detail in Chapter 1, some people argue that adults can make the relatively "free" decision to enter the sex sector, and they should be at liberty to do so, as they have the right to sexual self-determination.[4] Some studies have also emphasized that, morals aside, prostitution offers much higher incomes than other available alternatives for poor women with low levels of education, and that working conditions, especially in the better establishments and for some freelancers, are actually quite decent. However, children, and certainly younger children, cannot be considered to be capable of making such a decision. Prostitution exploits the immaturity and helplessness of children. While many women may voluntarily join the sex establishments and have some ability to negotiate the terms of their employment, children are commonly sold, trafficked, tricked or lured, and force and coercion are used to confine them and to induce them to entertain customers.

Of course, not all child prostitutes, especially teenagers, have been forced. "It has to be faced that not all children are forced by someone else into prostitution and that some sell themselves of their own accord, not because they want to, but because economic and social circumstances may dictate such a course of action (is this then voluntary?)" (Bruce, 1996, pp. 11-12.) Some surveys (e.g. Gray et al., 1996) have revealed that while there is a high degree of coercion involved in the commercial sexual exploitation of girls, prostitution involving boys rarely tends to be coercive. Girls are sold and trafficked, incarcerated in brothels, raped, deceived and abused. Boys involved in commercial sex, especially those in sex tourism, are more likely to do so as a matter of "choice" or through peer pressure, and the links with clients are more casually made (e.g. on streets and beaches, or in bars). The majority of children, however, do not voluntarily enter into prostitution. "Children in general do not enter the commercial sex sector on their own. Persuasion or deception from adults, threats, exploitation and acts of violence are committed mostly by adults seeking advantage from children." (National Committee for the Eradication of Commercial Sex, 1996, p. 1.)

These different perspectives influence the legal stance of national governments towards the commercial sex sector and individual prostitutes. Even in those countries where the commercial sex sector is legalized and/or where concern has focused on improving working conditions and the protection of prostitutes, child prostitution can never be sanctioned or condoned. Muntarbhorn recommends using the terms "child victims of prostitution" rather than "child prostitution" and "recovery and reintegration" rather than "rehabilitation" to emphasize that children should not be held responsible or discriminated against and stigmatized. The vulnerability of children has been the principal motivation for measures to protect them, and is one of the crucial factors distinguishing child prostitution from adult prostitution.

Experts have pointed out that vulnerability is a function of the bio-physiological, cognitive, behavioural and social changes that determine the growth and maturation of a person from infancy to adulthood. Even when a child is physiologically developed, he or she may not have the cognitive, psychosocial or emotional capacity, or self-perception, to make a voluntary choice to enter prostitution. Those girls who become physically mature at a young age, but are socially or psychologically immature, are particularly vulnerable to sexual exploitation.

Unless a child grows up in an enabling environment which caters to all the dimensions essential for developing into a healthy, fully functioning adult, he or she will be vulnerable to or at risk from sexual exploitation (Belsey, 1996). Unfortunately, many children live in environments characterized by extreme poverty, lack of educational opportunities, dysfunctional families, substance abuse, domestic violence and abuse. It is not only that children have limited autonomy over their own environments. Children are also more likely to be potential victims of their environments because of their vulnerability in terms of their psychosocial and cognitive development. Of course, it could be argued that, especially in developing countries, adults also face difficult economic, social or cultural contexts which may push them into prostitution. The difference, however, is that while children may also be in the same contexts, they do not have the mental, emotional or social maturity to deal with their circumstances.

Very importantly, child prostitution is an intolerable form of child labour. Whereas, in the case of adults, prostitution could be considered an occupation or a form of work, in the case of children it is a totally unacceptable form of forced labour. An important reason why the Thai government officially launched a campaign in 1992 to end child prostitution was because of the decision of the United States to place Thailand on a special list for the possible revocation of trade concessions, due to the problem of forced child labour. The 1989 United Nations Convention on the Rights of the Child stresses "the right of children to be protected from economic exploitation or from performing any work that is likely to be hazardous or to interfere with the child's education, or to be harmful to the child's health or physical, mental, spiritual, moral or social development". (Article 32.) The concern is also based on the fact that most countries now recognize, as stipulated in ILO Conventions and Recommendations (which are discussed below in the sub-section on legislation), that there should be a minimum age for work, especially hazardous work, and that children have the right to education and the development of their full human potentials.

A stronger view is that child prostitution is not just an intolerable form of forced labour but a contemporary form of slavery, which should accordingly be eliminated. Of course, certain forms of child prostitution are more akin to slavery than others (for instance, the plight of children sold to brothels and deprived of their freedom or right to retain their earnings is not the same as that of children who occasionally sell themselves for extra cash for themselves or their families), and some adult prostitutes too are enslaved. Nevertheless, the fact remains that all children should be protected from forced labour and sexual exploitation; they also have the right to education and the opportunity to reach their full physical and psychological development.

Children are more likely than adults to be victims of debt bondage and trafficking, which often accompany prostitution. As described in the next section, children, because of their young age and lack of control, are more vulnerable to being sold by parents or guardians and to being tricked, coerced, abducted or kidnapped by unscrupulous adults. Children and adults are, however, treated in much the same way when the trafficking is across national borders: immigration laws and enforcement agents deal with them as criminals to be deported, often after long prison stays, rather than as victims.

Various reports have also pointed out that children who are in residential or foster care, in orphanages or in children's homes are especially vulnerable to sexual exploitation. There are several cases of "orphanages" or "street shelters" for poor children which are actually fronts for paedophile organizations using them as centres to provide young children to visiting paedophiles.

Children, because of their immaturity, are also more easily susceptible to peer or group pressure (as in the case of street children) and to the influence of adult example (as in the case of children whose mothers are prostitutes). Children from poor urban communities and dysfunctional families are especially vulnerable to such influences. As succinctly expressed by social workers in the Philippines: "How can we talk about prevention when the mother is a prostitute, the father is a pimp, the uncles and brothers are pimps and often drug pushers as well, and sometimes even the grandmother was a prostitute. We are talking about generations that have had prostitution as the only avenue open to them for making a living." (Abreu, 1991, pp. 3-4.)

Children are also more likely than adults to be subjected to torture and physical violence to force them to succumb to prostitution. Although descriptions in the previous chapters suggest that most of the adult prostitutes knew what their work entailed, and that their working conditions were fairly reasonable, these descriptions do not hold true for the young girls who do not know the nature of the work into which they are being sold or trafficked. In interviews with young female victims of brothel prostitution, the pattern of rape, beatings, the threat or use of physical abuse, the threat of harm to their families, the withholding of food and water, and physical confinement tends to be consistently repeated. A study (Whaites, 1996) on street children drawn into prostitution found that many had been raped, initially when they were working in restaurants or factories, or as domestic maids. Others were sexually assaulted by other street children, who sometimes served as pimps.

In the case of the child victims of prostitution, there are what have been termed "a spiral factor" and a "chain effect" (Muntarbhorn, 1996b, p. 4). The "spiral factor" relates to the disturbing trend whereby the sex trade is spiralling towards younger and younger victims, not only because of the traditional belief among some customers that they can rejuvenate themselves by having sex with very young virgins, but also because of the more recent belief that they can protect themselves from the threat of HIV/AIDS by selecting children. The "chain effect" relates to the fact that one form of abuse tends to lead to another and often more serious form, so that there is a cumulation of negative consequences. For example, a child subject to sexual abuse at home often runs away and then resorts to prostitution and/or pornography as a means of subsistence. A child in such difficulties may become dependent on drugs, which in turn leads to greater dependence on prostitution and/or pornography to earn money for purchasing the drugs. The child's involvement in criminal patterns thus intensifies over time. A child who is sexually abused also often grows up to subsequently become an abuser.

Various studies have emphasized that the impact of commercial sexual exploitation is much more serious on children than on prostituted women. These impacts have most commonly been cited in terms of the physical health and psychological well-being of the children in prostitution. As starkly described by the ILO:

Commercial sexual exploitation is one of the most brutal forms of violence against children. Child victims suffer extreme physical, psychosocial and emotional abuse which have lifelong and life-threatening consequences. They risk early pregnancy, maternal mortality and sexually transmitted diseases. Case-studies and testimonies of child victims speak of a trauma so deep that many are unable to enter or return to a normal way of life. Many others die before they reach adulthood." (ILO, 1996, p. 17.)

A WHO report describes the health effects that directly result from sexual experiences or the circumstances that lead to sexual exploitation. The effects include "the consequences of infection, physical violence and/or sexual abuse, the toxic effects of substance abuse, pregnancy and the psychosocial impact of the experience according to the vulnerability and subsequent expression of psychological, emotional or mental development of the individual" (Belsey, 1996, p. 19).

More specifically, the health effects of commercial sexual exploitation on children are sexually transmitted diseases (STDs) including HIV/AIDS, psychological trauma and impaired development. STDs are the most common direct medical consequences of child prostitution, with HIV/AIDS the most serious of these infections, both for the child and public health. The effects of some of these infections may not be immediately apparent, and may not manifest themselves until the child is much older. Infertility is a common consequence of STDs.

Children face a much higher risk of contracting HIV/AIDS than adult prostitutes. They are much less likely to have access to information on the risks and consequences. They are also much less likely to have access to the means to prevent infection, including condoms. Even if they have such access, they tend to be powerless to negotiate safe sexual practices. Their immature reproductive tracts, the genital abrasions they suffer during sexual activity, and the hormonal fluctuations and permeability of key tissue walls increase the risk of transmission. Once exposed, they have limited protection against disease because their immune systems are not yet fully developed. The irony is that there has been a notable shift towards commercial sex with younger children – even where this is not the sexual preference of the clients – because of the belief that they represent a lower risk of HIV/AIDS, while in fact the reverse is more likely to be true.

Psychological trauma can have both immediate and long-term developmental consequences on child victims of prostitution. The younger the children, the more likely that their developmental process will be impaired. In the immediate term, the children suffer post-traumatic stress disorders.[5] In the longer term, their development is adversely affected by "impairment of attachment, self-esteem, and interpersonal relationships; and failure to acquire competence in peer relations, adoption of highly sexualized or highly aggressive behaviour or the use of drugs, dissociation, self-injury or other dysfunctional ways of dealing with anxiety" (Belsey, 1996, pp. 22-23).

Projects working with child prostitutes in five continents describe them as taciturn, introverted, distrustful and, sometimes, aggressive. They commonly "feel guilt and shame and truly believe they are worthless" (Bruce, 1996, p. 25).

Inter-generational health and human development effects have also been noted. Child prostitutes not only have a high risk of pregnancy; their babies tend to be born premature, exhibit postnatal growth deficiency and developmental delays in infancy and childhood, and face a high risk of perinatal mortality. The child prostitutes themselves are not likely to be able to care suitably for their infants or to be appropriate role models as mothers. Under these circumstances, they tend to be at great risk of perpetuating the behavioural cycle of physical, emotional or sexual abuse with their offspring, as part of the "chain effect" of an extending range of negative consequences.

The WHO has warned that child prostitutes may pose a greater danger to public health than adult prostitutes:

While there is no clear evidence, the involvement of children in commercial sex work could possibly increase the rate of transmission of HIV – first because of their increased biological vulnerability to STDs, and second, because of the lack of power in negotiating safe sexual behaviour. It is also reasonable to hypothesize that wherever trafficking of commercial sex workers takes place, the spread of HIV transmission from one locale to another is also facilitated (Belsey, 1996, p. 29).

A recent article describes whole villages in Myanmar that are dying because of the AIDS pandemic, which has escalated partly because young prostitutes found to have contracted the disease in Thailand are sent back to their places of origin, where they may continue the chain of transmission (Lintner and Lintner, 1996).

The organizational structures for child prostitution

While there are significant differences between child and adult prostitution, child prostitution is very much part and parcel of the commercial sex sector. The previous chapters highlight the diversified organizational structures and arrangements for adult prostitution in the commercial sex sector. Most child prostitutes are also part of these organizational structures and arrangements:

Although some children are prostituted by and/or specifically for paedophiles, the vast majority of child prostitutes are integrated into the mainstream sex industry which serves *all* those who wish to purchase commercial sex, rather than working in some isolated "market niche" which caters solely to the desires of paedophiles and preferential abusers. In both affluent and poor countries, it is not only the case that a significant percentage of prostitutes are under the age of 18, but also that younger prostitutes tend to be concentrated in the cheaper end of the prostitute market where conditions are worst and the "throughput" of customers is highest (O'Connell Davidson, 1996, p. 5).

There are, of course, paedophiles and preferential child sex abusers[6] who operate in non-commercial contexts to sexually abuse children (such as in cases of incest or abuse in orphanages or child-care centres). These individuals are characterized by long term and persistent behaviour patterns, and well-developed techniques in obtaining victims. They will often go to great lengths to satisfy their sexual preferences, including establishing long-term relationships with families in poor areas to gain access to their children, as well as establishing "orphanages" or "shelters" for street children. They do, however, also make use of the organized sex sector to gain access to young children; for example, paedophiles represent an important segment of the clientele of sex tourism. Public attention has focused on the paedophiles because of the tender age of the child victims. However, in terms of the numbers involved, the more serious problem is from the situational child sex abusers, who do not have a focused sexual interest in children *per se,* but who sexually exploit children because they are morally and/or sexually indiscriminate, or because they are in situations where child prostitutes are available to them. The commercial sex sector makes children available to situational child sex abusers, who appear to be increasingly taking advantage of the situation, particularly because of the belief that younger prostitutes are less likely to be infected by STDs or HIV/AIDS, or because of the myths associated with virginity and male virility.

As part of the commercial sex sector, child prostitution has become "a big money-making business that profits a lot of people – procurers, pimps, hotel operators, police and government officials, even parents of the youngsters themselves" (Otaganonta, 1992). It is important, therefore, to understand how the sector operates in the case of children. As with adult prostitution, it is possible to distinguish the organized and unorganized segments of the child sex trade. The organized structures include under-age girls working in bars, brothels, massage parlours and other entertainment establishments. There have been not only increasing numbers of young girls, but also a disturbing increase in the very young being employed in many of the sex establishments because of the growing demand from customers. More significantly, the organized sector includes links with the sale and trafficking of children and also child pornography, both often organized by well-connected underground syndicates. In recent years, there have also been direct linkages with sex tourism.

Unorganized child prostitution commonly involves street children selling sexual services, runaways from dysfunctional family backgrounds or from state institutions and school-going teenagers engaging in occasional sex for payment. The informal prostitution sector also often includes a large number of children who are "picked up" by sex tourists from beaches, parks and ordinary tourist bars and who serve as "companions" to the tourists for the period of their stay.

The trafficking and sale of children into prostitution

Trafficking in children includes all acts involving the capture, acquisition, recruitment and transportation of children within and across national borders with the intent to sell, exchange or use for illegal purposes, such as prostitution, servitude in the guise of marriage, bonded labour or sale of human organs, by means of violence or threat of violence. In the case of sexual trafficking, procurers and criminal organizations sell children to brothels or supply children directly to clients. Individual paedophiles may acquire children for their own uses. Paedophile organizations may also acquire children for their members. Increasingly, the trafficking is international; children are being transported from one country to another for the sex trade. Various methods are used to procure children for the purpose of trafficking and sale. It may take the form of outright kidnapping and abduction, sham marriages by pimps of young girls they then sell into prostitution, rape and the use of force, fake adoptions or false documentation in illegal migration. Often, traffickers entice children and their families with remunerative job offers and the advance payment of money. All too often, parents or guardians sell their children into debt bondage.

The recruitment of children into prostitution commonly involves the collusion of adults, often including parents and well-organized networks with official connections. A study by an NGO in the northern province of Chiang Rai, Thailand, described the "exploitation spiral" of young girls who are sold or trafficked into prostitution, as involving a range of people from parents to middlemen or agents, village leaders, school teachers, temple monks, government officers, drivers, check-point police, brothel owners, pimps, local policemen, mafia gangs, local doctors, bank officials, taxi drivers and tour operators (Saikaew, 1996, p. 71).

Although some families are not aware of the nature of the work that they are selling their daughters into, and although cases are reported where families have been tricked into believing that they are sending their daughters to work in restaurants or as domestic helpers, the sad truth is that children are still deliberately sold into the sex trade by parents or other family members. For instance, Chapter 2 reports that in Indonesia the selling by parents of young daughters into indentured servitude in brothels is not uncommon. A 1995 survey in Cambodia on child victims of prostitution found that 40 per cent were sold by their own families and another 15 per cent by "friends" (Gray et al., 1996)

In the Philippines, NGOs attempting to eradicate child prostitution – through efforts "to shatter the veil of ignorance of the children's activities that the parents sometimes refuse to acknowledge" – found, to their mortification, that the "veil of ignorance" was a myth and that, in fact, many families wholeheartedly accepted child prostitution. The NGOs reported that in several instances where they tried to press for the imprisonment or deportation of known foreign paedophiles, they met strong opposition from the families of the child victims, who came to the defence of the foreigners, many of whom give expensive presents to the children and often help to support their families. The Project Director of ECPAT in the Philippines describes how the families reason that "it is only through their children's 'occupations' that food is brought to their tables" and also how in several instances, the rescue efforts of NGOs and social workers were met with resistance and sometimes with jeers and outright hostility.

Some Filipino parents encourage their daughters to work as entertainers in Japan. Many young women go to Japan with fake passports that are arranged by unscrupulous recruitment agents and which show that they are of age, although they are often minors. In many cases, the girls knew they would be going into the sex trade. NGOs report that their workers have often been dismayed to find some of their young wards, hardly in their teens, sporting grown-up hairdos, revealing clothes and heavy makeup, and training to be dancers so they can apply for jobs as entertainers in Japan. Their peers, and even their own families, would encourage them to give up school and head straight for promotion agencies so they can start earning money (Abreu, 1991, p. 3).

Social workers report that *"tok khiew"* has been on the rise in poor Thai villages. *Tok khiew* is a common agricultural term that refers to a deposit for cash loans. Increasingly the same term is used when transacting "loans" for children. When an agent shows interest in a girl of about 9 or 10 years old, he or she will place a down payment with the girl's parents. When the girl reaches 12 or 13, the remainder of the agreed-upon loan is paid to the parents. The daughter must then leave with the agent to work off the payment, which is usually around US$800 to US$1,600. In 1996, it was estimated that some 2,000 children were under this type of arrangement in the two northern provinces of Phayao and Chiang Rai (Flamm, 1996, p. 20). Especially in the northern provinces, every year when 12-year-old schoolgirls graduate from the sixth grade, agents drive up in vans and recruit children for the sex trade. Youths are also recruited through village beauty contests and schools for dressmaking. The agents negotiate with the parents, pay them cash, and drive away with the daughters.

In some Thai rural families, the birth of a baby girl is celebrated as a golden opportunity for the family to become rich. One schoolteacher in a northern village reported that when he attempted to stop children going into prostitution, their parents lambasted him. He quoted a parent as saying: "Why do you tell my children not to go? You are just a teacher. How dare you teach like that? Look at yourself, can you buy a house, a pick-up truck for your parents like the girls?" (Rasakul, 1995.) The girls themselves also often say that they are willing to be sold, as a token of gratitude to their parents. Saisuree Chutikul, an adviser in the Prime Minister's Department and a prominent activist with regard to prostitution, explains that the willingness of young daughters to go along with the sale makes it easy on the parents: "obedience is something we treasure so much in our culture, so they do it. What the northerners treasure less is virginity. It is not as valued as in Muslim-dominated southern Thailand; a northern woman can still get married after having worked as a prostitute." (McNulty, 1994.)

Since their parents or relatives receive advance payments, the children are held in debt bondage by the brothel owners, agents or pimps. The payment received by their families is seen as credit against future earnings, which the girls must work off with interest. The girls normally have no idea of the nature and amount of the debt and interest they owe, nor what the terms for repayment are. Unscrupulous brothel owners or pimps keep the girls in prostitution by threatening them with the debts they owe or with retribution against their families.

The more serious cases of trafficking in children for prostitution involve ethnic minorities, such as children from the hill tribes in northern Thailand, or children trafficked from neighbouring countries, such as Cambodia, the Lao People's Democratic Republic, Myanmar and China. Though there are no reliable figures on the problem, the trafficking routes are well known. According to information gathered by the ILO's International Programme on the Elimination of Child Labour (ILO/IPEC), girls from Cambodia are brought through transit points at Poipet and Koh Kong and enter Thailand through Trat Province and Aranyaprathet district; children from the Lao People's Democratic Republic, are brought over the Mekong River into Chiang Rai, Nong Khai and Ubon Rachatani in Thailand; girls from

Myanmar are brought into Thailand through various border checkpoints, namely Tachilek-Mai Sai border, Myawaddy-Mae Sot border and the Three Pagodas' Pass in Kachanaburi Province; and girls from Sibsongpunna in the south of China are brought to Thailand through Myanmar.

The trafficking of women and girls from Myanmar into Thailand has been described in a special report by Human Rights Watch as "appalling in its efficiency and ruthlessness" (Asia Watch and the Women's Rights Project, 1993, p. 3). Driven by the desire to maximize profits and by the fear of HIV/AIDS, agents acting on behalf of brothel owners infiltrate ever more remote areas of Myanmar seeking unsuspecting recruits. Virgin girls are particularly sought after, because they bring a higher price and pose less of a threat of exposure to sexually transmitted diseases. Residents are well aware of the networks for selling young girls; they know a certain shop, a local agent or a temple where they can take the girls. The agents promise the girls jobs as waitresses or dishwashers, with good pay and new clothes. Family members or friends typically accompany the girls to the Thai border, where they receive a payment ranging from 10,000 to 20,000 baht (US$400 – 800) from someone associated with the brothel. This payment becomes the debt, usually doubled with interest, that the girls must work to pay off, not by waitressing or dishwashing, but through sexual servitude.

The Human Rights Watch report also highlighted official involvement in trafficking. Thai police and border guards are reported to be part of the network (Asia Watch and the Women's Rights Project, 1993). The report of the Special Rapporteur on the Sale of Children, Child Prostitution and Child Pornography also noted that "corruption and collusion among various law enforcement authorities [in Thailand] are widespread and pervasive" and that "many new reprehensible acts have also been identified on the part of child traffickers, for example, falsifying identification cards so as to classify children as adults; sending children home temporarily during police raids but forcing them back to brothels afterwards; using new facilities such as *karaoke* bars to sell children" (United Nations, 1994, p. 36).

Child prostitutes in brothels

Young child victims of prostitution are more likely to be found in brothels than in massage parlours, bars, nightclubs or other public entertainment places, mainly because the brothels are away from the public eye. The previous chapters show that those working in massage parlours, bars or nightclubs do not live on the premises and are normally free to come and go. But the brothels are often virtual prisons for the young prostitutes.

In the Philippines, for example, those working in brothels, or *casas,* are termed the "enslaved" because they are the lowest stratum and most exploited of the commercial sex workers. There are many known cases of young girls who are guarded and virtually owned by the brothel owners. Unlike women working in bars and nightclubs, they do not have regular working hours; they are on call whenever there are customers. They cannot choose their customers. They have no choice over the number they have to serve. They do not earn directly from customers; the brothel

owner decides the pay they will receive after the costs of their lodging and maintenance are deducted (Miralao et al., 1990, p. 6).

The field survey described in Chapter 5 reveals that customers frequenting the
brothels in Thailand had a definite preference for younger girls, while those going
to massage parlours did not express such a preference. However, only two out of 52
women surveyed in the rural brothels were below 18 years of age, partly because the
police had become increasingly strict on checking the ages of the prostitutes.
Nevertheless, the survey did find that nearly one-fifth of those currently working in
the brothels commenced work between the ages of 13 and 15.

Though the description in Chapter 5 does not focus specifically on the situation
in those brothels which offer child prostitutes, it does point out that working
conditions and the freedom of workers vary widely between brothels, and that some
areas, such as the town of Ranong in the south, have been well known for brothels
which imprison young girls from neighbouring Myanmar. The description below
clearly depicts "a modern form of slavery":

In the brothels, the owners use a combination of threats, force, debt bondage and physical confinement
to control the women and girls, force them to work in deplorable abusive conditions, and eliminate any
possibility of negotiation or escape. ... The Burmese women and girls we interviewed were determined
to pay off their debt as quickly as possible, knowing that it was the only way to get home. In addition to
the enforced compliance with the brothel owner's demands, therefore, there was also a financial incentive
to take as many clients as possible, do what they demanded, work every day possible, accept long hours
and avoid any additional expenses that might be added to their debt, especially health care with its
unpredictable costs. ... The brothels typically consist of a "selection" room or *hong du*; a room for virgins
or children (*hong bud boree sut*, literally, the "room to unveil virgins") and a series of cubicles where the
clients can take the girls. ... Girls and women who had been in the brothel for years still spoke in detail
about their first days in the brothel, how they tried to resist, the force used against them, how much it hurt,
and how they could not stop crying (Asia Watch and the Women's Rights Project, 1993, pp. 53-63).

Child sex tourism

Child sex tourism – "tourism organized with the primary purpose of facilitating the
effecting of a commercial sexual relationship with a child" (United Nations, 1995,
p. 13) – is a particularly serious form of child prostitution, partly because it attracts
paedophiles and also because it has been responsible for a palpable increase in the
violation of not only young girls but also young boys. Paedophiles and preferential
child abusers choose particular holiday destinations because they know that sexual
access to children in those places can be obtained relatively cheaply, easily and
safely. Unfortunately, Thailand and the Philippines have a reputation throughout the
world as two such places.

Underlying the increase in sex tourism is government promotion of tourism
per se as a major foreign exchange earner for developing countries. Efforts to
end child prostitution sometimes run into conflict with government support for the
tourist industry. As pointed out in Chapters 4 and 5, some government officials and
businessmen in the Philippines and Thailand still feel that the provision of every kind
of sexual service, including child prostitution, to foreign tourists is a necessary part
of tourist development. The Indonesian study in Chapter 2 also describes efforts by

some municipal governments in Indonesia to attract tourists through increasing the number of massage parlours, nightclubs, bars and striptease clubs.

A number of studies have explained why sex tourists represent such an important segment of the customers of child prostitutes, why paedophiles and preferential child abusers go to other countries to pursue their sexual urges, and why many "ordinary" tourists can become situational child abusers while they are out of their own countries. The set of circumstances peculiar to holidays, combined with attitudes to places and people identified as foreign, may easily lead to the sexual exploitation of a child by a tourist. The very fact that local children are made available allows the tourist to convince himself that the use of children for sex is somehow more acceptable, even "natural" to the host culture. The holiday-time loosening of inhibitions with respect to the treatment of others is exacerbated by the distance the tourist may feel between himself and a child in a developing country. An irony of the sex tourism industry is that the poverty which drives a child to offer sex for money offers the sex tourist an easy opportunity to avoid feelings of guilt. By paying for a child's services, he can convince himself that he is helping the child and his or her family to escape economic hardship and contributing to the economic development of the country.

The organization of sex tourism has been identified as involving both national and international elements. At the national level, the various organizational structures in the commercial sex sector – the pimps, taxi drivers, tour operators, hotel staff, brothel owners and entertainment establishments – also operate to supply child prostitutes to foreign tourists. "As in all other markets, their behaviour is partly a response to an existing demand for prostitution from tourists, and partly a pro-active attempt to generate such demand by creating and promoting an effective supply function. Sadly, many such forms of involvement rely on the existence of corruption among the police force (itself usually explained by the low pay of police officers)." (Staebler, 1996, p. 6.)

At the international level, the networks for child sex tourism have been identified as involving various individuals and groups. There are men and groups of men who appear to view the sexual exploitation of people in developing countries as a benign "hobby", and dedicate themselves to providing information for like-minded individuals on a non-profit-making basis. This may involve the exchange of information between men in sex tourist resorts or in bars and pubs back home. It is also achieved via the Internet, with some men contributing pornographic accounts of their sexual exploits and supplying details of sex establishments and prices in various destinations, including information on how to obtain child prostitutes (Staebler, 1996, pp. 6-7). Child sex tourism also involves tour operators who explicitly arrange child sex tours. Chapter 5 describes package sex tours to Thailand. Although such package sex tours appear to have declined as compared to the heyday in the 1980s, they are still operating. A recent report notes that the "business" has kept up with modern times. Whereas in the past, sex tours were relatively easy to identify, organizers now send their customers in a less obtrusive manner (Ram and Westwood, 1996, p. 2). Writers and publishers of travel guides which promote sex tourism, at least by implication, are also part of the networks. Some guides cater simply and solely to a sex tourist market, and provide a wealth of information for preferential child abusers.

The broader tourist industry, including airline companies, travel agents and package tour operators, also play a role in the sex industry. Although reputable travel companies may not intentionally wish to promote sex tourism, their marketing materials often help to sustain the flow, for example, by stressing the attractions of the "nightlife" of certain resorts or by promulgating certain stereotypes of women and children in developing countries. For instance, in 1992, the Thai government lodged a protest with an Austrian-based airline to withdraw its advertisements, which appeared to suggest that tourists should visit Thailand in order to avail themselves of the sexual services of children.

Within the informal sector, there is often a close link between sex tourism and street children (the phenomenon of street children in prostitution is described below). Street children who solicit independently from beaches, parks or ordinary tourist bars or hotels tend to be particularly attractive to tourists, especially situational child abusers. This is because the type of prostitute-client exchange which takes place in the informal sector is very different from that which takes place in the tourists' home country. The girls and boys are often willing to provide anything from 18 hours to two weeks of full access to their persons, and perform the kind of acts that in the West are taken to signify genuine affection (e.g. kissing, cuddling, sleeping in the bed with clients, providing physical care such as rubbing in suntan lotion, washing their hair or feet and so on, all things which an experienced Western prostitute would never do). The tourists do not have to go into a brothel or bar in order to pick up a prostitute, nor do they have to negotiate a "deal" in advance (the two things which they would commonly view as integral to "prostitution"). The situational child abuser can, therefore, interpret the process of being approached by a street child as a form of mutual attraction rather than as the initiation of a commercial sexual encounter. Later, when the child "confides" her or his desperate need for cash, the client constructs the act of giving them money not as payment for services rendered, but as a gesture of compassion or generosity. All of this makes it possible for some sex exploiters to tell themselves that the children are not really prostitutes, and thus that they themselves are not really clients (O'Connell Davidson, 1996, p. 14).

Street children and prostitution

The most common form of child prostitution in the informal sex sector is among street children. A street child has been defined as a girl or boy "for whom the street (in the widest sense of the word, including unoccupied dwellings, wasteland, etc.) has become his or her abode and/or source of livelihood; and who is inadequately protected, supervised or directed by responsible adults" (Belsey, 1996, p. 12). One estimate is that between 15 and 30 million children spend their days surviving on the streets of the urban landscapes of major cities of the world (Whaites, 1996, p. 3). The phenomenon of street children has been traced to abject poverty, the need to earn income, severe overcrowding in available housing, family breakdown and absentee parents (such as when their mothers have migrated overseas to work as domestic maids or entertainers), intra-family violence and substance abuse or sexual abuse. Of course, not all street children are prostitutes. But street children represent a high-risk group for going into prostitution, especially where links with their family or a significant adult have been cut, or where other means of survival do not bring in adequate incomes. A study on the sexual abuse of street children in several Asian countries, including the Philippines, Cambodia and India, concluded that the need for income is a powerful – possibly dominant – factor propelling children from poor urban families and migrant families newly arrived in cities into street work and eventually prostitution. "Street children accept any kind of work for a pathetically meagre return in order to stay alive. Even those street children who live mostly by illegitimate activities, such as theft, pickpocketing, prostitution, snatching chains, and running away with goods, etc. consider themselves legitimate workers" (Whaites, 1996, p. 4).

The path to prostitution among street children is frequently abuse and coercion, especially among the girls. They are introduced to the work through rape and deception, sometimes before they actually became street children (e.g. when they were working as domestic helpers). Other children who beg, hawk, collect rags and garbage for recycling and wash vehicles, may be sexually assaulted by other street children. In India, for example, social workers found that sexual assaults by older male street children against younger girls are relatively common. In some cases, the street child's pimp is another child. However, the child victims of prostitution are usually controlled by adults, who have support from an organized structure. Some children receive bonuses to trick or persuade others to become prostitutes.

A major survey in Cambodia found that while all the female victims had been sold and had worked in the sex sector under a high degree of coercion, among boys the entry into prostitution was rarely coercive (Gray et al., 1996). The boys reported that, unlike girls, they had done so "voluntarily", although at the time of the first encounter, they were normally naïve as to what would be expected of them. Commonly, the boys were introduced to customers by their peers, or they themselves knew where to go to make contacts on the street. Older boys sometimes procured younger ones for foreigners. While the girls were kept in prostitution through coercion or the desperate need for income, and wanted to leave if they could, a number of boys continued to prostitute themselves even while living at NGO centres where they were given food, shelter and clothes. Prostitution for them was not only a means of earning money, but also part of a street lifestyle that had its own "attractions". They spoke of the status of associating with relatively wealthy and well-travelled foreigners, of being taken on trips and given presents.

Those girls deceived into prostitution who remain on the streets tend to be worse off than their counterparts who are drawn into brothels. Some studies have pointed out that children involved in prostitution on the streets lack the very limited protection offered by brothel owners. Working on their own or with another child as a pimp, they can be taken by a customer away from any means of help or defence. In reality, the street child prostitute is usually a down-market choice for the customer, associated with low status and little respect.

For protection, street children sometimes operate in groups or gangs to sell sexual services on a freelance basis. Velasquez (1993a) describes the method of operation of teenage street prostitutes in the Philippines who cater mainly to local customers: the groups are led by a *bugaw* (pimp), though in some situations the teenagers serve as pimps for each other, and focus on certain areas. The group serves as a method of defence against violent customers and corrupt police officers. Pimps have reported paying police officers P100 (US$4) per night for each prostitute they manage, though these bribes only protect the pimps themselves, "who are the most visible link in the chain of teen prostitution". Such groups also provide a substitute family for the otherwise isolated street children. Experienced teenaged prostitutes can earn up to P500 (US$19) for an "all-nighter". However, it is common for them to earn as little as P50 (US$1.90) per customer. The pimps usually introduce the members of the group to customers, and take from 20 to 50 per cent of the payment.

Legal aspects of child prostitution

There is no question of legalizing child prostitution, and child prostitutes should be protected rather than treated as criminals. At the international level, there are several Conventions that seek to protect children from sexual exploitation and related problems such as trafficking and slavery. International Conventions provide the framework or basis for action, but their effectiveness depends on the extent to which they have generated or inspired national legislation and other policy measures, and law enforcement. In examining national laws pertaining to child prostitution, our focus is on the four Southeast Asian countries studied in the previous chapters. In the Philippines and Thailand, for instance, growing concernover child prostitution and the special problem of paedophilia has prompted the review of legislation covering prostitution in general, and the introduction of new and stricter laws that specifically address child prostitution and other forms of commercial sexual exploitation of children.

International Conventions

The most significant international legal instrument is the 1989 United Nations Convention on the Rights of the Child, which Indonesia, Malaysia, the Philippines and Thailand have all ratified, without reservation to Article 34, the key provision relating to the commercial sexual exploitation of children.[7] This is the most comprehensive treaty on the rights of children. Several provisions relate to the commercial sexual exploitation of children:

Article 19: "States Parties shall take all appropriate legislative, administrative, social and educational measures to protect the child from all forms of physical or mental violence, injury or abuse, neglect or negligent treatment, maltreatment or exploitation, including sexual abuse, while in the care of parent(s), legal guardian(s) or any other person who has the care of the child."

Article 32: "States Parties recognize the right of the child to be protected from economic exploitation and from performing any work that is likely to be hazardous or to interfere with the child's education, or to be harmful to the child's health or physical, mental, spiritual, moral or social development." A minimum age or ages are to be set and States are bound to "provide for appropriate penalties or other sanctions to ensure the effective enforcement of the present article."

Article 34: "States Parties undertake to protect the child from all forms of sexual exploitation and sexual abuse. For these purposes, States Parties shall in particular take all appropriate national, bilateral and multilateral measures to prevent: (a) the inducement or coercion of a child to engage in any unlawful sexual activity; (b) the exploitative use of children in prostitution or any other unlawful sexual practices; (c) the exploitative use of children in pornographic performances and materials."

Article 35: "States Parties shall take all appropriate national, bilateral and multi-lateral measures to prevent the abduction of, the sale of or traffic in children for any purpose or in any form."

Article 39: "States Parties shall take all appropriate measures to promote physical and psychological recovery and social reintegration of: a child victim of any form of neglect, exploitation or abuse; ... in an environment which fosters the health, self-respect and dignity of the child."

Other international treaties also provide binding texts or have "soft components" dealing explicitly or implicitly with child prostitution. For example, all four countries have ratified the Convention on the Elimination of All Forms of Discrimination Against Women, and the Philippines is a signatory of the Convention on the Suppression of the Traffic in Persons and the Exploitation of the Prostitution of Others. The Philippines and Malaysia have also ratified the 1956 Supplementary Convention on the Abolition of Slavery, the Slave Trade and Institutions and Practices Similar to Slavery. Article 1 of this Convention obliges States Parties to "take all practicable and necessary legislative and other measures to bring about progressively and as soon as possible the complete abolition or abandonment of ... [*inter alia*] ... any institution or practice whereby a child or young person under the age of 18 years is delivered by either or both of his natural parents or by his guardian to another person, whether for reward or not, with a view to the exploitation of the child or young person or of his labour."

Although ILO standards were not drawn up to deal specifically with the problem of child prostitution, certain Conventions and Recommendations, especially those dealing with exploitative child labour, are relevant. These ILO Conventions have been the focus of renewed attention, largely as a result of the efforts of the IPEC. The Minimum Age Convention, 1973 (No. 138), obliges ratifying States to fix a minimum age for admission to employment or work, to undertake to pursue a national policy designed to ensure the effective elimination of child labour, and to raise progressively the minimum age for admission to employment or work to a level consistent with the fullest physical and mental development of young persons. Recommendation No. 146, which supplements the Convention, provides the broad framework and essential policy measures for both the prevention of child labour and its elimination. To date, however, none of the four Southeast Asian countries has ratified the Convention. [*Editor's note*: Malaysia ratified the Convention on 9 September 1997.]

The ILO Conventions that deal more directly with the worst forms of exploitation of child labour are the Forced Labour Convention, 1930 (No. 29), and the Abolition of Forced Labour Convention, 1957 (No. 105). Forced or compulsory labour is defined as "work or service which is exacted from any person under the menace of any penalty and for which the said person has not offered himself voluntarily". Certainly the descriptions above confirm that child prostitution represents one of the most intolerable forms of forced child labour. The ILO Committee of Experts and the Conference Committee on the Application of Standards have singled out the exploitation of children for prostitution and pornography as one of the worst forms of forced labour, and have called for action not only by States in which the problem occurs, but also by other countries, to assist in the eradication of such practices, especially by tourists and foreign visitors (ILO, 1996, p. 27).

The 1996 International Labour Conference adopted a Resolution concerning the Elimination of Child Labour which called upon member States and employers' and workers' organizations to "develop formal policies and set priorities so as to immediately proceed to put an end to the most intolerable aspects of child labour, namely the employment of children in slave-like and bonded conditions and in dangerous and hazardous work, the exploitation of very young children, and the commercial sexual exploitation of children".

In 1998, the International Labour Conference will hold a first discussion to consider the adoption of a new ILO standard at the 1999 Session of the Conference, aimed at putting an end to the most intolerable forms of child labour. The new Convention would complement existing instruments and would focus on the most extreme forms of child labour. The aims of the proposed new standard, which would apply to all children under the age of 18, are to set clear priorities for national and international action, to require member States to provide for and strictly enforce adequate criminal penalties, and to encourage member States to assist each other by means of international judicial and technical assistance or other types of cooperation to target the intolerable.

National laws

National legislation relating to child prostitution can be discussed in terms of: (a) whether general laws pertaining to prostitution apply also to children, or whether they distinguish between adults and minors; (b) whether child prostitutes are treated as criminals or as victims in need of protection; (c) the types of provisions to criminalize sexual relations with minors even outside of a commercial arrangement, or even with the consent of the child; (d) whether boys or under-age males are adequately covered under existing legislation; (e) the age limit set for a child to be deemed capable of consenting to sexual relations, as distinguished from the age limit set for a person to legally be a commercial sex worker; (f) whether there are specific laws or regulations relating to child prostitution or other forms of the commercial sexual exploitation of children, or whether child prostitutes are covered under comprehensive laws to protect children; (g) the groups held criminally liable, for example, whether parents, guardians or caretakers – or those accepting sexual services offered by a child – are punishable; (h) whether national criminal laws can be applied extraterritorially, such as to deal with child sex tourism and foreign paedophiles; and (i) the procedures for obtaining evidence from a child, including the evidence requirements concerning the age of a child and the rights of the accused versus the rights of the child to protection.

In all the four countries studied, the law distinguishes between adults and children, although the definition of minors or under-age persons differs. In Indonesia and Malaysia, where the act of prostitution is legal, the law seeks to protect those under 21 years of age. In Malaysia, the Women and Girls Protection Act has provisions for detaining an under-age prostitute for up to three years for her own protection. By order of a magistrate, made after an inquiry, she may be removed to a place of refuge, although institutional rehabilitation is normally a last resort. The first step would be counselling and supervision by social workers while the girl resides at home. Sex workers of 21 years and above cannot be detained, and are not forced to undergo counselling or training for alternative employment, but programmes are available to those who want to participate in them. In Indonesia, there is some ambiguity because the legal age of entry into the official brothel complexes is 17 years, but a girl is not considered under age if she is married and holds a residential registration identification card. In the Philippines, prostitution is illegal, but Republic Act 7610, which came into force in 1992 (and is described in greater detail below), specifically classifies prostitutes below 18 years of age as victims of exploitation rather than as criminals. In Thailand, the 1996 Prostitution Prevention and Suppression Act distinguishes between prostitutes above 18 years, those between 15 and 18 years and those below 15, and imposes more severe penalties on procurers, employers and clients the younger the child they commercially sexually exploit.

The four countries also attempt to protect children by criminalizing sexual relations with minors without referring specifically to prostitution. The crime is normally defined in terms of "committing indecent acts with" or "corrupting" minors, regardless of the consent of the child. However, the age when a child is deemed capable of consenting to have sexual relations is normally lower than the age limit for prostitution. In Malaysia, for instance, the Women and Girls Protection Act makes it an offence to "have carnal knowledge of a female below the age of 16 years". In Thailand, section 277 of the Penal Code provides that "any person who commits an act of rape on a girl aged under 15 years, who is not his wife, with or without the consent of such a girl, shall be liable to imprisonment from 4 to 20 years and fine from 8,000 to 40,000 baht. For wrongdoing pursuant to the preceding paragraph against a girl aged under 13 years, the perpetrator shall be liable to imprisonment from 7 to 20 years and fine from 14,000 to 40,000 baht". In the Philippines, perpetrators are prosecuted for rape or lascivious conduct when the child is under 12 years of age.

The countries prohibit the sale and trafficking in children, procurement for prostitution and profiteering from child prostitution. Although the legislation refers to offences in general and covers both adults and children, there are some provisions for heavier penalties where minors are involved. Recent legislation and proposed legal amendments seek to ensure protection for children of both sexes. Previously, boys were sometimes omitted from legal provisions. Especially in the light of the growing number of boys in child sex tourism, protection for children of both sexes is crucial. For example, Thailand has introduced a new law to replace the Anti-Trafficking Act of 1928, which covered women and girls but not boys. The proposed bill on Traffic in Women and Children extends offences to cover selling, purchasing, trading of women and children (defined as any person under 18 years of age), taking them from or sending them to any place, receiving, holding or detaining them or making them do acts, even with their consent, for the purpose of satisfying the sexual desires of others or exploiting them for unjust gain (Rayanakorn, 1995, p. 56).

Growing determination to take effective action has motivated the countries to tighten laws and introduce new legislation dealing directly with child prostitution and other forms of commercial sexual exploitation of children. The Philippines Republic Act 7610 specifically addresses the Special Protection of Children against Child Abuse, Exploitation and Discrimination. Article III of this Act deals with child prostitution and sexual abuse, article IV with child trafficking and article V with obscene publications and indecent shows. Article III, section 5, provides that:

Children, whether male or female, who for money, profit or any other consideration or due to the coercion or influence of any adult, syndicate or group, indulge in sexual intercourse or lascivious conduct, are deemed to be children exploited in prostitution and other sexual abuse.

The penalty of reclusion temporal in its medium period to reclusion perpetual shall be imposed upon the following:

(a) those who engage in or promote, facilitate or induce child prostitution which include, but are not limited to, the following:

- acting as a procurer of child prostitute;
- inducing a person to be a client of a child prostitute by means of written or oral advertisements or other similar means;
- taking advantage of influence or relationship to procure a child prostitute;
- threatening or using violence towards a child to engage him as prostitute; or
- giving monetary consideration, goods or other pecuniary benefit to a child in prostitution. (quoted in ILO, 1996, p. 67.)

Thailand has drawn up a national policy and plan of action for the prevention and eradication of the commercial sexual exploitation of children; this covers not only legislation but also policies and social and administrative measures. The new Prostitution Prevention and Suppression Act and other proposed amendments to existing legislation are part of these multidisciplinary national efforts. Although the new Act covers all forms of prostitution, the focus is clearly on "the total elimination of entry into the commercial sex business by children of both sexes under 18" (National Committee for the Eradication of Commercial Sex, 1996, p. 2). The Act reduces the punishment on the prostitutes themselves to only a fine, but raises the penalties for those involved in procurement, trafficking, profiteering and advertising, and, most significantly, distinguishes between offences committed against those aged 18 and above, those below 18 and those below 15. The younger the child involved, the heavier the penalties. The Act also deems that prostitutes under 18 years of age should first be sent to a primary shelter to determine whether the girls should be sent to a suitable protection and vocational development institute, or released.

Another important aspect of the new Prostitution Prevention and Suppression Act in Thailand is the identification of culpable parties. Three provisions are especially significant. The Act specifically targets clients of child prostitutes. Section 9 states:

Whoever commits sexual intercourse or any other act for sexual gratification of that person or of the third party against the other person who is over 15 years but not yet over 18 years of age in the place of prostitution, with or without consent of the other person, shall be punished with imprisonment of one to three years and a fine of 20,000-60,000 baht.

If the commission of the offence as specified in the first paragraph is against a child not over 15 years of age, the offender shall be punished with imprisonment of two to six years and a fine of 40,000-120,000 baht.

If the commission of the offence as specified in the first paragraph is against the marriage partner of the offender, and is not committed for sexual gratification of the third person, the offender is not guilty.

Another section of the Act provides that if the perpetrator, aider or abetter of trafficking in or procurement for prostitution is "an administrative official, police official, government official, or worker in the primary shelter or in the protection and vocational development place according to this Act, such perpetrator, aider or abetter shall be punished with imprisonment of 15-20 years and a fine of 300,000-400,000 baht". The Act also targets the father, mother or guardian of child prostitutes. It provides that those found guilty of any offence under the Act can have their guardianship revoked, and the court can appoint another guardian to replace them.

It has been increasingly recognized that national legislation may not be adequate to protect children from sexual exploitation by tourists or foreign visitors, cross-border trafficking, abductions from one country to another, or abuses of inter-country adoption of children. Efforts have therefore been made to tighten national legislation in the countries where the problems are serious. For example, the Philippines' Republic Act 7610 has provisions which control foreign travel by children and the adoption of children in return for a consideration, as well as any acts of trading and dealing with children for money. Thailand has proposed amendments to its Penal Code so that it can prosecute any offender "who procures, deceives or traffics an adult or child of either sex for an indecent sexual act for the purpose of sexual gratification of another person, no matter where the offence is committed, and what nationality the offender is" (National Committee for the Eradication of Commercial Sex, 1996, p. 26). The Thai Extradition Act and Mutual Legal Assistance in Criminal Matters Act also allow the Thai Attorney-General to provide assistance in criminal matters to foreign states, such as in the prosecution of foreign paedophiles who have committed crimes in Thailand and escaped back to their home countries.

Other countries have also introduced extraterritorial legislation to allow the application of their national laws to crimes committed abroad, and to give their domestic courts extraterritorial jurisdiction to deal with their nationals who go abroad as tourists or business visitors in order to exploit children in countries such as Thailand or the Philippines. Australia's Crimes (Child Sex Tourism) Amendment Act of 1994 specifies in section 50BA that "a person must not, while outside Australia, engage in sexual intercourse with a person who is under 16". Other countries, such as the Scandinavian countries, New Zealand, Germany, Belgium, France and Japan, also have similar extraterritorial provisions to deal with their nationals who are paedophiles or who engage in child sex tourism. Some countries have also introduced legislation to deal specifically with tourism for the purpose of sex with minors. The 1994 United States Violent Crime Control and Law Enforcement Act criminalizes domestic or foreign travel with the intent to engage in sexual acts with a minor. Australia's Crimes (Child Sex Tourism) Amendment Act and legislation adopted by New Zealand in 1995 also make it an offence to benefit from or encourage such travel. In Italy, the government passed an Order of the Day in 1995 that requires travel agents to comply with the Convention on the Rights of the Child, especially with those articles against the commercial sexual exploitation of children.

Enforcement of legislation on child prostitution

The World Congress against the Commercial Sexual Exploitation of Children, held in August 1996, noted that concern over the growing incidence of sexual exploitation of children, and the international character of several of its manifestations, has triggered new and amended legislation, but that law enforcement now poses the major challenge. Creating the political will and commitment for governments to take effective action at national and international levels is still a key hurdle. The problems of law enforcement relating to adult prostitution are also relevant in the case of child prostitutes. In addition, there are problems particular to extending protection to children.

Among the factors which deter effective enforcement of legislation is the problem of establishing the real age of the children involved (United Nations, 1995, p. 14). The problem relates not only to the evidence requirements concerning the age of the person. Unscrupulous brothel owners often use forged papers or identification cards for minors. Especially with trafficked children, determining age can be very difficult. Interestingly, Thailand's new Prostitution Prevention and Suppression Act seems to be having some success in this regard. Research conducted two months after the Act came into force found that brothel and massage parlour owners in northern Thailand were sending home women and girls from Myanmar and the hill tribes because they did not have any identification cards. The concern was not that they were illegal migrants, but rather that it was not possible to establish their ages. The establishment owners feared the law, which is very strict regarding those who procure or employ sex workers under the age of 18 years.

Part of the problem is also that, in many countries, it is a legal defence to plead that the accused had reason to believe the victim in question was above the legal age.[8] It is also often the case that the legal age for marriage is lower than the age of consent, as in Indonesia, where those who are married can legally obtain residential cards even if they are below 17 years of age, and can thus work in the official brothel complexes. In Thailand, an additional paragraph was added by the Senate in its discussion of the draft Prostitution Prevention and Suppression Act, to provide that if the person having sexual intercourse with an individual between 15 and 18 years of age is the marriage partner, and sexual gratification of a third person is not involved, then an offence has not been committed.

There may also be difficulties relating to proof of an offence. Child victims are not likely to lodge complaints, and it is also unlikely that an offender will be caught in the very act of sexually abusing a child. It has therefore been suggested that "there appears to be merit in shifting the burden of proof when the protection of a child is at issue, and in so framing the laws that the onus is on the accused to justify his being in the company of a child who is not a relative" (O'Brian, 1996, p. 20). The Philippines Republic Act 7610, for example, stipulates that merely to be found alone with a child who is not a relative inside a hotel, vehicle or other place constitutes an attempt to commit prostitution, which is an offence under Article III, section 6. Under section 5 (a), the mere verbal offer of a child for purposes of prostitution constitutes the offence of sexual abuse.

Another factor relates to the procedural difficulties of obtaining admissible evidence from a child. The age of the child, and his or her lack of education, may undermine the quality of a child's evidence. There is also the need to protect the child from the trauma of court proceedings and of confronting their abuser. Thailand has proposed revising its Criminal Procedure Code to ease the burden on the child of giving evidence. For instance, the draft Criminal Procedure Amendment Act provides that if the child is below 15 years of age, his or her statement should be given in a room specifically arranged for the purpose, separate from other adults and in the presence of a psychiatrist, social worker or any other person whom the child requests to be present. The statement shall be videotaped and the video used as evidence in court. Cross-examination of the child on the contents of the video will only be allowed through a psychiatrist. The proposed amendments also allow for pre-trial depositions by victims who may be vulnerable to delays in the proceedings, such as street children or trafficked children. Once the deposition has been taken and the alleged offender has had the opportunity to confront the witness, the deposition can be used in court. The Criminal Procedure Amendment Act has gone before Parliament, but as of July 1997 had not been adopted.

There are also more practical problems of law enforcement. In the Philippines, for example, a number of NGOs working with children have reported that efforts to press charges against foreign paedophiles have met with strong resistance from the families of the children. A rally that a Filipino NGO staged to press for the imprisonment of a known foreign paedophile met with opposition from members of the urban poor community from where most of his 34 victims came; the parents of some of these children defended the man because of the material benefits that he gave the children and their families. Even local officials criticized the NGOs for their efforts, reasoning that poor families, including children, should not be denied any means to survive.

Enforcement is particularly problematic when international elements are involved. Sex tourists or paedophiles may travel to another country to sexually exploit children with impunity if they manage to return to their country of origin. Extradition is one means of punishing an offender. Some countries have extradition treaties which allow a child exploiter to be extradited back to the country where the crime was committed. But the procedures are long, complicated and expensive. An increasing number of countries have, therefore, extended their criminal jurisdiction to cover the criminal acts of their citizens committed against children in countries such as the Philippines and Thailand and have also adopted measures to prohibit the organization of travel with the intent to sexually exploit children. Again, there are difficulties of enforcement. Even when law enforcement officials from the two countries have cooperated and succeeded in bringing offenders to court, there is still the issue of how the crime is to be punished. There is a risk that offences against foreign children will be seen as less serious than the same offences committed against nationals, and that the penalties imposed will be less severe for a crime committed abroad.

Another issue is how children who are sold or trafficked into a country for prostitution are treated by law enforcers. They are commonly dealt with under the immigration and alien laws of the receiving country, and treated as lawbreakers who are deported, although under international covenants and anti-trafficking laws they should be considered as victims, and thus exempt from fines or imprisonment, and be granted safe repatriation back to their countries of origin. The receiving country tends to treat them as criminals on at least two counts: as illegal immigrants and as prostitutes. Studies of women and children trafficked from Myanmar into Thailand for prostitution show that they are arrested and imprisoned, often for long periods, without charge or trial. Even if they are brought to trial, they face language and communication barriers and have no idea of their rights; the process of deportation often involves a new round of exploitation and sexual abuse. Prostitutes from Myanmar who are picked up in Thailand are mandatorily tested for HIV/AIDS; if they are found positive, they are deported home, where they are segregated by the Myanmar authorities and left to die (Lintner and Lintner, 1996; Muntarbhorn, 1996b, p. 22). In Malaysia, foreign prostitutes and procurers picked up in raids are detained in an immigration centre and subsequently deported.

Since all the country studies noted that a major problem is corruption among the police, immigration officers and government officials, the issue of the quality of law enforcers is an important one. Muntarbhorn (1996b) pointed out that low pay, poor selection processes and insufficient training of law enforcers concerning child rights often result in weak law enforcement and corruption. He recommends that they be given incentives and improved in-service training, and that those who indulge in malpractices should be severely penalized. He also suggests other measures to improve law enforcement, including the establishment of a national central bureau to oversee enforcement, police training and the setting up of special task forces within the police, as well as extradition orders in the case of foreign offenders.

However, enforcement of legislation on the commercial sexual exploitation of children is not just the responsibility of the police or law enforcers. Within a country, it is common for several government agencies – the police, immigration authorities, social welfare, education and health authorities – to cooperate closely to deal with exploited or abused children. These official bodies are also increasingly cooperating with NGOs concerned with children or other vulnerable groups, especially in the collection and sharing of information on known sex abusers and foreign paedophiles. In the Philippines, under Republic Act 7610, the Departments of Justice and of Social Welfare and Development have cooperated to develop a comprehensive programme to protect children from commercial sexual exploitation. Enforcement of the Act also imposes mandatory reporting by hospitals, doctors, nurses, teachers and law-enforcement officials about cases of sexual abuse of children. In Thailand, a national-level committee, comprising representatives of various government departments and the private sector, has been established within the Office of the Prime Minister to coordinate efforts to eliminate child prostitution. A Child Rights Protection Division has been established within the Office of the Attorney-General to monitor child sexual abuse cases. This division has developed a network that includes NGO representatives. Private sector initiatives have also helped in law enforcement. NGOs and associations of business organizations have been increasingly active in information and awareness-raising campaigns to educate all sectors of society on children's rights. They also encourage community watches of children at risk and the reporting of crimes against children.

Given the international dimensions of the commercial sexual exploitation of children, enforcement mechanisms also require cooperation at an international level or on a bilateral basis. The International Criminal Police Organization (Interpol) maintains a database of criminals, and serves as a focal point for the systematic collection and exchange of information among countries. Recent efforts have been made to establish a register of convicted paedophiles, which can be used as an "early warning system" to alert national authorities, including border police, customs and immigration officers, of the movement of known criminals. Another cooperative method is the placement by States of police liaison officers in countries to which their nationals travel in large numbers. Although such liaison officers have been used mainly in the fight against drug trafficking, there is now a growing focus on training them to prevent, or assist in the detection of, crimes of sexual exploitation of children committed by their countrymen in other countries. Some 64 countries now have a system of police liaison officers to detect and report crimes against children. These officers are trained by Interpol to focus on children as victims and as witnesses in investigations. They report to the Standing Working Party on Offences Committed against Minors, which has recommended that, at the national level, countries should maintain registers of missing children, and set up specialized centres where children who are found can be debriefed and cared for before the issue of return to their families is settled.[9] The Working Party has also recommended that children missing for more than six months should be made the subject of international missing persons notices at Interpol headquarters.

Policies and programmes aimed at eliminating child prostitution

The Convention on the Rights of the Child calls for integrated, cross-sectoral strategies both to prevent and to remedy the situation of the commercial sexual exploitation of children. As a complement to the Convention, a Programme of Action for the Prevention of the Sale of Children, Child Prostitution and Child Pornography was adopted by the United Nations Commission on Human Rights in 1992. Emphasizing that the commercial sexual exploitation of children has both economic and social roots, the Convention and Programme of Action call for a broad range of multifaceted responses, not only from international and national government agencies, but also from parents, families, NGOs, the business sector and the community. The cooperation and coordination between the public and private sectors is critical because both state and non-state actors are potentially the guardians as well as the exploiters of children. This multi-pronged approach by all social partners is evident in the Agenda for Action adopted at the World Congress against the Commercial Sexual Exploitation of Children, in Stockholm in August 1996:

- *Coordination and cooperation at local/national levels:* Government and non-government sectors are called upon to work closely together to develop national agendas for action, involving comprehensive, cross-sectoral and integrated strategies and effective implementation and monitoring mechanisms to end the commercial sexual exploitation of children and to nurture an environment, attitudes and practices responsive to child rights.
- *Coordination and cooperation at regional/international levels:* States, national, regional and international organizations should together press for full implementation of the Convention on the Rights of the Child and advocate and mobilize support for child rights, including ensuring that adequate resources are available to protect children from commercial sexual exploitation.
- *Prevention:* Measures to prevent children from being lured, coerced and trafficked into commercial sexual exploitation include gender-sensitive communication, media and information campaigns, as well as national social and economic policies and programmes to assist children vulnerable to sexual exploitation, to encourage and assist families and communities to resist acts that lead to child prostitution, to promote the value of children as human beings, and to reduce poverty.
- *Protection:* Action to protect children from commercial sexual exploitation includes measures to establish the criminal responsibility of service providers, customers and intermediaries in child prostitution; measures to create safe havens for children trying to escape from commercial sexual exploitation; and measures to establish or strengthen networks between national and international law-enforcement authorities and civil society for various forms of cooperation.
- *Recovery and reintegration:* Such measures – which are based on a non-punitive approach to child victims of commercial sexual exploitation – aim to provide social, medical, psychological and other support as well as alternative means of livelihood to child victims and their families. They also aim to prevent and remove societal stigmatization of child victims, and to facilitate their reintegration in communities and families.

• *Child participation:* Action against child prostitution should involve the active participation of children, child victims, young people, their families, peers and others who are potential helpers of children.

Efforts at the international level

In addition to the international Conventions, there is a growing number of programmes at the international level to combat the commercial sexual exploitation of children. Regional or sub-regional initiatives are, however, still lacking.

The Programme of Action for the Prevention of the Sale of Children, Child Prostitution and Child Pornography calls for better law enforcement and more effective cooperation between key organizations, and includes measures for raising public consciousness and concern; improving sources of information and monitoring of the situation; providing alternative educational programmes for street children; tackling poverty and improving the economic conditions of those at risk; imposing severe punishments on procurers, intermediaries and clients; and assisting in the rehabilitation and reintegration of child victims and their families. A Special Rapporteur examines the situation throughout the world and provides regular updates to the United Nations Commission on Human Rights.

The ILO's International Programme on the Elimination of Child Labour (IPEC) started in 1992, and is now operational in more than 25 countries. In addition to the promotion of the ILO standards described above, IPEC provides support to countries in developing their capacity to appraise the nature and extent of child labour, identify priority target groups, and formulate and implement policies and programmes which aim at the elimination of child labour. Countries identify the most serious forms of child labour and the most pressing needs, and IPEC provides:

assistance in fields such as: appraising the problem, development of national policies and programmes of action, strengthening of law enforcement, preventing child prostitution and child trafficking, and rehabilitating victims through social mobilization, awareness raising and the provision of alternatives to parents and the children. At the institutional level, the set-up of cooperation and coordination mechanisms is emphasized, because it is clear that it is only through joint efforts among all key actors that concerted action can be implemented. These include the family units, teachers, the medical profession, social welfare and legal aid personnel, the police, religious and community leaders within certain geographical areas and between sending and receiving locations. (Boonpala, 1996b, p. 7.)

Some national initiatives supported by IPEC in participating countries are described in the next section of this chapter.

Some NGOs have established effective national and international networks and conducted media campaigns to end the sexual exploitation of children. Perhaps the best known and most active is the campaign run by End Child Prostitution in Asian Tourism (ECPAT), which was established in 1991 by a group of concerned individuals and NGOs. There are now some 250 groups in the coalition which forms the ECPAT network in over 25 countries worldwide (ECPAT, 1995). It has campaigned at both national and international levels for legal reforms, education, information and media coverage, and political action. ECPAT national groups, such as in the Philippines and Sri Lanka, have organized workshops to facilitate the exchange of experiences among those working directly with sexually exploited children. ECPAT has also set up a fund to sponsor training for groups working to rehabilitate child victims of prostitution. It was largely due to ECPAT's efforts that the first World Congress against the Commercial Sexual Exploitation of Children was held, in Stockholm in August 1996.

The International Catholic Child Bureau (ICCB) has also played a major catalysing and coordinating role in the fight against child prostitution. The ICCB first took up the issue of children in prostitution in the mid-1980s at the request of the then United Nations Special Rapporteur on the Trafficking in Persons and the Exploitation of Others. Since then, it has been active in advocacy work through its offices in South America, West Africa, Asia, Europe and the United States. In Southeast Asia, it is closely associated with ECPAT. It has also carried out research on the types and effectiveness of projects and services for young victims of prostitution (Bruce, 1996).

As early as 1985, the World Tourism Organization adopted the Tourism Bill of Rights and Tourist Code, which includes exhortations to States, tourism professionals, suppliers of tourism and travel services, as well as tourists themselves to prevent or refrain from the exploitation of others for prostitution purposes. More recently, in October 1996, the World Tourism Organization passed a resolution on the prevention of organized sex tourism, which "denounces and condemns in particular child sex tourism, considering it a violation of Article 34 of the Convention on the Rights of the Child [United Nations, 1989] and requiring strict legal action by tourist sending and receiving countries". The resolution also appeals to the travel trade to adopt practical, promotional and commercial measures to help eliminate child sex tourism. The World Tourism Organization also announced at the World Congress against Commercial Sexual Exploitation of Children that it was setting up a joint public-private sector task force, the Tourism and Child Prostitution Watch, to encourage self-regulation in the tourism industry by increasing awareness of the problems of sexual exploitation in tourism, and by collecting and disseminating information on successful measures for dealing with the problems.

Other actors in the tourist trade have also been taking direct action to fight child sex tourism. In December 1994, the Universal Federation of Travel Agents' Associations (UFTAA) adopted the Children's and Travel Agents' Charter, in which members and affiliates "pledge to combat the prostitution of children related to so-called 'sex tourism' and to protect the child victims of such tourists by supporting the measures taken by governments to counter the sexual exploitation of children; by informing their foreign colleagues of the penalties imposed on tourists who commit acts which involve the use of children for the purpose of sexual gratification". In June 1995, the International Union of Food, Agricultural, Hotel, Restaurant, Catering, Tobacco and Allied Workers' Associations adopted a Resolution on Child Prostitution which "recommends that hotel affiliates, tour guide affiliates and other tourism services workers in destinations where child sex prostitution is practised, engage in a dialogue with their employers to ensure that the facilities of the undertaking are not available for child prostitution, and that the fact be publicized".

Another recommendation is that "such policies developed by tourism service trade unions and enterprises should include the following elements: (a) a statement that the hotel, travel operator, or other enterprise, opposes the practice of child prostitution, and will take all measures to prevent the use of its services to facilitate such activity; this policy to be made known to clients/customers/guests; (b) a statement that any staff member abused or criticized by clients/guests for refusing to give assistance in the procuring or provision of facilities for child prostitution will be supported by management and will not face any discipline".

Among the most common initiatives to deal with child sex tourism are those to educate tourists and warn them against the commercial sexual exploitation of children. Staebler (1996, pp. 10-14) describes some of these measures. A principal means is through brochures, cards or leaflets that warn tourists against child sex tourism. The tourist industry, governments and NGOs often cooperate to produce and distribute these. For example, the Swedish aid agency Radda Barnen helped to produce a card which is distributed by the Swedish Travel Agency Association. One side of the card, which is inserted in airline tickets to Asia, gives the "bright side" of tourism, while the other side describes the "dark side", and warns tourists that they should protect rather than exploit children. The French travel industry and several government ministries also produced a leaflet warning against child prostitution, for distribution through travel agents. Educational materials are also distributed by customs officers at airports, at travel fairs and in-flight by the airline companies. On the ground, groups in Thailand concerned about the sexual abuse of children helped to distribute widely a pamphlet to foreign tourists through hotels and shops. Produced by the National Commission on Women's Affairs, the pamphlet carries the message that sex with children is a crime.

Efforts at the national level

Thailand and the Philippines are among the countries that have adopted national policies and programmes for dealing with child labour in general and with child prostitution in particular. There is growing recognition among countries that, because of the multifaceted nature of the problem and the various vested interests involved, comprehensive programmes and concerted action by a wide range of key actors are needed.

Thailand's National Policy and Plan of Action for the Prevention and Eradication of the Commercial Sexual Exploitation of Children spells out the official policy in terms of: (a) the total elimination of entry into the commercial sex business by children of both sexes under 18 years of age; (b) prohibition of luring, threats, exploitation and acts of violence in the operation of the commercial sex business; and (c) imposition of punishment on all persons with a part in bringing children into the commercial sex industry, and punishment of officials negligent in, or choosing to ignore, their duty to enforce compliance with relevant policies, laws, rules and regulations (National Committee for the Eradication of Commercial Sex, 1996, pp. 2-10).

Detailed strategies and plans are set out for the period 1997-2006 to eliminate the commercial sexual exploitation of children through specific measures for prevention; suppression; assistance and protection; recovery, reintegration and adjustment to a normal life; and the establishment of structures, mechanisms and systems for supervision, control, follow-up and rapid implementation.

Preventive measures include:

- surveillance, survey, research, follow-up and monitoring on a regular basis;
- a campaign to stop the luring or seduction of children and women inside the country and abroad, especially from Myanmar, the Lao People's Democratic Republic, China and Cambodia;
- a public information campaign to promote values and to mobilize public participation on a wider scale in the prevention and solution of these problems;
- nine years of quality basic education for all children;
- improvements in the quality of education and vocational training and in the quality of teachers;
- appropriate family education and sex education; and
- provision of other social and economic services accessible to target groups, so that children can develop appropriately according to their age group.

Measures for the suppression of child prostitution include:

- promulgation of the new Prostitution Prevention and Suppression Act and amendments to other relevant legislation;
- improvement of law enforcement through providing law-enforcement officials with better knowledge;
- compilation, analysis and dissemination of information on children and cases of arrests of entrepreneurs and exploiters;
- reduction and elimination of overt and hidden commercial sex businesses, including taking action against unregistered job recruitment agencies and other agencies sending women and children to work as prostitutes abroad;
- inspections of major bus and railway terminals and highway police checkpoints on routes connecting with border areas; and
- support of foreign governments in the enforcement of laws imposing punishment upon their citizens committing sex offences against Thai children and children from other countries.

Measures for assistance and protection outlined in Thailand's Plan of Action include:

- expanding the system through which complaints can be lodged, assistance given and facilities provided to children who have been lured or forced into prostitution;
- encouraging the public to play a role in providing information on child sexual abuse, such as through the setting up of a complaint-lodging system;
- improving coordination with Thai embassies and consulates when Thai children abroad are found in the commercial sex business; and
- setting up a system through which foreign children lured into prostitution can be sent home with the cooperation of concerned agencies.

Recovery and reintegration measures include:

- provision of full-scale assistance services, including temporary lodging, education and vocational training, job placement and counselling services;
- provision of lodging for street children and sexually abused children;
- participation of the private sector, such as through income-generation training for women and children, including bidding, subcontracting and joint ventures; and
- in the case of sending foreign children back to their home countries, coordination with the government and NGOs in the country and abroad to ensure the children's physical and mental rehabilitation, and adjustment to a normal life.

The plan also calls for:

- establishment of a national-level committee within the Office of the Prime Minister to specify direction, policy, planning, coordination, follow-up and assessment at the national level;
- coordination by the Office of the National Commission on Women's Affairs;
- participation and coordination of concerned agencies, in particular the Department of Local Administration, Community Development and Public Welfare, with NGOs and local communities, in surveillance campaigns and other actions;
- follow-up and monitoring of implementation at the provincial level by the Committee for the Promotion of Social Welfare;
- financial and technical support to NGOs working with child prostitutes; and the creation of mechanisms for cooperation with international organizations and NGOs abroad working for children's rights and against the commercial sexual exploitation of children.

A number of programmes are already operational in Thailand, supported by the Office of the National Commission on Women's Affairs. The IPEC Programme in Thailand has also supported several initiatives at the provincial and community levels to prevent trafficking and the commercial sexual exploitation of children. One of these is the Daughters' Education Programme (DEP), which operates in the north of Thailand. Girls at a high risk of being sent into prostitution are given temporary shelter and access to education.[10] The DEP offers various educational programmes: educational sponsorship for girls to attend primary and secondary school; vocational training so that they can learn income-generating skills; youth leadership training so that they can play a more active role in the community; and day care and basic literacy for young children from very poor and troubled families who have no nationality or identity papers, and therefore have difficulty enrolling in the formal education system (Saikaew, 1996, pp. 68-69). The DEP also conducts awareness-raising among the communities prone to sending their children into prostitution. Recognizing that the families also need assistance, the DEP has started training programmes and provides a revolving fund for parents to embark upon simple forms of income generation.

Another project initiated in 1987 by a Thai NGO, the Foundation for Women, developed reading books for the last grade of primary school to inform children about the dangers of prostitution and to prevent them from being lured into the sex sector.

Two books, which are now well known, are *Kamla*, the story of a northern village girl who had been deceived, forced into prostitution and finally met a tragic end, and *Kamkaew*, a similar story for children in the northeast. In close cooperation with the education department, the books were distributed to schools in several provinces, and served as an eye-opener for children, teachers and communities. To encourage discussion and continue activities, the Foundation for Women has also produced various kinds of educational materials, including handbooks, videocassettes and posters, for rural communities. The foundation has also organized exposure trips to red-light districts and meetings with women in prostitution for rural teachers, community leaders and youth leaders. Some teachers reported bringing their pupils from hill tribes with them on the exposure trips or to view the awareness-raising materials, and on the impact of these activities. When agents went to the village to recruit girls to work in Bangkok, some refused on the grounds of what they had seen.

In the Philippines, the objectives of eliminating child labour in hazardous work and of protecting and rehabilitating abused and exploited children are included in the Philippine Plan of Action for Children, which was adopted in 1990. In mid-1994, a national planning workshop sponsored by IPEC brought together representatives from a wide range of government institutions and NGOs, employers' and workers' organizations, as well as local government officials and academics from the capital and rural areas, to develop an Indicative Framework for Action to Attack Child Labour. Victims of child trafficking as well as children trapped in prostitution were identified as priority target groups for action. Filipino NGOs have long been very active in preventive, rehabilitation and advocacy programmes for child victims of commercial sexual exploitation. The programmes operate mainly at three levels: community-based, street- or workplace-based and institution/centre-based.

Many programmes focus on the communities, such as slum areas, military complexes, tourist destinations and poor villages, where children are at high risk of being drawn into prostitution. The underlying rationale for measures to strengthen community involvement is that it is not enough to work with children only; there must be active involvement of parents and families, local officials and authority figures, as well as changes in the economic and social environment, in order to eliminate child prostitution. Some of these community-level programmes are described by Abreu (1991).

For example, a Filipino NGO, Bahay Tuluyan (Alternative Education Programme for the Street Children and Women of the Malate Parish), gives slide presentations and theatrical productions in local communities, to show how paedophiles prey on the young and what kinds of sexual abuse their victims are subjected to. Members of the NGO also meet regularly with parents and children and with district officials to discuss problems of child prostitution, as well as to make families aware of the dangers of sending their daughters to Japan as entertainers. In its community organizing programme, Bahay Tuluyan recruits street children as volunteers for its participatory research team. These street children can gather facts and information more freely from their peers and communities, which Bahay Tuluyan uses to better understand and respond to their problems.

Another Filipino NGO, Caritas Manila, runs a preventive programme in about ten parishes. Its Morning Glory Programme works with children and their parents in slum areas. Children are given back-to-school grants, while the parents are provided with training in marketable skills and help in finding jobs or starting income-generating activities. The programme believes that "the more crucial aspect of prevention is the training of parents who will ultimately keep the children from returning to the streets". Regularly, parents and their children attend value-formation sessions, bible study and prayer sessions. In Pagsanjan, a favourite tourist destination, information dissemination campaigns have been launched to raise the community's awareness of the nature and danger of paedophilia.

Another programme, Bantay-Bata, or the Child Watch Hotline, was developed by the Bureau of Child and Youth Welfare of the Department of Social Welfare and Development. An information and education campaign has used broadcast and print media to generate public awareness and understanding of the plight of abused, abandoned, neglected and exploited children; to encourage the public to advocate, promote and protect the rights of children through involvement in projects or activities; and to ensure the provision of appropriate services and facilities for the affected children. The radio hotline is used by listeners to report cases of abused and exploited children. The radio stations then pass the reports on to the Department of Social Welfare and Development. To ensure that people knew about the hotlines, stickers were conspicuously displayed in theatres, markets, churches and grocery stores (Manahan, 1991, pp. 39-40).

Other programmes operate in the children's milieu – on the streets, in bars, brothels or other "hangouts" of the children. They provide on-site services through outreach activities to meet the children's needs for food, clothing and recreation. Outreach workers also help to put the children in touch with other services, such as those provided at drop-in centres where, for instance, children may stay for a few days so that they can immediately leave violent or hazardous home situations, or can have time to sleep. The outreach workers also help in street organizing and in providing alternative or non-formal education to street children. The non-formal education aims to "help the children understand their life experiences and socio- economic situation – why they are poor – and in this way help them know how to make decisions and to devise ways and means to resolve their poverty" (Abreu, 1991, p. 7).

The centre/institution-based programmes are of different types. Some NGOs operate drop-in centres in the community. The Bahay Tuluyan runs a 24-hour drop-in centre where children can come for emergency assistance, medical aid and a temporary place to relax or sleep. It is not a rehabilitation centre where a child can reside for any length of time. Caritas Manila also has a drop-in centre for children roaming the Ermita-Malate area. The centre offers counselling and tutoring, and provides services for locating the families of the children and then working with them in exploring possibilities of reconciliation.

There are also residential centres which offer rehabilitation services. Most children in the residential centres are referred there by the legal system or by agencies seeking solutions for the children. One such centre is New Beginnings, a home for sexually abused girls and child prostitutes. Administered by professional social workers, the home provides residential care for child victims in a family-type environment where they are taught Christian values, receive education and learn alternative ways to support themselves and their families. Where possible, the cooperation of the natural parents, which is described as "often the most difficult part", is sought. Where the child's reconciliation with the family is not deemed possible or advisable (since the family is in many cases part of the original problem), the programme works for the child's adoption. Another residential project is the Childhood for Children Project set up by the Preda Human Development Centre in Olongapo in 1989. In the residential centre, the children are given access to alternative education. They also mingle with poor urban residents from surrounding communities who come to the centre's workshop to train and work in handicraft production. The centre uses supportive therapists to encourage the child victims to release their feelings of anger, hostility, pain and frustration.

Notes

[1] Ofreneo and Ofreneo (Chapter 4) put the figure at between 50,000 and 60,000. ECPAT (1995) estimates that there are 60,000 child prostitutes, while Bruce (1996, p. 31) estimates 30,000 to 50,000.

[2] The Task Force to End Child Sexploitation in Thailand (TECST) was set up in 1990 by NGO representatives, to coordinate the efforts of various local groups working with women and children, especially in the areas of child prostitution.

[3] In a special issue of the newsletter of the National Commission on Women's Affairs, produced for the Fourth World Congress on Women, the Commission estimated that 15 to 20 per cent of the 150,000 to 200,000 prostitutes in Thailand are children under 18 years of age (National Commission on Women's Affairs, 1995, p. 8).

[4] The Government of the Netherlands, for example, has adopted this position in its policy towards prostitutes. In its submission to the United Nations, the Netherlands stated that "it follows from the right of self-determination ... that he or she is at liberty to act as a prostitute and allow another person to profit from his or her earnings" (United Nations Doc. E/1990/33 as quoted in Reanda, 1992, p. 203).

[5] Post-traumatic stress disorder has been described as a psychological response to an event threatening injury or death that entails: (a) a sense of re-experiencing the trauma and the intrusion of memories or feelings; (b) a pattern of avoidance, a numbing of responsiveness or reduced involvement in the external world; and (c) a persistent state of psychological arousal, reflected by such problems as difficulty with sleeping, startle responses and angry outbursts (Belsey, 1996, p. 23).

[6] Paedophiles are defined as adults with a personality disorder involving a specific and focused sexual interest in pre-pubertal children, while preferential child sex abusers are those individuals whose preferred sexual objects are children who have reached or passed puberty (O'Connell Davidson, 1996, p. 3).

[7] None of the 187 countries which have ratified this Convention as of 31 July 1995 has registered a reservation to this article. Duties of States in connection with this Convention were reinforced in 1992 by the adoption of the United Nations Programme of Action on the Sale of Children, Child Prostitution and Child Pornography, which provides a multidisciplinary framework for establishing measures to implement the rights of the child in this area. The Programme of Action provides, for instance, that special educational measures should be directed towards the general public, especially men and parents; States should establish their own databases and should improve reporting; and international, regional and national information campaigns are required to raise public awareness at all levels. In addition, the Commission on Human Rights decided in early 1995 to draft a protocol to the Convention on the Rights of the Child, on the Sale of Children, Child Prostitution and Pornography. It remains to be seen whether this protocol will actually lead to more effective measures at the national level.

[8] Some countries outside Asia have responded to this problem. For example, a recent amendment to the law in Belgium removed the right to use such an excuse, and shifted the burden of proof to the suspect, who has to demonstrate an "insurmountable error", such as the minor using a false identification card.

[9] This recommendation is based on growing evidence that "missing children" may have been running away from sexual abuse or exploitation, and that they should not be returned to their families without prior investigation of the reasons for their disappearance.

[10] Such girls have been identified as belonging to or living near families of former prostitutes, from broken homes, from families with debts, from families of drug addicts and tribal girls (Boonpala, 1996b, p. 11).

WHITHER THE SEX SECTOR? SOME POLICY CONSIDERATIONS 7

Lin Lean Lim

The economic and social bases of prostitution remain strong. In spite of substantial recent economic progress in Indonesia, Malaysia, the Philippines and Thailand, there has been an increasing supply of and demand for both adult and child prostitutes. Further economic development and increasing prosperity are not likely to lead to a substantial decline in prostitution in the near future. Indeed, the growth of the sex sector is linked to economic development processes. Although the organizational structures and arrangements within the sex sector have been evolving and adapting to changing economic, legal and health circumstances, the total numbers involved in prostitution do not appear to have decreased significantly.

The significance of the sector in local, national and international economies – and the seriousness of the inherent problems – require that policy makers confront the issues and adopt clear and sustainable official positions for dealing with prostitution. To assist policy makers, this chapter reviews the main issues and concerns, and assesses the legal, policy and programme options. The considerations discussed, and the policy and legal stances suggested, are relevant not only for the four Southeast Asian countries but also for other countries concerned with problems related to prostitution.

Socio-economic development and the growth of the sex sector

If absolute poverty was the sole root cause or major context for prostitution, then the sex sector should have declined in Indonesia, Malaysia, the Philippines and Thailand. The four countries have all recorded substantial economic progress in recent years. However, the country studies show that the pattern of development and the types of macroeconomic policies adopted can have much to do with the continued expansion of the sex sector. Although absolute poverty has declined, social safety nets are still largely absent and income inequalities remain wide. Recent macroeconomic policies have emphasized export orientation and industrialization while encouraging rapid urban development; they have contributed either directly or indirectly to the relative neglect of rural areas, reduced agricultural employment, and increased gaps between rural and urban incomes. Rural families remain larger than urban ones, with more mouths to feed. Since social welfare programmes are generally rudimentary or inaccessible to rural families, these families still rely on survival strategies that can include selling children into prostitution.

Even for families above the absolute poverty line, relative poverty is still an important underlying factor, especially with the spread of new forms of consumerism and increasing materialism to remote rural areas. Various field studies and newspaper articles in Thailand report that it is possible to walk into a poor agricultural village in the northeast and often to guess correctly which are the houses of families who have sent their daughters into the sex sector. Houses that have been renovated or extended and have television aerials and new electrical appliances are likely examples, although some of them may have benefitted from remittances from migrant workers in other sectors. The same situation applies in both Thai and Filipino communities where women have gone overseas to work in the entertainment sector. The demonstration effect serves as an incentive for other families to also send their children into the sex sector.

These factors have tended to be powerful, especially because recent macro-economic policies have reduced agricultural employment opportunities while creating mainly low-wage jobs in manufacturing and services for women. Policies that have encouraged rapid urban development and migration from rural areas have also tended to augment the potential supply of commercial sex workers. The Thai study (Chapter 5) argues that economic restructuring emphasizing export-led industrialization has implied the relative neglect of agriculture, and the contrasting patterns of urban and rural development have increased regional inequalities and relative poverty in the north and northeast of Thailand, which are the main sources of supply of workers for the sex industry. Young women leave these areas to look for work in the cities, only to find that remunerative employment opportunities are limited. The Indonesian study (Chapter 2) makes the point that workers in the textile, garment, tobacco and electronics industries, who are 90 per cent female, often do not earn enough money to cover their own living expenses, much less to allow them to remit money to their families. The Malaysian study (Chapter 3) notes that the lure of easy and plentiful money– coupled with new social norms, the relative anonymity and freedom from familial and village surveillance, growing materialism and the increasing cost of living a more conspicuous lifestyle – provides the motivation for some young female migrants to enter prostitution.

All the country studies confirm that earnings from prostitution are often more than from alternative employment opportunities open to women with no or low levels of education. A striking finding from the surveys is that although many women indicated that they would like to move to other jobs, they were conscious of the income loss they would face.

On the demand side, recent economic development has created increasing prosperity and an expanding middle class. This has enhanced the capacity and, very likely, the motivation of men to buy sexual services in a much wider and more sophisticated range of settings. Economic growth over the last three decades has increased the disposable incomes of a growing number of Thai men. While the practice of taking a minor wife continues for some, their increased purchasing power is now more commonly used to obtain sexual services on a temporary basis under enjoyable and luxurious circumstances. This has resulted in the widening of the diversity of settings in which sexual services are offered, and in the establishment of new and more luxurious types of sex establishments.

It has certainly not been the intentional policy of these countries to promote prostitution as an economic activity. Nevertheless, some macroeconomic policies have undoubtedly influenced the growth of the sex sector. For instance, aggressive and successful measures to promote tourism as a major source of foreign exchange earnings have been linked to the expansion of prostitution, including child prostitution. Chapter 4 describes how – with the Philippine tourism promotion drive – the number of "hospitality women" in Manila issued with health cards jumped from 1,700 in the early 1980s to more than 7,000 in 1986. Especially in the late 1970s and 1980s, a common perception among policy makers was that an active entertainment sector, including the availability of commercial sex services, enhanced the attractions of the country as a tourist destination. Chapter 5 notes that every Thai government in recent times has espoused national policies of active support for tourism, and that the implications and strength of such support were evident in the attempts of some government officials to minimize the threat of HIV/AIDS, so as not to scare away the tourists. It cannot be denied that government policies of support for tourism spawned not just sex tours, but also contributed to the growing numbers of women, girls and boys drawn into the sex sector. Numerically, tourists account for only a small proportion of the market; locals account for the bulk of the demand. But foreign clients influence policy makers, some of whom view commercial sex as a major factor in attracting tourists and adopt the stance that prostitution should be ignored or, in some cases, supported, but not banned. The tourist industry itself has very substantial vested interests, since it is a major earner of foreign exchange and involves enormous investments in hotels, resorts, entertainment and transport. In the past few years, however, adverse publicity, especially in the international media, has encouraged these countries to try to improve their tourism image so that they are not seen merely as sex destinations.

The government policy of earning foreign exchange through the export of labour has also encouraged overseas prostitution. While it has not been the deliberate policy of the Thai or Philippine governments to send their women into prostitution in other countries, the procedures, networks and institutional structures, including the employment agencies, that have been set up to facilitate the legal flow of contract migrant labour have directly or indirectly facilitated the migration of women who have gone into or been forced into prostitution in the receiving countries. The Philippines, for instance, has training and orientation programmes for women going into the "entertainment industry" in Japan, Europe and elsewhere. The Philippines and Thailand have also allowed a system of "mail order brides". Indonesia sends its women overseas for employment, but almost exclusively into domestic service. Although these three countries have imposed various regulations and restrictions on recruitment agents and foreign employers – as well as improving awareness-raising and orientation programmes – ineffective enforcement has meant that even women going overseas for domestic service are often tricked or coerced into prostitution and are victims of commercial sexual exploitation. On a brighter note, however, macro-economic policies of outward orientation and emphasis on international trade may have helped to motivate these countries to take action against the more abusive aspects of the commercial sex sector, especially child prostitution. For example, one of the factors which prompted Thailand's announcement in 1992 of its commitment to eradicate child prostitution was the decision of the United States government to put Thailand on a watch list for possible revocation of trade concessions, because of the use of forced child labour.

The future of the sex sector

Whether economic development and increasing prosperity in these countries can reduce prostitution largely depends on the market for sexual services. While improved economic conditions may yield employment alternatives for those likely to be drawn into the sector, they may also contribute to an increase in demand for commercial sex.

On the supply side, in terms of the availability of a pool of young women prepared, or under some circumstances forced, to engage in prostitution, there is a demographic consideration. Jones et al. (1995) point out that the number of Indonesian women aged between 15 and 24 years will soon cease its rapid growth. After increasing by 23 per cent between 1985 and 1995, the growth over the 20 years following 1995 will be less than 9 per cent. The declining proportion of young people looking for work is also a factor in the other Southeast Asian countries, which have experienced falling population growth rates (especially Thailand, where the birth rates have declined the most rapidly). With rising levels of education in all these countries, the number of poorly educated young women within the 15 to 24 age group should also decline drastically. The increasingly better-educated young job-seekers should have access to better work prospects as the economies continue to grow and diversify. Therefore, the pressure on women and children to enter prostitution as a means of escaping absolute poverty should lessen.

However, substantial numbers of people in the population will remain relatively poor, materialism and consumerism will continue to spread, and the attractive earnings in many parts of the sex sector will continue to provide a strong incentive to take up prostitution. Although there is certainly a universally recognized tendency for the uneducated and poorly educated to be over-represented in the ranks of the commercial sex workers, reasonably high levels of education do not prevent women from entering the sex sector. In the Philippines, over 60 per cent of the prostitutes interviewed had completed their secondary education. The push of absolute poverty may lessen over time, but the pull of promises of easy affluence may grow with economic prosperity.

Furthermore, the sex sector is a big money-making business for many vested interests. This economic base is not easy to dismantle; the powerful commercial and sometimes political as well as criminal elements involved will not willingly give up this lucrative line of business. They are likely to attempt to adapt and adjust rather than to abandon their operations. The Malaysian study reports that operators in the sex sector have been making increasing use of sophisticated communications technology to avoid police raids. Although the police have been intensifying their efforts, the efficacy of the raids has been declining. The Thai study notes that although the official figures show a fall in the number of registered commercial sex workers after 1990, they do not reflect a shrinking sex sector, merely a shift from direct to indirect and less easily detected prostitution.

On the demand side, poverty has never stopped men from paying for sexual services but growing prosperity certainly increases the capacity to buy sexual services. In some contexts, such purchases are associated with the ability to enjoy an improved or modern lifestyle. More significantly, customers have become more discriminating about the settings in which sexual services are purchased. Therefore, it is likely that, among the wide range of settings in which the sex sector operates, the balance will tend to tip away from the "basic" settings, and towards more luxurious and discreet environments. For example, the urban sex sectors in Malaysia and Thailand, which are at higher levels of development than the other two countries, and which have been experiencing record rates of economic growth, have moved to private members clubs and messes, the extensive use of mobile telephones to arrange sexual transactions and indirect forms of prostitution, such as at golf courses. In Indonesia and the Philippines, however, brothels and massage parlours are still very much the norm.

However, whether the overall supply and demand for commercial sex will increase or decrease will, in the final analysis, be strongly influenced by social norms and government policy. The potential role of government policy should not be underestimated.

In looking at social norms, the previous chapters suggest that religion has so far not been a dominant influence in either reducing the supply of or demand for prostitutes. Recent fundamentalist religious movements have, however, put pressure on the government authorities to step up raids and preventive checks. Whether religious movements strongly opposed to commercial sex gain in further influence remains to be seen.

There are some signs of positive changes in social norms which are likely to be associated with declining prostitution. There is a growing awareness of gender equality issues and the human rights of women, spurred to a large extent by the activities related to the build-up to and the follow-up on the Fourth World Conference on Women in 1995. High-profile campaigns against child labour have stirred the social conscience about the obligations of parents and other adults towards children. In all four countries, the women's movement has been in the forefront of efforts to end both the commercial sexual exploitation of women and children and sex tourism; their continued efforts should bear fruit. In Thailand, for example, the National Commission on Women's Affairs spearheaded the adoption of the new Prostitution Prevention and Suppression Act. The Philippine Development Plan for Women 1989-1992 and the Philippine Plan for Gender-Responsive Development 1995-2025 specifically address the issue of prostitution. Rising educational levels may also slowly change patriarchal views.

An obvious influence on the future of the sex sector is the threat of HIV/AIDS. The studies note that there have been shifts towards a demand for younger and younger children, in the belief that they are not likely to be infected with the disease. But there are also several reports of declining numbers of customers, because many have been scared off. The surveys show that employers/owners are seriously concerned about the business impact of the disease. For example, the number of Malaysian men going to Hat Yai in the south of Thailand for commercial sex appears to have dropped sharply since the beginning of the AIDS scare. Whether the fear of contracting the disease has actually reduced the supply of workers is not evident, but it has clearly prompted changes in the organization of the sex sector. The Thai survey found that brothel owners in a rural area had taken a concerted stand to reject customers who refused to use condoms. In bars and other entertainment areas, the owners make available large supplies of condoms (e.g. in glass jars on bar counters). There has also been much greater attention given to regular health checks, by the health authorities, the employers and the prostitutes themselves. Very importantly, the threat of the spread of HIV/AIDS through commercial sex has prompted public debate and calls for more effective regulation and reform of the sex sector, as well as galvanizing efforts to review existing legislation and programmes.

Adopting a policy stance on the sex sector

Given the magnitude and significance of the sex sector and the urgency of related problems, such as the threat of HIV/AIDS and the victimization of children, it is crucial that legislators and policy makers adopt a clear position on prostitution, as the basis for the review and formulation of effective legal, policy and programme measures. A major hurdle, to date, is that policy makers have shied away from directly dealing with prostitution as an economic sector. Coherent and effective government policies and programmes targeting prostitution are lacking. To a large extent this is due to ambivalent, inconsistent or contradictory perceptions and approaches. To help policy makers to confront the challenges facing them, this section summarizes some main considerations that could provide the basis of a coherent or more definitive position on prostitution.

- First, and crucially, in view of the differences between child prostitution and adult prostitution, separate measures for each, rather than a single or unified policy stance, are recommended. Although both adult and child prostitution are part of the commercial sex sector and have strong economic and social founda- tions, the position on child prostitution is unequivocal, whereas there could be different considerations for adult prostitution. Children are victims of prosti- tution, whereas adults could choose sex work as an occupation. International conventions all treat child prostitution as an unacceptable form of forced labour; the goal is its total elimination. In the case of adults, the position is less obvious because it is possible to make a distinction between enforced and voluntary prostitution.

- Child prostitution should be treated as a much more serious problem than adult prostitution. Because of their age and immaturity (not only physiological but also social, psychological and cognitive), children are clearly much more vulnerable and helpless against the established structures and vested interests in the sex sector, and much more likely to be victims of debt bondage, trafficking, physical violence or torture. Commercial sexual exploitation is such a serious form of violence against children that there are lifelong and life-threatening consequences. There are also chain effects, with sexual abuse leading to other forms of abuse, such as drug abuse, and cumulative negative consequences. The health effects are more serious on children than adults, and, in fact, child prostitutes may pose a greater danger to public health than adult prostitutes.

- Successful efforts to eliminate child prostitution would reduce the problem of adult prostitution. Many adult prostitutes actually enter the sex sector when they are still children. Moreover, their continued involvement in commercial sex tends to compound rather than minimize the trauma and problems they encounter as children.

- A realistic and feasible approach would be to take into account the heterogeneity and complexity of the sex sector and to address the needs of different groups of prostitutes accordingly. Those who enter the sex sector as adults do so for a range of reasons. Some freely choose sex work as an expression of sexual liberation, or as an economically rational decision based on income potentials, costs involved and available alternatives. Others are pressured by poverty and dire economic circumstances. Still others are subject to overt coercion from third parties, in the form of deception and/or physical violence or threats. At the same time, a range of circumstances exists among those working in the sex sector. In part depending on the methods of entry, the terms and conditions of work can differ greatly among the prostitutes. The national surveys confirm that earnings could be much higher than from available alternatives and, at the upper end of the market, terms and conditions of work could be relatively very good. On the other hand, there are prostitutes working under conditions akin to bondage or slavery or who are subject to severe exploitation and abuse.

- For those adult individuals who freely choose sex work, the policy concerns should focus on improving their working conditions and social protection, and on ensuring that they are entitled to the same labour rights and benefits as other workers. For those who have been subject to force, deception or violence, the priority should be their rescue, rehabilitation and reintegration into society. In between these two ends of the spectrum, measures should aim at prevention, development and amelioration. These measures should try to ensure that potential prostitutes, their families and communities are more aware of the pros and cons of the sex sector so that they are less likely to be deceived, that those in the sector have proper working conditions and labour rights, and that those who wish to leave the sector have access to social supports and rehabilitation facilities and, importantly, the skills and means to take up alternative employment opportunities.

- Those developing policies focusing on the terms and conditions of work in the sex sector should take into account some important facts about prostitutes' realities. For instance, the higher incomes earned are supposed to offer a premium to make up for the stigma, health risks and other unpleasant aspects of the occupation. Further, prostitution is one of the most alienated forms of labour; the surveys show that women worked "with a heavy heart", "felt forced" or were "conscience-stricken" and had negative self-identities. A significant proportion claimed they wanted to leave sex work if they could.

- The non-moralistic view is that individual prostitutes should not be treated as criminals, nor punished for making a living. Such a view recognizes that prostitutes take up the profession mainly for poverty-related reasons or because they have been coerced. It also recognizes that prostitutes do not coerce or exploit clients. However, the stance does not mean at all that the criminal elements involved in the sector should be ignored. Rather, the approach should be to distinguish between the individual prostitute and the organizational structures and relations within the sector, and to impose criminal sanctions, not on the prostitutes, but on those who traffic in, procure, exploit or abuse prostitutes. Attention should especially be given to the most vulnerable workers in need of special protection, such as the very young, those who are illegal international migrants and the "enslaved".

- Any meaningful approach to the sex sector cannot focus only on individual prostitutes. An effective response to the issues of the sex sector requires measures directed at the economic and social bases. A stance focusing on individual prostitutes tends to emphasize moralistic and human rights concerns, which are undoubtedly important, but which will not have a major impact on changing or reducing the sector. The stark reality is that the sex sector is a "big business" that is well entrenched in national economies and the international economy, with highly organized institutional structures, widespread linkages with many other types of legitimate economic activities, networks of dependencies involving significant parts of the population, and powerful vested interests. Prostitution is also deeply rooted in a double standard of morality for men and women, as well as in a sense of gratitude or obligation that children feel they owe their parents. These economic and social foundations are not easy to dismantle.

- Given that the economic and social foundations are not easy to change, the sex sector is not going to disappear in the foreseeable future. Especially in view of its size and significance, the official stance cannot be one of neglect or non-recognition. Currently, in most countries, the sex sector is not recognized as an economic sector in official statistics, development plans or government budgets. It is worth considering, for example, the possibility that official recognition of the sector, including maintaining records about it, would be extremely useful for assessing the health impacts of the activities associated with the sector, for determining the scope and magnitude of labour market policies needed to deal with workers in the sector, and for extending the taxation net to cover many of the lucrative activities connected with it.

- It is also important that policy makers recognize that macroeconomic policies and a country's pattern and pace of development can have much to do with the growth of the sex sector. The indirect effects of development policies can significantly influence the supply of and demand for commercial sex workers. Some policies, especially those related to the promotion of tourism and the export of female labour for overseas employment, can be directly linked to the increase in prostitution. In evaluating the impact of macroeconomic policies, it is thus crucial not to neglect the consequences for the sex sector.
- The health dimensions of the sex sector are too serious and urgent to ignore. Although all governments are aware of the seriousness of the HIV/AIDS threat, many state agencies still keep their distance from the sex sector, partly because of concern over objections from religious groups, or because they have not developed effective measures to address and contain the problems. Any health programme targeting the sex sector cannot, however, cover only the prostitutes. Measures should also be directed towards clients, especially since the chain of transmission from the sex sector to the population at large involves clients who also have unprotected sex with their spouses or others.

Legal approaches to the sex sector and the enforcement of legislation

If the policy stance recognizes the scale and economic significance of the sex sector, a legal approach based on total prohibition would not be realistic or truly enforceable. A strong prohibitionist approach would mean banning the sector and criminalizing all those involved. As discussed above, criminalizing prostitutes for sex work *per se* would be highly unfair. In most cases individual prostitutes are themselves subject to or victims of highly organized institutional structures and arrangements. Criminalization may punish the prostitutes, but not necessarily stop them from such work, especially if there are no viable alternatives. Should sex work be declared illegal, prostitutes may be discouraged from openly seeking safer sex education and health services, thereby merely exacerbating the health threats both to themselves and the larger population. Any attempt to ban the sector should consider that, to date, operators have been able to circumvent stricter law enforcement through the use of modern communications technology. Where a ban serves only to drive the sector underground, the danger is that those most in need of protection from exploitation and abuse would be totally marginalized.

It should be strongly emphasized that the proposal that there should be decriminalization of prostitutes does not at all imply that decriminalization should also apply to the institutions of the sex sector that thrive on the coercion, exploitation or abuse of women and children. As a legal approach, decriminalization should involve: (a) reform or review of laws and regulations that sanction, penalize or discriminate against sex workers on the basis of their work; (b) recognition of prostitution as a legal occupation, so that individuals working in the sector have access to the same labour rights and social protection as other workers; (c) special measures to protect the most vulnerable in the sex sector; (d) tightened and stricter enforcement of criminal sanctions against those trafficking in, exploiting or abusing prostitutes; and (e) penal provisions against corrupt enforcement authorities and clients of under-age prostitutes.

It is also critical that a decriminalization approach, to be effective, should deal not only with the manifestations but also with the fundamental causes of prostitution. This means that the legal approach has to be part and parcel of more comprehensive programmes which address the economic and social bases of the sex sector and which target both those who are already in the sector and those at risk of being drawn into it.

The third legal approach – legalization through registration and regulation of the sex sector, often including compulsory health checks – is the one that has been commonly adopted. While both the decriminalization and the "regulationist" systems involve recognition of the legal status of commercial sex workers, they differ in so far as the latter system imposes greater restrictions and rules. Under a regulationist system, both sex establishments and sex workers are subject to a compulsory system of registration and health checks, and, significantly, are usually confined to specifically designated geographical areas or red-light districts. This approach undoubtedly has practical benefits, especially for enforcement authorities. It provides a legal framework for the regulation of a sector that is economically significant but has inherent problems, and for the regulation of the labour rights of sex workers. A regulated commercial sex sector would also bring it within the taxation net of the economy. In deciding whether to adopt a regulationist approach, policy makers should take into account the objections of prostitutes' rights groups, that compulsory registration and health checks or segregation in specially designated red-light districts discriminates against and stigmatizes the sex workers. It is also important to ensure that all sex workers are registered. To the extent that some are not registered, the aim of compulsory health checks or of protecting vulnerable workers would be thwarted.

Whether decriminalization or legalization would lead to an increase or decrease in the supply of and demand for sex workers is obviously an important consideration. If currently the incentive for a sex worker to take on a job that carries a social stigma is the significant wage differential between the sex sector and the rest of the economy, the recognition of prostitution as another occupational category may reduce the wage differential, and hence the incentive to become a sex worker. Of course, the other side of the argument is that, although earnings may no longer provide a premium, those who previously refrained because of the social stigma may enter the sector after the change and increase the numbers working there. On the demand side, too, those who previously refrained because of the illegality of the activity may be tempted to indulge.

Regarding the specific issue of the child victims of prostitution, the international Conventions and Recommendations described in Chapter 6 provide a comprehensive legal framework. Bringing national legislation in line with these international instruments and enhancing the effectiveness of national laws dealing with the commercial sexual exploitation of children involves numerous considerations. A country's general laws to protect children (which almost all countries have, in accordance with the United Nations Convention on the Rights of the Child) may not adequately deal with the commercial sexual exploitation of children. Where the problem of the child victims of prostitution is serious, it would be more effective to formulate specific laws covering the various aspects of the commercial sexual exploitation of children. Legal provisions dealing with prostitution in general should distinguish between adults and minors, and should impose heavier penalties the younger the victim of child prostitution. By international definition, children under the age of 18 years should be dealt with as "victims" of prostitution engaged in an intolerable form of forced labour. It is crucial to ensure that the legislation covers not only girls but boys (for instance, Malaysia's Women's and Girls' Protection Act needs to be revised accordingly). It is important to eliminate inconsistencies between the legal ages of consent to sexual relations, for prostitution and for marriage.

Although laws dealing with adult prostitution often do not sanction clients, legislation dealing with child prostitution should cover penalties against clients, even where there has been "consent" of the child. Legislation should have clear provisions for penalizing not only clients, pimps and procurers, but others as well. To offer effective protection to children, it is important that their parents, guardians and caretakers, as well as law-enforcement agents should also be held responsible. (Thailand's new Prostitution Prevention and Suppression Act, for example, has provisions that parents or guardians found guilty of any offence under the Act can have their guardianship revoked. It also imposes heavy fines and jail sentences on civil servants found guilty of any offence under the Act.) Because of the young age and immaturity of the child victims of prostitution, the legal procedures for obtaining evidence from a child should be simplified and should protect the child.

Since sex tourism tends to be an important source of commercial sexual exploitation of children, there should be provisions for extraterritorial application of laws, so that perpetrators from other countries can be brought to justice (several countries have now extended their criminal jurisdiction to cover the criminal acts of their citizens committed against children in other countries). With international trafficking an important aspect of the problem of commercial sexual exploitation of children, it is also important to review immigration laws, to ensure that children and others who are the victims of trafficking are not dealt with as criminal aliens, but are instead given the necessary protection and assistance to return to their home countries. It may also be necessary to look more carefully at adoption laws, since intermediaries and paedophiles sometimes "adopt" children from poor families for commercial sexual exploitation purposes.

Effective enforcement of legislation is a major problem. The difficulties of law enforcement relating to adult prostitution are also relevant in the case of child prostitutes. There are additional problems specific to the extension of protection to children. Some suggestions for the improvement of enforcement follow.

* Inconsistent attitudes on the part of governments towards the sex sector are a very important reason for poor enforcement and explain why corruption is able to

persist. The country chapters provide various examples of conflicting laws and regulations. A consistent policy stance on the sex sector is critical.

- Political will and commitment are also crucial. Initiating an active campaign against child prostitution is a major and courageous move, since it involves an admission that children are being abused and exploited in the country.

- Low pay, poor selection processes and insufficient training of law enforcers concerning human rights and especially children's rights often result in corruption and weak law enforcement (Muntarbhorn, 1996b, p. 30). Providing better incentives, improving training and raising awareness among law enforcers is recommended. In countries where the problems related to prostitution in general – or to child prostitution in particular – are especially serious, it may be effective to set up a special task force within the police and to have specially trained officers who liaise closely with Interpol.

- Enforcement should not be the responsibility of the police or law enforcers alone. Efforts should be made to set up other enforcement mechanisms, including a task force of relevant government officials from the police, immigration authorities and social welfare, education and health departments, in order to coordinate efforts for dealing in a comprehensive manner with the commercial sexual exploitation of children. Effective law enforcement is a social responsibility that requires local communities to play their own "watchdog" role. Programmes to train village and community leaders, teachers, doctors, nurses and religious leaders to set up community-watch groups, to carry out surveillance, to report crimes against children and to seek assistance for children whom they consider to be at a high risk of being drawn into the sex sector have proven to be effective.

- Enforcement of legislation should be well coordinated with other efforts to ensure that there are no unanticipated or adverse consequences. Chapter 4 describes how police crackdowns on prostitution in Manila were not coordinated with the activities of the Department of Health or NGOs, making it impossible to trace those who went underground or moved to other areas, as well as rendering STD and HIV/AIDS monitoring much more difficult. Coordination is also especially important between the police, the social welfare authorities and relevant NGOs, so that children who are rescued are given the proper assistance for recovery and reintegration.

- Since child prostitution involves transnational dimensions, cooperation and coordination at the international level or on a bilateral basis is needed. Cooperation and coordination between law enforcement agencies can be effective. The system whereby police liaison officers are placed by states in countries to which their nationals travel in large numbers is one example. There are also very successful examples of cooperation between NGOs in different countries, of measures taken by international trade union movements, and of initiatives by the business community, especially those involved in the tourist industry. High-profile media coverage – at both national and international levels – of the problems of child sex prostitution and paedophilia also helps to galvanize action by various organizations and governments.

Social programmes targeting the sex sector

To be effective, law enforcement needs to be supplemented with a range of social policies and programmes. A multi-pronged approach that combines preventive measures, health services, recovery and reintegration or rehabilitation measures and development measures is necessary, to address both the root causes and the manifestations of prostitution, especially child prostitution. Social programmes should not be solely the responsibility of the government. They tend to be most effective when they combine and coordinate the efforts of government agencies, NGOs, the private sector and the media, and when they are implemented in contexts of broad political and social support as well as public awareness and concern about the issues.

The main types of programmes address health, "rehabilitation" and prevention.

- Health programmes should cover the provision of information and advice on health risks and preventive measures as well as health checks and treatment for sex workers. Where health systems are implemented through a system of compulsory registration and monitoring, there would be a measure of control over the health status of the prostitutes, but this would be effective only if all sex workers were covered and if there were also measures covering the customers.
- Since the term "rehabilitation" could imply that those in need of such programmes have been guilty of some wrongdoing, the terms "recovery" and "reintegration" are preferred, especially when referring to measures to assist the child victims of prostitution. Such programmes can be community-based or centre/institution-based (including residential programmes).
- To reduce the number of women and children at risk of being drawn into the sex sector, preventive programmes normally cover education, awareness-raising and advocacy. There should also be developmental efforts to give women and children and their families alternative sources of income. The targets of educational and sensitization programmes should be poor families and the women and children at risk, law enforcers and government officials, community leaders, and other para-professionals, such as teachers and religious leaders. Developmental efforts need to target not only the women and children at risk but also their families and communities. The task is a difficult one, requiring sustained efforts to tackle root causes related to poverty, family breakdowns, socio-cultural traditions and other factors.

No comprehensive or systematic assessment of the effectiveness of the different programmes targeting commercial sex workers, especially those who are under age, has been conducted. Nevertheless, various reviews and programme evaluations suggest some general conclusions about their efficacy.

- Strong political commitment as well as close cooperation and coordination among agencies are essential to carry out effective, multidisciplinary and coordinated action that leads to social alliances against commercial sexual exploitation, especially of children. More successful alliances involve government agencies, NGOs, women, youth and child groups, professional organizations, the business community and the media. The multifaceted nature of the factors underlying prostitution and the consequences of commercial sexual exploitation, especially of children, mean that measures are needed to address not only the children, but also the various vested interests (including parents, clients and intermediaries), those responsible either directly or indirectly for law enforcement, and the wider community and society.

- The overall capacity of the various programmes has tended to be very small compared to the potential target groups. This is mainly due to the limited public funds that are normally allocated to such programmes. In the case of health programmes, this may be due to government concerns over objections from religious groups. Especially in view of the threat of HIV/AIDS, the need for more comprehensive health programmes covering both prostitutes and clients should be obvious.

- Preventive programmes are more important than rehabilitation programmes, especially in the case of children (but the scope and magnitude of the sex sector normally means that attention has to be given to both prevention and rehabilitation). Effective programmes combine, for instance, basic education for boys and girls (including various types of support to enable poor children to go to school and to keep them in school), income-generating activities for poor parents to help relieve the economic pressures that push them into sending their children into the sex sector, and various types of awareness-raising aimed at the community and law enforcers. The experience of social workers in the Philippines and Thailand clearly demonstrates that there is often no "veil of ignorance" on the part of parents. Unless programmes address the economic reasons why parents allow or encourage their children to go into prostitution, prevention cannot be effective.

- At the local level, active community participation, such as through community-watch programmes to protect children, is important. Active community participation is more likely to ensure not only concerted action but also, and more importantly, changes in social attitudes and the creation of "child-centred caring environments" (Bruce, 1996). There are various examples of successful community-watch programmes where, especially with the help of the local media, concerned individual citizens have been encouraged to report cases of child abuse or of children or families at risk, and where action has been taken through cooperation between government and non-governmental organizations.

- Various reviews have emphasized the important role of para-professionals – village leaders, religious leaders and teachers, who have first-hand knowledge or a store of traditional knowledge and who have access to people in the community – in establishing links between organized programmes and the community. The communities tend to have more confidence and faith in their own members than in outsiders, no matter how well-intentioned the outsiders may be.

- Prostitutes, and child victims of prostitution themselves, can play an important role in terms of reaching out to families and children at risk, or working with victims of commercial sexual exploitation. Through their own first-hand experience, they can more starkly demonstrate the problems and realities; they can also reduce the reticence of people who may be wary of outsiders. Ex-prostitutes and ex-victims of child prostitution can become important role models for others in the process of rehabilitation and reintegration into society.

- While preventive (and also rehabilitation) programmes aim to work simultaneously with the family and the child at risk or the child victim, it must be recognized that sometimes families are the cause of the problem. Efforts to improve family ties, to help parents provide for the psycho-social needs of the child and to help in reintegration of the child into the family are all important, but where the return of the child to the family is judged to be inadvisable, measures including fostering and adoption have been tried.

- The rehabilitation impact of encouraging or enabling the women and girls to take up alternative employment is often questionable. Rehabilitation is mainly successful among those women who have voluntarily sought to get out of the sector and those rescued from forced prostitution. The country surveys indicate that most prostitutes were motivated by strong economic factors, and earned more in the sex sector than in previous or alternative jobs. Training in alternative job skills is an important part of rehabilitation programmes, especially in giving commercial sex workers a stronger sense of choice in whether they continue to do sex work or find other occupations. But providing basic vocational skills in home economics and handicrafts, or grooming the women to be good housewives, is unlikely to provide them with access to economically viable alternatives. Given the economic realities, viable job retraining has to be accompanied by effective job development to create alternatives. Where alternative jobs pay less than subsistence wages, are boring or demeaning, the women are not likely to go into them. Alternative jobs could attempt to make use of the skills that the women possess, such as skills in negotiating with or pleasing others, and entertainment skills.

- For both adult and child prostitutes, rehabilitation programmes have to offer more than just educational and employment opportunities. In order to be successful in helping the women and children to take up alternative lifestyles, rehabilitation programmes also need to focus on measures to build up participants' self-esteem and dignity, and to discover or rediscover their self-worth and confidence. The national surveys found that most prostitutes had poor self-images. In the case of children, "sex-role counselling for youthful prostitutes is more effective than job training, employment or institutionalization. No matter what jobs, money or educational opportunities are made available, young people are unable to change their response patterns if they continue to view themselves as 'whores and faggots'." (ILO/IPEC, n.d.) Experienced programme workers report that the first few months of rehabilitation tend to be the most difficult, because the sex workers have been cut off from their income source, they cannot think clearly in terms of a future, and they have not as yet learnt to see themselves as worthy human beings.

- Legal aid and counselling should be part of rehabilitation programmes. The women and children may need assistance in dealing with the police, with taking cases against pimps or employers, and with domestic problems, including abusive spouses, demanding parents, and so on, if they are successfully to leave prostitution.
- Rehabilitation programmes that are linked to law enforcement or that involve residential stays for a specified period of time tend to stigmatize those attending the programmes, who generally dislike the programmes' involuntary nature. For example, the Thai and Malaysian studies indicated that many commercial sex workers view the rehabilitation programmes with apprehension, because of the fear of being institutionalized for a length of time and the associated stigma.
- Assessments have been made of residential or institutionalized programmes for child victims of prostitution, as compared to community-based programmes, outreach approaches or drop-in centres. Field workers speak of children who abuse the system of drop-in centres because they never decide to make a clean break with the streets or with the prostitution milieu. There are also children who move from one drop-in centre to another to make use of the facilities, but not to change their way of life. The institutionalized approach has also been linked to more serious weaknesses. The children themselves, like adult women, often resent residential rehabilitation or care because of the mandatory nature of stay, and the rules or prohibitive measures that have to be observed. The centres are also costly to maintain and cater for relatively few children. More importantly, an institutionalized approach may be limiting and ineffective when the children are cut off from community, family or school support. The importance of community and family involvement is emphasized in most evaluations. Instead of attempting to recreate community or family structures in an institutional setting, it may be more effective to encourage communities, families and schools to recognize and deal with the problems of children as an integral part of their activities. Ideally, institutional care should be combined with community-based services and family support.
- Monitoring, follow-up and aftercare of those who have left the rehabilitation programmes is crucial in order to ensure that they do not return to their old occupation. Support services at the community level can assist in resocialization. Surveys by the International Catholic Child Bureau found that about a quarter, sometimes more, of the children passing through projects returned to prostitution after months or even years in rehabilitation or care (Bruce, 1996, p. 36). Recovery and reintegration will never be complete unless efforts are made to monitor and follow up on the children to ensure, for example, that when they are returned to their families, they are not sold back into prostitution or subjected to pressure from pimps. However, aftercare services are often the weakest part of the programmes. Inadequate funding, limited numbers of social workers in the community and the mobility of families in slum areas help to explain why many programmes or projects are unable to keep track of the women and children, or to assist them once they leave rehabilitation centres.

A multi-pronged approach – in line with the wisdom of international conventions and experience, and emphasizing a clear legal stance and effective law enforcement – is necessary to deal with the many issues involved in the sex sector. Such an approach must recognize the indirect effects of macroeconomic policies. Social programmes must address both the root causes and the consequences of prostitution. All social partners must be involved at community, national and international levels. Clearly, political and social will and commitment are crucial.

BIBLIOGRAPHY

Abdul Hadi bin Zakaria. 1975. *Some patterns of high class prostitution in Kuala Lumpur and Petaling Jaya.* Master of Arts dissertation, University of Malaya, Kuala Lumpur.

—. 1980. *Pelacur dan pelacuran di Malaysia* (Prostitutes and prostitution in Malaysia) (Kuala Lumpur, Utusan Publications).

—. 1987. "Pelacuran di kalangan wanita dan gadis" (Prostitution among women and girls), *Jurnal Antropologi dan Sosiologi* (Kuala Lumpur), Vol. 15, pp. 41-62.

—. 1990. "The reactions of teenage prostitutes towards their detention in rehabilitation centres in Malaysia", *Asian Profile* (Hong Kong), Vol. 18, pp .427-440.

Abreu, L.M. 1991. *Overview of prostitution in the ESCAP region and review of efforts to promote community awareness for its prevention in the Philippines.* Paper prepared for the ESCAP Workshop on the Promotion of Community Awareness for the Prevention of Prostitution in the ESCAP Region, Lampang, Thailand, 20-27 August.

Ahlburg, D.; E.R. Jensen; A.E. Perez. 1997. "Determinants of extramarital sex in the Philippines", *Health Transition Review* (Canberra), supplement to Vol. 7, pp. 467-479.

Andaya, B.W.; L.Y. Andaya. 1982. *A history of Malaysia* (London, Macmillan).

Anoneuvo, C. 1987. "Prostitution in the Philippines", in National Council of Churches in the Philippines, *Cast the first stone* (Quezon City, National Council of Churches).

Arasaratnam, S. 1979. *Indians in Malaysia and Singapore* (Kuala Lumpur, Oxford University Press).

Asia Watch and the Women's Rights Project. 1993. *A modern form of slavery: Trafficking of Burmese women and girls into brothels in Thailand* (New York and London, Human Rights Watch).

Azizah, K.; et al. 1987. "Social amenities and the quality of life in squatter areas of Kuala Lumpur: Some preliminary findings", in Population Studies Unit, *Population and the quality of life in Malaysia* (Kuala Lumpur, Population Studies Unit, Faculty of Economics and Administration, University of Malaya).

—. 1993. *Women's rights as human rights.* Paper presented at the Human Rights Conference on the Trafficking of Asian Women, Ateneo de Manila University, Quezon City, 2 April.

Belsey, M. 1996. *Commercial sexual exploitation of children: The health and psychosocial dimensions.* Paper submitted by the World Health Organization for the World Congress against the Commercial Sexual Exploitation of Children, Stockholm, Sweden, 27-31 August.

Bhatiasevi, A. 1997. "Health Ministry denies estimate of two million sex workers", *Bangkok Post*, 29 July, p. 4.

Bindman, J. 1997. *Redefining prostitution as sex work on the international agenda* (London, Anti-Slavery International and Network of Sex Work Projects).

Blanc-Szanton, M.C. 1990. "Gender and inter-generational resource allocation among Thai and Sino-Thai households", in L. Dube (ed.), *Structures and strategies: Women, work and family* (New Delhi, Sage).

Boonpala, P. 1996a. "The role of the International Labor Organization", in US Department of Labor, Bureau of International Labor Affairs, *Forced labor: The prostitution of children* (Washington, DC, United States Department of Labor, Bureau of International Labor Affairs).

—. 1996b. *Strategy and action against the commercial sexual exploitation of children.* Paper prepared for the World Congress against the Commercial Sexual Exploitation of Children, Stockholm, Sweden, 27-31 August.

Brinkmann, U. 1991. *The AIDS epidemic in Thailand* (Boston, Massachusetts, Harvard University School of Public Health).

Bruce, F. 1996. *Children and prostitution: "Don't give up on me..."* (Geneva, International Catholic Child Bureau).

Buklod Centre. 1992. *Hospitality: What price?* (Olongapo City, Arbee Printhouse).

Bureau of Women and Minors. 1980. *A study of the daily and monthly cash earnings of women workers in night clubs, saunas, cocktail lounges, discos/beer houses, etc.* (Manila, Department of Labour and Employment).

Calalang L.M. 1985. *Situation of young women in prostitution-related occupations in the Philippines* (Manila, Department of Labour and Employment, Bureau of Women and Minors).

Camagay, M.L.T. 1988. "Prostitution in 19th century Manila", *Philippine Studies* (Manila), Vol. 36, pp. 241-245.

Chan, P. 1983. "The political economy of urban squatting in metropolitan Kuala Lumpur", *Contemporary Southeast Asia* (Singapore), Vol. 4, pp. 486-508.

Chong, K.S. 1991. *Overview of prostitution in the ESCAP region and review of efforts to promote community awareness for its prevention: Malaysia.* Paper presented at the ESCAP Workshop on the Promotion of Community Awareness for the Prevention of Prostitution in the ESCAP Region, Lampang, Thailand, 20-27 August.

Cohen E. 1988. "Tourism and AIDS in Thailand", *Annals of Tourism Research* (Elmsford, New York), Vol. 15.

Cueto, D.S. 1997. "375,000 Filipino women, kids into prostitution, says UNICEF", *Philippine Daily Inquirer* (Manila), 26 July.

D'Cunha J. 1992. "Prostitution laws: Ideological dimensions and enforcement practices", *Economic and Political Weekly* (Bombay), 25 April.

De Dios, A.J. 1988. *Military prostitution in the Philippines*, mimeograph (Manila).

—. 1990. "The case of Japayuki-san and the Hanayome-san", in M. Evasco, A.J. De Dios and F. Caagusan (eds.), *Women's springbook: Readings on women and society* (Quezon City, Women's Resource and Research Centre and Kalayaan).

—. 1991. *Struggle against sexual exploitation and prostitution: A Philippine perspective*, mimeograph (Manila).

Dery, L.C. 1991. "Prostitution in colonial Manila", *Philippine Studies* (Manila), Vol. 39, pp. 475-489.

Dick, H. 1993. "The economic role of Surabaya", in H. Dick, J.J. Fox and J. Mackie (eds.), *Balanced development: East Java in the New Order* (Singapore, Oxford University Press).

Economic and Social Commission for Asia and the Pacific (ESCAP). 1991. *Indonesia.* Background paper prepared for the Workshop on the Promotion of Community Awareness for the Prevention of Prostitution in the ESCAP Region, Lampang, Thailand, 20-27 August.

Encyclopaedie van Nederlandsch-Indie. 1902. "Prostitutie (Prostitution)" (The Hague, Martinus Nijhoff).

Encyclopaedie van Nederlandsch Oost-Indie. 1919. "Prostitutie (Prostitution)", Vol. 3 (The Hague, Martinus Nijhoff).

End Child Prostitution in Asian Tourism (ECPAT). 1993. "Why development can combat child prostitution", *ECPAT Australia Bulletin*, No.3.

—. 1995. *A short introduction to ECPAT and the issue of child sexual exploitation* (Bangkok, ECPAT), mimeograph.

Flamm, M. 1996. "Silencing bells in Thailand", *Together: A Journal of World Vision International* (Monrovia, California), No.52, October-December, pp. 20-21.

Fong, C.O. 1984. *Urban poverty in Malaysia: Policies and issues* (Kuala Lumpur, Population Studies Unit, Faculty of Economics and Administration, University of Malaya).

Gabriela Commission on Violence against Women. 1987. *A situationer, philosophy and program of action* (Manila, Gabriela), mimeograph.

Godley, J. 1991. "Prostitution in Thailand", in Institute for Population and Social Research, *NIC: Free zone for prostitution*. IPSR Publication No. 148 (Salaya, Nakhonpathom, Mahidol University) (in Thai).

Goonesekere, S.W.E. 1993. *Child labour in Sri Lanka: Learning from the past* (Geneva, ILO).

Gray, L.; S. Gourley; D. Paul. 1996. "Cambodia's street children prostitutes: a case study", *Together: A Journal of World Vision International* (Monrovia, California), No. 52, October-December, pp.6-12.

Guest, P. 1992. *Gender and migration in Southeast Asia*. Paper presented at the International Colloquium on Migration, Development and Gender in Southeast Asia, organized by the Population Studies Unit, University of Malaya, Kuantan, October.

—. 1993. *Guesstimating the unestimateable: The number of child prostitutes in Thailand*. Paper presented at the Seminar on Child Prostitution, Bangkok, November.

Haga, J. 1901. "De schaduwzijden van het reglement op de prostitutie in Nederlandsch-Indie" (The drawbacks of the prostitution regulations in the Dutch Indies), *Geneeskundig Tijdschrift voor Nederlandsch-Indie*, Vol. 41, pp. 531-538.

Hantrakul, S. 1985. "Prostitute: At the heart of sex domination", *Ban Mai Roo Rai*, Vol. 1, No. 2, pp. 42-59 (in Thai).

Haslani, H. 1988. *Program pemulihan akhlak wanita dan gadis: Satu penilian di Taman Seri Puteri, Cheras* (The moral rehabilitation programme for women and girls: An evaluation at Taman Seri Puteri, Cheras). Project Paper, Faculty of Law, University of Malaya, Kuala Lumpur.

Havanon, N.; J. Knodel; T. Bennett. 1992. *Sexual networking in a provincial Thai setting*. AIDS Prevention Monograph Series Paper No.1 (Bangkok, AIDSCAP).

Hill, A.H. 1955. *The Hikayat Abdullah: An annotated translation* (Singapore, Malaya Publishing House).

Hong, E. 1983. *Tourism: Its environmental impact in Malaysia*. Paper presented at the Seminar on Problems of Development, Environment and the Natural Resource Crisis in Asia and the Pacific, organized by Sahabat Alam Malaysia, Penang, 22-25 October.

Hongladarom, C.; J. Guyot. 1983. *The changing role of women in the political economy of Thailand*. Paper of the Human Resource Institute (Bangkok, Thammasat University).

Hugo, G.; L.L. Lim; S. Narayanan. 1989. *Malaysian human resources development planning project module II: Labour supply and processes study No.4: Labour mobility* (Kuala Lumpur, Economic Planning Unit).

Hull, T. n.d. *Preventing AIDS in Batam: Challenges and responses in the Indonesian health system*, mimeograph.

Husna, S.; Y. Nurizan. 1987. "Provision of housing and the quality of life of urban low-income households", in Population Studies Unit, *Population and the quality of life in Malaysia* (Kuala Lumpur, Population Studies Unit, Faculty of Economics and Administration, University of Malaya).

Hutaserani, S. 1990. "The trends of income inequality and poverty and a profile of the urban poor in Thailand", *TDRI Quarterly Review* (Bangkok, Thailand Development Research Institute), Vol. 5, No. 4, pp. 14-19.

Ingleson, J. 1986. "Prostitution in colonial Java", in D.P. Chandler and M.C. Ricklefs (eds.), *Nineteenth and twentieth century Indonesia: Essays in honour of Professor J.D. Legge* (Melbourne, Monash University).

Institute for Population and Social Research (IPSR). 1991. *NIC: Free zone for prostitution*. IPSR Publication No. 148 (Salaya, Nakhonpathom, Mahidol University) (in Thai).

Institute of Population Studies (IPS). 1993. *The demographic and behavioral study of female commercial sex workers in Thailand*. IPS Publication No. 210/93 (Bangkok, IPS, Chulalongkorn University).

International Labour Office. 1996. *Child labour: Targeting the intolerable* (Geneva, ILO).

225

International Programme for the Elimination of Child Labour (ILO/IPEC). n.d. *Highlights of the review of literature of the project: A research and intervention programme to create a child-focused environment for children with experiences in prostitution*, An IPEC Progress Report, mimeograph (Geneva).

Jamnarnwej, W. 1984. *Women and the law in Thailand*. Paper presented at the Seminar on Women and the Law, Kuala Lumpur, 29 April-1 May.

Joginder, S.J. 1964. *History of Malaya 1400-1959* (Penang, United Publishers).

Jones, G.W. 1994. *Marriage and divorce in Islamic Southeast Asia* (Singapore, Oxford University Press).

—; Y. Asari; T. Djuartika. 1994. "Divorce in West Java", *Journal of Comparative Family Studies* (Calgary, Canada), Vol. 25, No. 3.

—; E. Sulistyaningsih; T.H. Hull. 1995. *Prostitution in Indonesia*. Working Papers in Demography No. 52. (Canberra, Research School of Social Sciences, Australian National University).

Keyes, C. 1984. "Mother or mistress but never a monk: Buddhist notions of female gender in rural Thailand", *American Anthropologist* (Washington, DC), Vol. 11, No. 2, pp. 165-184.

Kinsey, A.; B. Wardell; B. Pomeroy; C.E. Martin. 1953. *Sexual behaviour in the human female* (Philadelphia, W.B. Saunders).

Kobkitsuksakul, S. 1988. *Miss Thailand Beauty Contest, 1934-1987*. Unpublished thesis submitted to the Graduate School, Thammasat University (Bangkok) (in Thai).

Koentjoro. 1989. *Melacur sebagai sebuah karya dan pengorbanan wanita pada keluarga ataukah penyakit sosial* (Is prostitution an occupation and a woman's sacrifice for her family, or is it a social disease?). Paper presented to the Second National Seminar on Indonesian Women, Facts and Characteristics. Faculty of Psychology, Gadjah Mada University, Yogyakarta.

Kompas. 1993. "Di Kodya Bandung, penghasilan WTS Rp. 200,000 - Rp. 6 juta", 21 April.

—. 1994. "WTS di JABAR meningkat, penampungannya terbalas", 29 March.

Krisna, Y.A.N. 1979. *Menyusuri remang-remang Jakarta* (Observing nightlife in Jakarta) (Jakarta, Sinar Harapan).

Kunto, H. 1993. "Nyi dampi, de bloem van kebon kelapa", *MATRA Magazine* (Jakarta), May.

Lee, P.P. 1978. *Chinese society in nineteenth century Singapore* (Kuala Lumpur, Oxford University Press).

Lerman, C. 1983. "Sex-differential patterns of circular migration: A case study of Semarang, Indonesia", *Peasant Studies* (Salt Lake City), Vol. 10, No. 4, pp.251-269.

Levinson, M. 1994. "Off to work", *Newsweek*, 17 October, pp. 38-43.

Lim, L.L. 1996. "The migration transition in Malaysia", *Asian and Pacific Migration Journal* (Manila), Vol. 5, Nos. 2-3, pp. 319-337.

—; N. Oishi. 1996. International labour migration of Asian women: Distinctive characteristics and policy concerns, *Asian and Pacific Migration Journal* (Manila), Vol. 5 No. 1, pp. 85-116.

Limanonda, B. 1992. *Women, population and development*. Paper prepared for the Conference on Population Programme Policies: New Direction, Chiang Mai, October.

Lintner, B.; H.N. Lintner. 1996. "Blind in Rangoon: AIDS epidemic rages, but the Junta says no to NGOs", *Far Eastern Economic Review* (Hong Kong), 1 August, p. 21.

Mak, L.F. 1981. *The sociology of secret societies: A study of Chinese secret societies in Singapore and Malaysia* (Kuala Lumpur, Oxford University Press).

Malaysia Department of Statistics. 1990. *Survey of manufacturing industries 1990* (Kuala Lumpur, National Printing Department).

Malikaman, S., et al. 1983. *Prostitution problem: Searching for better legal and social welfare measures for prostitutes in Thailand*. Chulalongkorn University Series of Publications for Community Service Publication No.2 (Bangkok, Chulalongkorn University) (in Thai).

Manahan, B.C. 1991. *Promotion of community awareness for the prevention of prostitution in the Philippines*. Paper presented at the ESCAP Workshop on the Promotion of Community Awareness for the Prevention of Prostitution in the ESCAP Region, Lampang, Thailand, 20-27 August.

Matra. 1993. "De bloem van indische bergsteded: Kembang kembang malam di Bandung", May. pp. 59-64.

—. 1994. "Bursa seks ala Medan" (The sex market Medan style), April, p. 93.

Matsui, Y. 1980. "Economy and psychology of prostitution tourism", *Asian Women's Liberation* (Tokyo), Vol. 3, No. 6, p. 9.

MacBeth, J. 1993. "Sin under seige", *Far Eastern Economic Review* (Hong Kong), 11 March.

McNulty, S. 1994. "Prostitution is not a moral question", *Asian Wall Street Journal* (Hong Kong), 25 October.

Mettarikanond, D. 1983. *Prostitution and the policies of the Thai Government from 1868 to 1960*. Unpublished thesis submitted to Graduate School, Chulalongkorn University, Bangkok (in Thai).

Ministry of Health. 1988. *Plan of action for the prevention and control of AIDS* (Kuala Lumpur, Ministry of Health).

Miralao, V.A.; C.O. Carlos; A.F. Santos. 1990. *Women entertainers in Angeles and Olongapo: A survey report* (Manila, Women's Education, Development, Productivity and Research Organization and Katipunan ng Kababaihan para sa Kalayaan).

Moselina, L.M. 1981. "Olongapo's R and R industry: A sociological analysis of institutionalized prostitution", *Ang Makatao* (Manila), Vol. 1, No. 1, January-June.

Muecke, M. 1989. *Mother sold food, daughter sells her body: Prostitution and cultural continuity in the social function of Thai women*. Paper presented at the Annual Meeting of the American Anthropological Association, Phoenix, Arizona.

—. 1990. "The AIDS prevention dilemma in Thailand", *Asian and Pacific Population Forum* (Honolulu), Vol. 4, No. 4, pp.1-8.

Muntarbhorn, V. 1992. "A scourge in our midst", *Bangkok Post*, 13 November, p. 4.

—. 1996a. "International perspectives and child prostitution in Asia", in US Department of Labor and Bureau of International Labor Affairs, *Forced labor: The prostitution of children* (Washington, DC, United States Department of Labor, Bureau of International Labor Affairs).

—. 1996b. *Sexual exploitation of children* (New York and Geneva, United Nations Centre for Human Rights)

Murray, A.J. 1991. *No money, no honey: A study of street traders and prostitutes in Jakarta* (Singapore, Oxford University Press).

—. 1993. *Dying for a fuck: Implications for HIV/AIDS in Indonesia*, mimeograph.

Mu'thi, A. 1965. "Sedikit tentang hukum perzinaan" (A little about the laws on adultery), *Gema Islam*, Vol. 4, Nos. 79-80, pp. 13-16.

Nagaraj, S. 1994. "The sex sector in Malaysia: Report of research and a workshop", *Network Notes* (Kuala Lumpur), Vol. 2, No. 2, pp. 26-43.

Nagayama, T. 1992. "Clandestine migrant workers in Japan", *Asian and Pacific Migration Journal* (Manila), Vol. 1, Nos. 3-4, pp. 623-636.

National Commission on the Role of Filipino Women. 1995. *Philippine Plan for Gender-Responsive Development 1995-2025* (Manila, National Commission on the Role of Filipino Women).

National Commission on Women's Affairs. 1985. *Women's development in Thailand* (Bangkok, National Committee for International Cooperation).

—. 1995. *Women of Thailand*, Special issue of the *Newsletter of the National Commission on Women's Affairs* (Bangkok), September.

National Committee for the Eradication of Commercial Sex. 1996. *National policy and plan of action for the prevention and eradication of the commercial sexual exploitation of children* (Bangkok, National Commission on Women's Affairs, Office of the Prime Minister, Thailand).

Nitimihardjo, C., et al. 1994. *Orientasi nilai budaya yang melatarbelakangi perilaku sosial klien tuna susila Sasana Rehabilitasi Wanita Silih Asih Palimanan Cirebon* (Cultural value orientation underlying the social behaviour of immoral clients of the Silih Asih Women's Rehabilitation Centre, Cirebon) (Bandung, Sekolah Tinggi Kesejahteraan Sosial).

Nyland, B. 1995. "Child prostitution, and the new Australian legislation on paedophiles in Asia", *Journal of Contemporary Asia* (Stockholm), Vol. 25, No. 4, pp. 546-560.

O'Brian, M. 1996. *The international legal framework and current national legislative and enforcement responses*. Paper submitted by the ECPAT Working Group on Law Reform and Law Enforcement, to the World Congress against the Commercial Sexual Exploitation of Children, Stockholm, Sweden, 27-31 August.

O'Connell Davidson, J. 1996. *The sex exploiter*. Paper submitted by the ECPAT Working Group on The Sex Exploiter, to the World Congress against the Commercial Sexual Exploitation of Children, Stockholm, Sweden, 27-31 August.

Ofreneo, R.; R.P. Ofreneo. 1993. *The sex sector: Prostitution and development in the Philippines: A revised research report* (Diliman, University of the Philippines), mimeograph.

—; —. 1994. *The sex sector: Prostitution and development in the Philippines*. A Summary of a Research Report presented at the Workshop on Policies and Programme Issues for Action on the Sex Sector, Bangkok, 31 October-1 November.

Ong, J.H. 1993. "Singapore", in N.J. Davis (ed.), *Prostitution: An international handbook on trends, problems and policies* (Westport, Connecticut, Greenwood Press).

Otaganonta, W. 1990. "Child prostitution in Thailand: Turning a blind eye", *Bangkok Post*, 1 August.

—. 1992. "Battle to protect the children of Asia", *Bangkok Post*, 8 April.

Panyacheewin, S. 1992. "How severe is Thailand's prostitution problem?", *Bangkok Post Outlook*, 29 August.

Papanek, G.V. 1975. "The poor of Jakarta", *Economic Development and Cultural Change* (Chicago), Vol. 24, No. 1, pp.1-28.

Perpinan, S.M.S. 1981. *Prostitution tourism*. Paper presented at the Church and Tourism Conference, Stockholm, 2-6 November.

—. 1982. *The geopolitics of prostitution*. Paper presented at the Workshop on the Promotion of Procedures for the Implementation of Internationally Recognized Human Rights, Tagaytay City, Philippines, 14-19 February.

Pheterson, G. 1989. *A vindication of the rights of whores* (Seattle, Seal Press).

Phongpaichit, P. 1982. *From peasant girls to Bangkok masseuses* (Geneva, International Labour Office).

—. 1993. "The labour market aspects of female migration to Bangkok", in United Nations, *Internal migration of women in developing countries* (New York, Department for Economic and Social Information and Policy Analysis).

Phurisinsith, W. 1976. "An article about prostitutes", *Journal of Sociology* (Bangkok), April-December. pp. 108-129.

Podhisita, C. 1985. *Peasant household strategies: A study of production and reproduction in a northeastern Thai village*. Unpublished Ph.D. dissertation, University of Hawaii, Department of Anthropology (Honolulu).

Potter, S. 1977. *Family life in a northern Thai village: A study in the structural significance of women* (Berkeley, University of California Press).

Pramualratana, A. 1990. *Changing support systems of the old in a rural community in Thailand*. Unpublished Ph.D. dissertation, Australian National University (Canberra), Department of Demography.

Prukpongsawalee, M. 1991. *NIC and the commercial sex worker*. Paper presented at the Seminar on NIC: Free Zone for Prostitution, Institute for Population and Social Research, Mahidol University, Salaya, January.

Purcell, V. 1948. *The Chinese in Malaya* (London, Oxford University Press).

Purnomo, T.; A. Siregar. 1985. *Dolly: Membedah dunia pelacuran Surabaya, kasus Kompleks Pelacuran Dolly* (Dolly: Exploring the prostitution world in Surabaya – The case of the Dolly prostitution complex) (Jakarta, Graffiti Press).

Ram, E.; D. Westwood. 1996. "Beyond Stockholm", *Together: A Journal of World Vision International* (Monrovia, California), No. 52, October-December, pp.1-2.

Rasakul, S. 1995. "Innocence lost", *Bangkok Post*, 15 January.

Rattanawannathip, M. 1991. "Prostitution: Necessity or naked greed", *Centre for Women and Development Networker* (Bangkok), January.

Rayanakorn, K. 1995. *Special study on laws relating to prostitution and traffic in women* (Bangkok, Foundation for Women's Research and Action Project on Traffic in Women).

Reanda, L. 1991. "Prostitution as a human rights question: Problems and prospects of United Nations action", *Human Rights Quarterly* (Baltimore), Vol. 13, No. 2, pp. 202-228.

Rohana, A. 1985. *Retrenchment: An exploratory study of the retrenchment experience of the textile and electronic workers in Penang* (Penang, School of Social Sciences, Universiti Sains Malaysia), mimeograph.

Rutnin, M. 1992. *Child prostitution in Thailand.* Paper presented at the Conference on Youth in the Asia-Pacific Region, Bangkok, 30 June-4 July.

Sabaroedin, S. 1991. *Promotion of community awareness for the prevention of prostitution in Indonesia.* Paper presented to the Workshop on the Promotion of Community Awareness for the Prevention of Prostitution in the ESCAP Region, Lampang, Thailand, 20-27 August.

Sahasakul, C. 1992. *Lessons from the World Bank's experience of structural adjustment loans (SALs): A case study of Thailand.* Research Monograph No.8. (Bangkok, Thailand Development Research Institute).

Saikaew, L. 1996. "A non-governmental organization perspective", in US Department of Labor, Bureau of International Labor Affairs, *Forced labor: The prostitution of children* (Washington, DC, United States Department of Labor, Bureau of International Labor Affairs).

Saisawat, S. 1986. *Attitude of Senator Assembly on solving the prostitution problem in Thailand.* Unpublished thesis submitted to the Graduate School, Mahidol University, Salaya (in Thai).

Santasombat, Y. 1992. *Women trafficking: Community and prostitution in Thai society* (Bangkok, Local Development Institute) (in Thai).

Sattaporn, C. 1975. *The prostitution problem in Thailand* (Bangkok, Faculty of Public Administration, Thammasat University) (in Thai).

Sereewat-Srisang, S. 1987. *Migration, tourism and women* (Bangkok, Foundation for Women) (in Thai).

Shamin, I. 1997. *Trafficking in children and child prostitution.* Paper presented at the National Workshop on Child Labour organized by ILO/IPEC and the Ministry of Labour and Manpower, Dhaka, 5-7 January.

Sinar. 1993. "Gemerlap satu miliar semalam", "Mengangguk untung di remang malam", 26 August, pp. 16-19.

—. 1994. "Merebaknya kerajaan Hartono", pp. 15-17; "Bermula dari sopir omprengan", pp. 18-19; "Kami terbaik di Asia", p. 19; "Banyak pasal menjerat germo", p. 20; "Saya ini 'kayak' orang sosial saja", p. 21; "Akan muncul Hartono-Hartono lain", pp. 22-23; "Yang disalahkan selalu pelaurnya", p. 25; "Saya tahu itu dosa", p. 26; "Kenapa cari yang exstra di luar?", p. 27; 25 July.

Sinha, I. 1996. *Commercial sexual exploitation of children.* Country Paper prepared for World Congress against the Commercial Sexual Exploitation of Children, Stockholm, Sweden, 27-31 August.

Sittitrai, W.; T. Brown. 1991. *Female commercial sex workers in Thailand: A preliminary report* (Bangkok, Thai Red Cross Society).

Skinner, G.W. 1957. *Chinese society in Thailand: An analytical history* (Ithaca, New York, Cornell University Press).

Skrobanek, S. 1986. *Strategies against prostitution: The case of Thailand* (Bangkok, Foundation for Women).

Soedjono, D. 1977. *Pelacuran: Ditinjau dari segi hukum dan kenyataan dalam masyarakat* (Prostitution: Seen from the viewpoint of law and social realities) (Bandung, Karya Nusantara).

Soesilo, R. 1960. *Kitab undang-undang hukum pidana* (Guide to the criminal law) (Bogor, Politeia Publishers).

Soewarso, T.I. 1988. "Epidemiologis sifilis, frambusia dan Regular Mass Treatment (RMT)" (The epidemiology of syphilis and framboesia and Regular Mass Treatment), in S.F. Daili et al. (eds.), *Perkembangan terakhir penanggulangan sifilis dan frambusia* (Recent developments in the control of syphilis and framboesia) (Jakarta, Faculty of Medicine, University of Indonesia).

Soonthorndhada, A. 1992. "Individual role behaviour, expectations and adaptations: Past to present", in B. Yoddumnern-Attig et al. (eds.), *Changing roles and statuses of women in Thailand: A documentary assessment.* Institute for Population and Social Research Publication No.161 (Salaya, Nakhonpathom, Mahidol University).

Srisang, L. (ed.). 1990. *Caught in modern slavery: Tourism and child prostitution in Asia.* Report and Proceedings of the Chiang Mai Consultation of the International Campaign to End Child Prostitution in Asian Tourism (Chiang Mai, Thailand, Ecumenical Coalition on Third World Tourism), 1-9 May.

Staebler, M. 1996. *Tourism and children in prostitution.* Paper submitted by ECPAT for the World Congress against the Commercial Sexual Exploitation of Children, Stockholm, Sweden, 27-31 August.

Stearn, V.W. 1987. *The bar economy: A social investigation in the Malate Parish of Manila,* mimeograph (Manila).

Suarmiartha, E.; et al. 1992. *Perilaku seksual berisiko terhadap penularan AIDS pegemudi truk Denpasar-Surabaya* (Risky sexual behaviour for the spread of AIDS among truck drivers from Denpasar to Surabaya). Paper presented at the annual JEN Meeting, Jakarta, 29 November-4 December.

Sudibyo, R.M.S. 1937. "Bahaja pelatjoeran boeat pemoeda" (The danger to youth of prostitution), *Pemandangan,* 18 October.

Sulistyaningsih, E.; Y. Swasono. 1993. "The sex industry: Prostitution and development in Indonesia". A report submitted to Mahidol University, Bangkok, mimeograph.

Sunindyo, S. 1993. *She who earns: The politics of prostitution in Java.* Unpublished Ph.D. thesis, University of Wisconsin, Madison.

Sureeman, N. 1988. *Beautiful girls in a glass room: The process of becoming masseuses in Thai society* (Bangkok, Thammasat University Thai Study Institute) (in Thai).

Sussangkarn, C., et al. 1988. *The long-term view on growth and income distribution* (Bangkok, Thailand Development Research Institute).

Tan, M.L. 1987. *Prostitution in the Philippines: Health aspects* (Quezon City, College of Social Sciences and Philosophy Department of Anthropology), mimeograph.

—. 1990. *Synthesis of an AIDS KAP (Knowledge, Attitudes and Practices) survey among sentinel groups in Metro Manila* (Quezon City, College of Social Sciences and Philosophy Department of Anthropology).

Tempo. 1993. "Bisnis prostitusi", p. 21; "Menyingkap jaringan perdagangan wanita", pp. 22-25; "Dari karaoke sampai ranjang", pp. 25-26; "Ayam kampus", pp. 27-28; "Wanita dari Indonesia dan sake di kabukicho", p. 28; 13 November.

Thailand Development Research Institute (TDRI). 1992. "The political crisis and Thailand's macroeconomic outlook", *TDRI Quarterly Review* (Bangkok), Vol. 7, No. 3, pp. 22-25.

—. 1993. *Thailand economic information kit* (Bangkok, TDRI).

Thaipakdhi, Y. 1973. *Factors affecting work in massage parlours.* Unpublished Masters Thesis, Thammasat University, Faculty of Social Administration (in Thai).

Thitsa, K. 1980. *Providence and prostitution: Image and reality of women in Buddhist Thailand* (London, Calvert North Star Press).

Truong, T.D. 1983. "The dynamics of sex tourism: The case of Southeast Asia", *Development and Change* (London), Vol. 14, pp. 533-553.

—. 1985. *Virtue, order, health and money: Towards a comprehensive perspective on female prostitution in Asia.* Paper presented at the Workshop of Experts on Prevention and Rehabilitation Schemes for Young Women in Prostitution and Related Occupations, Bangkok, 17-21 June.

—. 1990. *Sex, money and morality: Prostitution and tourism in South-east Asia* (London, Zed Books).

Tunsarawuth, S. 1996. "Thailand's $44 billion underworld prostitution heads list of lucrative illegal businesses, says study", *Straits Times* (Kuala Lumpur), 3 December.

Ungphakorn, J. 1990. *The impact of AIDS on women in Thailand.* Paper presented to the Conference on AIDS in Asia and the Pacific, Canberra, 5-8 August.

United Nations. 1994. *Promotion and protection of the rights of children: Sale of children, child prostitution and child pornography: Note by the Secretary-General.* Doc. A/49/478 (New York, United Nations General Assembly).

—. 1995. *Promotion and protection of the rights of children: Sale of children, child prostitution and child pornography: Note by the Secretary-General.* Doc. A/50/456 (New York, United Nations, General Assembly).

—. 1996. *Fourth World Conference on Women, Beijing, China, 4-15 September 1995, Platform for Action and the Beijing Declaration* (New York, United Nations Department of Public Information).

United Nations High Commission on Human Rights. 1996. *Rights of the child: Report of the Special Rapporteur on the Sale of Children, Child Prostitution and Child Pornography* Doc. E/CN.4/1996/100 (New York, United Nations).

United Nations Economic and Social Council. 1996. *Rights of the child: Question of a Draft Optional Protocol to the Convention on the Rights of the Child, on the Sale of Children, Child Prostitution and Child Pornography, as well as Basic Measures needed for their Eradication: Report of the Working Group on its Second Session.* Doc. E/CN.4/1996/101 (New York, United Nations).

United Nations Fund for Children (UNICEF). 1995. *Extracts from CRC Documents (Sexual Exploitation, Child Prostitution, Sex Tourism, Child Pornography)* (Geneva, UNICEF).

Uwiyono, A., et al. 1992. *Lokalisasi dan Hukum: Suatu Tinjauan Yuridis Terhadap Prektek Bertahannya Pelacuran di DKI Jakarta* (Jakarta, National Epidemiology Network, Health Research Centre, University of Indonesia).

Velasquez, L.M. 1993a. "60,000 teens engaged in sex trade", *Philippine Daily Inquirer* (Manila), 29 March.

—. 1993b. "Who can teenage prostitutes turn to?", *Philippine Daily Inquirer* (Manila), 30 March.

Warren J.F. 1993. *Ah Ku and Karayuki-san. Prostitution in Singapore 1870-1940* (Singapore, Oxford University Press).

Weniger, B.; et al. 1991. "The epidemiology of HIV infection and AIDS in Thailand", *AIDS* (Bangkok), Vol. 5, Supplement 2. pp. 571-575.

Whaites, A. 1996. "The path to prostitution among street children", *Together: A Journal of World Vision International* (Monrovia, California), No. 52, October-December, pp. 3-5.

White, M.C. 1990. "Improving the welfare of women factory workers: Lessons from Indonesia", *International Labour Review* (Geneva, ILO), Vol. 128.

Wibowo, S.; A. Gunawan; D. Merina; Anisah; D. Aziz. 1989. *Penelitian descriptif mengenai sebab-sebab kota Indramayu sebagai produsen utama wanita tuna susila* (Descriptive study of the reasons why Indramayu is a prominent source of prostitutes) (Jakarta, Pusat Penelitian Kemasyrakatan dan Kebudayaan, Lembaga Penelitian, Universitas Indonesia).

Wihtol, R. 1982. "Hospitality girls in the Manila tourist belt", *Philippines Journal of Industrial Relations* (Manila), Vol. 4, Nos.1-2

Wongburanavart, C. 1994. "Thailand's lost virtue", *Asian Wall Street Journal* (Hong Kong), 25 October.

Wongchai, Y., et. al. 1988. *Socio-economic factors affecting going to work in the sex sector of other countries.* Unpublished report from Thammasat University (Bangkok), Faculty of Social Welfare (in Thai).

Working Group on Public Welfare. 1989. *Problems, causes and strategies in protection and solving of prostitution in Thailand.* Paper prepared for the Special Committee on Prostitution, Solving Problems in Thailand, for the Representative Assembly (Bangkok) (in Thai).

World Bank. 1995. *Malaysia meeting labor needs: More workers and better skills.* Report No. 13163-MY (Washington, DC, World Bank).

World Congress against the Commercial Sexual Exploitation of Children. 1996. *Draft declaration and agenda for action,* Stockholm, Sweden, 27-31 August.

Yeow, M.S. 1992. *Malaysia* (Singapore, MPH and Sun Tree).

Yoddumnern, B. 1985. *Continuity and change in a northern Thai village: Determinants and consequences of fertility decline on northern Thai family structure.* Unpublished Ph.D. dissertation, University of Illinois, Department of Anthropology (Champaign, Illinois).

The sex sector

Yoddumnern-Attig, B., et al. (eds.). 1992. *Changing roles and statuses of women in Thailand: A documentary assessment.* Institute for Population and Social Research Publication No.161 (Salaya, Nakhonpathom, Mahidol University).

Zainah, I. 1975. *Rehabilitation of juvenile prostitutes: A case study of the Women and Girls Rehabilitation Centre, Cheras.* Project Paper, Diploma of Public Administration, Faculty of Economics and Administration, University of Malaya, Kuala Lumpur.